D1316742

NIAGARA FALLS PUBLIC LIBRARY
1425 MAIN ST
NIAGARA FALLS NY 14305

ALSO BY EMMANUEL CARRÈRE

The Adversary

Class Trip

The Mustache

Gothic Romance

I Am Alive and You Are Dead

MY LIFE AS A
RUSSIAN NOVEL

MY LIFE AS A RUSSIAN NOVEL

A MEMOIR

EMMANUEL CARRÈRE

Translated by Linda Coverdale

METROPOLITAN BOOKS • HENRY HOLT AND COMPANY • NEW YORK

Metropolitan Books
Henry Holt and Company, LLC
Publishers since 1866
175 Fifth Avenue
New York, New York 10010

Metropolitan Books® and ® are registered trademarks of
Henry Holt and Company, LLC.

Copyright © 2007 by P.O.L. éditeur
Translation copyright © 2010 by Linda Coverdale
All rights reserved.
Distributed in Canada by H. B. Fenn and Company Ltd.

Originally published in France in 2007 under the title
Un Roman russe by P.O.L. éditeur, Paris.

Library of Congress Cataloging-in-Publication data

Carrère, Emmanuel, 1957–
  [Roman russe. English]
  My life as a Russian novel : a memoir / Emmanuel Carrère.—1st U.S. ed.
    p. cm.
  ISBN 978-0-8050-8755-0
  I. Title.
  PQ2663.A7678R6613 2010
  843'.914–dc22   2010001717

Henry Holt books are available for special promotions and
premiums. For details contact: Director, Special Markets.

First U.S. Edition 2010

Designed by Kelly S. Too

Printed in the United States of America
1 3 5 7 9 10 8 6 4 2

MY LIFE AS A
RUSSIAN NOVEL

· 1 ·

The train is humming along, it's nighttime, Sophie and I are making love in the berth and it really is her. In my erotic dreams, my partners are usually several women at once and difficult to identify, but this time, no: I recognize Sophie's voice, her words, her spread legs. In the sleeping car compartment where we have so far been alone, another couple turns up, the Fujimoris. Mme Fujimori hops right into bed with us. The entente is immediately cordiale, with much merriment. Supported by Sophie in an acrobatic position, I enter Mme Fujimori, who soon comes ecstatically. M. Fujimori now announces that the train has stopped. It's sitting in a station and has been there for perhaps some time. Motionless in the glare of the sodium lights, a policeman is watching us. Convinced that he's about to get on the train to reprimand us, we hastily close the curtains, then rush to tidy up the compartment and put our clothes back on so we'll be ready, when he opens the door, to assure him blithely that he hadn't seen a thing, that he'd been dreaming. We imagine his suspicious, disappointed face. All this takes place in an exciting blend of panic and helpless giggling. I do point out, however, that there's nothing to laugh about: we might get arrested, hauled off to the police station while the train goes on its way, at which point God knows what will happen. Vanishing without a trace in this muddy back of beyond, we'll die in some dungeon deep in the Russian heartland with no one to hear our screams. My warnings send Sophie and Mme Fujimori into fresh gales of mirth and I end up laughing with them.

The train has stopped, as in my dream, at a deserted but brightly lit platform. It is three in the morning, somewhere between Moscow and Kotelnich. I have an achy head and parched throat—too much to drink at the restaurant before going to the station. Taking care not to wake Jean-Marie, stretched out in the other berth, I make my way among the crates of equipment cluttering the compartment and out into the corridor in search of a bottle of water. The dining car where we sluiced down our last vodkas a few hours ago is closed, the only illumination a single dim light at each table. Four soldiers, having planned ahead, are continuing to get plastered. As I go by they offer me a drink; I decline and, walking on, I recognize Sasha, our interpreter, sprawled on a banquette, snoring sonorously. I sit down a bit farther away, calculate the time difference—midnight in Paris, still okay—and try to call Sophie on my cell phone to tell her about this dream that seems to me extraordinarily promising. When I can't get through, I take out my notebook instead and write it down.

Wherever did M. and Mme Fujimori come from? That's not hard to figure out. Fujimori is the name of the former president of Peru, the subject of an article I skimmed on the plane. The corruption scandals that turned him out of office didn't interest me much, but an article on the facing page caught my eye. It was about missing people in Japan whose families are convinced they've been kidnapped and held secretly in North Korea, some for as long as thirty years. No recent event had triggered the article, no demonstration organized by the families, no anniversary, no new development in the case, closed ages ago, if indeed it had ever been opened. It isn't clear at all why the article appeared yesterday rather than some other day, this year rather than some other year; perhaps the journalist had run into a few people—in the street, in a bar—whose relatives had simply vanished back in the seventies. To bear up under the torment of uncertainty, families had come up with the kidnapping story and then, much later, told it to a stranger, who was now telling it to the world. Was it plausible? Was there any evidence—if not proof—to support the claim, or at least a likely explanation? If I had been the newspaper editor, I would have asked the journalist to dig a little deeper. But no, he simply reported that some Japanese families believed their relatives had disappeared into prison camps in North Korea. Dead or alive, who could say? Dead, most likely, of hunger or beatings by their jailers. And if alive, they probably no longer at all resembled the young men and women who vanished thirty years ago. If they were ever found, what would one say to them? And they, what would they say? Should one even want to find them?

The train sets out again, through forests. No snow. The four soldiers have finally gone off to bed. There's no one left in the dining car, with its flickering table lamps, but Sasha and me. At one point, Sasha bestirs himself, sits halfway up. His big rumpled head appears suddenly above the backrest of his banquette. Seeing me at the table writing, he frowns. I gesture soothingly in his direction, as if to say, Go back to sleep, there's plenty of time, and down he goes again, doubtless certain he's been dreaming.

When I was a foreign aid worker in Indonesia twenty-five years ago, travelers used to pass around terrifying and mostly true stories about the prisons stuffed with people who'd been caught with drugs. In the bars of Bali, there was always some bearded guy in a sleeveless T-shirt going on and on about how he'd survived a close call that had left a less fortunate buddy serving 150 years of slow death in Bangkok or Kuala Lumpur. One evening after we'd been carrying on this way for hours with jaunty nonchalance, some guy I didn't know trotted out another story, perhaps true, perhaps not. This was back when the Soviet Union was still around. When you take the Trans-Siberian Railway, he explained, you're strictly forbidden to get off along the route, to stop at a station to do some sightseeing, for example, and then get on the next train. Well, it seems that in certain backwater towns, near the railroad tracks, you can find exceptionally hallucinogenic mushrooms (or really cheap rare carpets, jewelry, precious metals, whatever), so sometimes travelers dare to ignore the rule. The train stops for three minutes in a little station in Siberia. Bitter cold, no town, just a bunch of huts, a sinister mud hole that looks abandoned. Without anyone's noticing, the adventurer gets off the train, which departs. Alone, he shoulders his pack and leaves the station—a platform of rotting planks—to flounder through muck and puddles, past wooden fences and barbed wire, wondering if the whole thing was such a good idea. The first person he meets is some sort of degenerate who, in a cloud of appallingly bad breath, delivers a speech in which all nuance is lost (the traveler knows only a few words of Russian, which might not even be what the wretch is speaking), but the gist is clear: he can't go wandering around like that, he'll get himself picked up by the police. *Militsiya! . . . Militsiya!* Then comes a torrent of incomprehensible language, but thanks to some mimicry, the traveler decides that the derelict is offering him shelter until the next train. It's not a very appealing prospect, but what choice does he have and, who knows, maybe he'll get a chance to talk mushrooms or jewelry. Following his host, he enters a disgusting hovel heated by a smoky stove, where he finds a gathering of even more sinister characters. A bottle of rotgut appears, they drink and stare at him while they argue, and the word *militsiya* crops up frequently, the only word he recognizes, so, rightly or wrongly, he figures they're talking about what will happen if he falls into the clutches of the police. He won't get off with *just* a stiff fine, oh no! They laugh till they fall over. No, he'll never be seen again. Even if there are people waiting for him at the end of the line, in Vladivostok, they'll simply decide he's gone missing, that's all. No matter how big a stink his family and friends make, they'll never find out or get anyone else to find out what happened to him. The traveler attempts to calm down: maybe that's not really what they're saying, maybe they're discussing their grandmothers' homemade jams. But he knows perfectly well that's not it. He knows they're talking about what's in store for him, he realizes he'd have been better off running into the corrupt police they're threatening him with so merrily, in fact *anything* would have been better than this drafty shack, these jolly toothless vagrants now closing in on him, beginning—still in fun—to pinch his cheeks, give him little shoves, punches, to show him what the police will do, until the moment when they knock him senseless and he wakes up later, in the dark. He's naked on a dirt floor, shaking with cold and fear. Reaching out, he discovers that they've locked him into some kind of shed and that it's all over. Every now and then the door will open, the happy half-wits will slap him around, stomp on him, sodomize him—have a little fun, basically, which is hard to find in Siberia. Nobody knows where he got off the train, nobody will come to save him, he's at their mercy. The bums probably hang around the station whenever a train is due, hoping some idiot will break the rules: that guy, he's theirs. They find all sorts of uses for him until he croaks, then they wait for the next one. He comes to this conclusion not by thinking things through, of course, but more like a man regaining consciousness in a narrow box where he can't see a thing, can't hear a sound, can't move. Only slowly does he understand that he's been buried alive, that the whole dream of his life was leading to this, and that this is reality, the last reality, the true one, the one from which he will never wake.

There he is.

And in a way, there I am as well. I've been there all my life. To imagine my own situation, I've always turned to stories like that. I told them to myself as a child, and then I just told them. I used to read them in books, and then I wrote books. For a long time, I enjoyed doing that. I took pleasure in suffering in my own particular way, a way that made me a writer. But I don't want that anymore. I can no longer bear to be locked into that bleak, unchanging scenario, can't bear to find myself, no matter how I begin, always spinning a tale of madness, frozen immobility, imprisonment, fine-tuning the workings of the trap that will crush me. A while ago I published such a book, *The Adversary*, which held me captive for seven years and bled me dry. I thought: Now it's over; I'll do something else. I'll go toward the outside, toward others, toward life. And a good way to do that would be to return to reportage, to shoot another film.

I spread the word and was soon offered a project. Not just any project: the story of an unfortunate Hungarian taken prisoner at the end of World War II who spent more than fifty years in a psychiatric hospital in the Russian hinterland. We thought it was just the thing for you, a reporter friend told me proudly, which of course exasperated me. That everyone thinks of me whenever there's some poor soul shut up for life in an insane asylum—that's exactly what I don't want anymore. I don't want to be the guy intrigued by that story. Which doesn't prevent me, obviously, from being intrigued. Plus it takes place in Russia, not where my mother was born but where they speak her mother tongue, the one I spoke a little as a child and then forgot completely.

I said yes. And a few days later I met Sophie, which in another way made me feel I was moving on to something new. Over dinner at the Thai restaurant near the place Maubert, I told her the Hungarian's story, and tonight, on the train taking me to Kotelnich, I think back on my dream, recognizing that everything that paralyzes me is in there: the policeman watching me as I make love, the threat of imprisonment, the certainty of a trap closing in. Yet the atmosphere in the dream, I reflect, is light, lively, joyous, like the knees-up party improvised with Sophie and the mysterious Mme Fujimori. I resolve that, yes, I will tell one last story of imprisonment, which will also be the story of my liberation.

Everything I know about my Hungarian comes from a few wire stories dated August and September 2000. After being dragged along by the retreating Wehrmacht, this nineteen-year-old country boy was captured by the Red Army in 1944. Interned at first in a POW camp, he was transferred in 1947 to the psychiatric hospital in Kotelnich, a small town five hundred miles northeast of Moscow. There he spent fifty-three years, forgotten by everyone, hardly speaking, because no one around him understood Hungarian and he, strangely enough, never learned Russian. He was discovered this summer, completely by chance, and the Hungarian government organized his repatriation.

I saw a few pictures of his arrival in Budapest, a thirty-second news item on television. The automatic glass doors of the airport slide open to admit a wheelchair in which huddles a frightened old man. The people around him are in short sleeves, but he is wearing a thick wool cap and shivering beneath a lap robe. One leg of his trousers is empty, folded back and fastened with a safety pin. The photographers' flashbulbs crackle, blinding him. He is bundled into a car mobbed by elderly women, who gesture wildly and shout different names: Sándor! Ferenc! András! More than eighty thousand Hungarian soldiers were reported missing after the war and everyone gave up waiting for them long ago, but now here's one of them coming home, fifty-six years later. Basically, he's an amnesiac; even his name is a mystery. The patient records of the Russian hospital, which constitute his only identification papers, refer to him variously as András Tamas, or András Tomas, or Andreas Tomas, but he shakes his head if someone addresses him by those names. He either cannot or will not say his name. This explains why at his repatriation, covered by the Hungarian press as a national event, dozens of families think they recognize him as their long-lost uncle or brother. In the weeks following his return, the press provides almost daily updates about him and the search for his identity. The authorities welcome and interview the families who claim him, while at the same time questioning the old man to try to awaken his memory, repeating to him the names of people and villages. One report mentions that the doctors at the Psychiatric Institute of Budapest, where the patient is being held under observation, have arranged for a steady procession of antiques dealers and collectors to show him military caps, gold braid, old coins, objects intended to evoke the Hungary he once knew. He reacts very little, grumbles more than he speaks. What serves him as language is no longer really Hungarian but a kind of private dialect born of the interior monologue he must have kept up throughout his half century of solitude. Scraps of sentences emerge, mutterings about crossing the Dniepr River, about shoes stolen from him or that he fears might be stolen, and especially about the leg that was cut off, back there, in Russia. He would like them to give it back or give him another one. A wire story headline declares, "The Last Prisoner of WW II Demands a Wooden Leg."

One day someone reads him "Little Red Riding Hood," and he weeps.

At the end of September, the investigation is closed, the result confirmed by DNA testing. The man back from the dead is András Toma (although in Hungary one says Toma András, Bartók Béla, the last name first, as in Japan). He has a younger brother and sister living in a village at the eastern tip of the country, the same village he left fifty-six years earlier to go off to war. They are ready to welcome him home.

Rooting around for more information, I learn that András will not be moved from Budapest to his native village for another few weeks and that the psychiatric hospital in Kotelnich will be celebrating its ninetieth anniversary on October 27. That is the place to start.

The train stops in Kotelnich for only two minutes, not much time for unloading our crates of equipment. I'm used to print journalism, which means working alone or occasionally with a photographer; a television crew, right off the bat that's more cumbersome. Even though we're the only passengers getting off and no one is getting on, the platform is fairly crowded, mostly with old women eager to sell buckets of blueberries; they shout at us when we point to all our stuff, indicating that we have enough to lug around as it is. The place looks a lot like the Trans-Siberian station in my story: beaten earth, mud puddles, flaking wooden fences behind which guys with shaved heads watch us with a curiosity that is frankly unpleasant. I find myself thinking it's good that there are four of us here rather than just one. Jean-Marie grabs his camera, Alain pops his mike onto its boom, the old women get grumpier. Sasha goes in search of a car and soon returns with someone named Vitaly, who drives us in his Zhiguli of indeterminate age to the town's only hotel, the Vyatka.

Vyatka is both the original and the recently restored name

of Kirov, the next stop on the rail line and the capital of this region. During lunch at my parents' apartment a few days before my departure, we discussed the places I would be visiting and my mother mentioned that the town was named Kirov during the Soviet era, in homage to the Bolshevik leader whose assassination triggered the purges of 1936. My father, who takes a passionate interest in my mother's family, told me that in 1905 my great-granduncle Count Viktor Komarovsky was the vice governor of the city when it was still called Vyatka. The Hotel Vyatka, in any case, is one of those places familiar to travelers in Russia, where not only does nothing work (heating, television, elevator, all kaput), but you get the feeling that nothing has ever worked, not even on the first day. Two out of three lightbulbs are burned out. Tangles of poorly insulated electric wires snake along leprous paneling. Instead of standing upright against the walls, the useless radiators stick out horizontally toward the center of the rooms at the end of long pipes that bend in strange directions. Threadbare grayish sheets so small they seem like towels half cover the sagging single beds, and a coating of greasy dust clings to whatever passes for furniture. No hot water. The day before, when I'd naïvely asked Sasha if we could use a credit card to pay for the hotel, he'd looked at me in mock astonishment, shaking his head. A credit card . . . pfft. And since I speak a little Russian (*chut'-chut'*: just a tiny bit), he'd said, *Tut, my na dne*: We're in the sticks here.

The pilgrimage to the places of András Toma's lost life begins in the psychiatric hospital, in the office of the chief surgeon and director, Dr. Petukhov, who clearly feels that ideally our journey should end there as well. Not that Yuri Leonidovich, as he invites us to call him, is hostile to journalists. On the contrary, he proudly flips through the packet of business cards left by the representatives of various Russian and foreign media organizations: Izvestia, CNN, Reuters . . . But having perfected his spiel on the subject, he doesn't really see what more we could possibly want. So: on January 11, 1947, the patient was transferred to the psychiatric hospital in Kotelnich from Bystryag, some twenty-five miles away, from a prison camp torn down in the fifties. The patient was received right here, in this well-heated little wooden house painted in pretty pastel colors and gleaming with polish, by Dr. Kozlova. She opened a file on him . . . and with a slightly theatrical gesture, Yuri Leonidovich in turn opens that file and invites Jean-Marie to zoom in for a close-up (as his predecessors have undoubtedly done) of Dr. Kozlova's notes. Yellowed paper, faded ink, small, even handwriting. The patient was registered under the name of Tomas, Andreas, born in 1925, of Magyar nationality. The extra *s* and *e* caused much confusion after his return to Hungary, but it would be hard to hold Dr. Kozlova responsible since the patient answered none of her questions, seeming not even to hear them, so we must assume that any replies were given by the soldiers in his escort. His clothes were torn, dirty, too small, and, above all, not warm enough for January. The patient remained stubbornly silent but sometimes laughed for no reason. Back at the military hospital attached to the prison camp, he had wept, had trouble sleeping, often refused to eat, and occasionally been violent, behavior that had led to the diagnosis of "psychoneurosis," justifying his transfer to a public hospital. Without much hope, I ask if Dr. Kozlova is still alive. Yuri Leonidovich shakes his head:

no, there are no witnesses left to the arrival of András Toma or to the early years of his residency. When he himself took up his position about ten years ago, he continues, the patient was of no interest to a psychiatrist. Subdued, silent, withdrawn. In 1997, they'd had to amputate one leg.

And then, on October 26, 1999, exactly one year ago, some big shot in the department of health came to visit the hospital. Showing his guest around, Yuri Leonidovich paused to introduce the one-legged old man as their senior patient. Moved by the memory of that scene, the director smiles. I can just imagine him pinching Toma's cheek, like Napoleon teasing his Old Guard veterans. A fine old fellow, nice and quiet, been here since the war and speaks only Hungarian, ha ha ha!

A local reporter happened to be covering the occasion, which wasn't exactly a thrilling one, so she gave her story a theme: the last prisoner of the Second World War lives among us. The rallying cry was launched, one news agency picked it up, then another, and soon it was making the rounds. Alerted, the Hungarian consul came out from Moscow, followed by psychiatrists from Budapest, who wound up taking András Toma away. Yuri Leonidovich has since heard only excellent news of his former patient and is delighted by his progress, of which he is regularly informed by his Hungarian colleagues. I'm astonished at how casually he mentions that progress. He seems completely untroubled by the fact that within two months a man can return to life and language after fifty-three years in Soviet care, essentially reduced to a bump on a log, and it doesn't occur to the good doctor that visiting journalists might therefore draw some cruel conclusions regarding psychiatry in his country in general or his hospital in particular. I see nothing defensive in the way Dr. Petukhov lays out Toma's case, and although he won't allow us to consult the file, I have the impression that his refusal springs less from distrust than from the desire to maintain his monopoly over the only newsworthy story that has ever turned up in Kotelnich.

Chief surgeon, director of the hospital, and deputy of the local Duma (as we will learn), Yuri Leonidovich hardly ever leaves his cozy wooden house and only rarely sees the patients. Vladimir Alexandrovich Malkov, to whom he consigns us after we insist on seeing a little more of the place, is the attending physician in charge of the wing where Toma spent so many decades of his life. Very tall, very blond, very pale, in a white lab coat and lightly tinted glasses, he has the cold demeanor that might have led a nineteenth-century novelist to remark that he looked like a German. Less jovial and cooperative than Yuri Leonidovich at first, he seems to have mixed feelings about the various crews of reporters whose business cards his boss collects. How can you live without hot water? a cameraman had asked him. His reply, with a shrug: You, you live. Us, here, we survive.

Ward 2. Nine beds. Toma's was the first one to the left of the door, against the wall in a corner, and his former roommates are still assigned to the beds they had when he left. Slippers and sweats, and the gaunt faces of men stripped of everything. Some walk in the narrow spaces separating the beds, shuffling their feet and twitching their hands as they shuttle between the window and the door. Some sit on the edges of their beds, hour after hour. Some just lie there: one beneath a blanket drawn up over his face, which we never see; another stretched out like a recumbent figure on a tomb, arms crossed over his chest, face frozen into a rictus that has become his sole expression. They have washed up here because life outside was too hard, the alcohol too strong, their heads too filled with threatening voices, but they are not dangerous or even agitated. Stabilized, explains Vladimir Alexandrovich. The hospital's budget has been steadily shrinking over the past ten years, so they have had to reduce the number of patients, sending away as many as possible, everyone who was doing better and had families to take them in, but these men here have no one, so what can you do? They keep them. They don't really treat them or talk to them, but they keep them. It's not much. It's better than nothing.

They kept András Toma even though he had a country—and as it turned out, a family—to which they could have sent him; in theory there was no reason they could not have informed the Hungarian consulate in Moscow of his existence, but no one thought of that. It's so far away, Moscow, let alone Hungary . . . He'd landed where he was and had remained there, like a package waiting to be picked up, and little by little even the pain of waiting had faded away.

But Toma had not spent his days lying on his bed like a stone figure on a tomb; he had preferred the carpentry shop, the locksmith's workshop, the garage, and during the period when the hospital had a farm, you could always find him there. Quite clever with his hands, constantly busy, he came and went freely, that's why Vladimir Alexandrovich thinks that business about his being the last prisoner of the war is a bit much. He wasn't a prisoner at all, wasn't even sick; he lived here, felt at home here, and that's it. Sasha jumps right in: Not even sick, really? Not for years. He'd been diagnosed as schizophrenic when he arrived, but he'd been in a state of shock, a man who had known the horrors of war and spent three years in a prison camp. The psychotic period he went through had been a reaction to those traumas, and it never recurred. Toma must have decided, more or less consciously, that the best way to avoid a relapse was to lie low, unnoticed, mute, not understanding what was said to him. Melting into the background.

Back in Yuri Leonidovich's office, whenever I could figure out a few words of the Russian, I had interrupted Sasha's translation, saying, *Da, da, ya ponimayu*: Yes, yes, I understand. After we left, Sasha, exasperated, had told me, Listen, either you understand and you don't need me, or you let me do my job, okay? I'd said okay, but now, talking to Vladimir Alexandrovich, I can't help breaking in again. I explain as best I can that my mother is of Russian extraction, that I spoke Russian as a child, and that I've read—in Russian—"Ward No. 6," a story by Chekhov that takes place in a provincial mental asylum. Irritated by my increasing fluency, Sasha is sulking, but Alain and Jean-Marie are impressed, while Vladimir Alexandrovich has thawed completely. I'm speaking Russian, I've read "Ward No. 6"! We're friends now and, still on a roll, I boldly ask if there might be some way to consult the Hungarian's file or, ideally, make a copy of it. Sure, of course, you have to ask Yuri Leonidovich. Yes, but the problem is, Yuri Leonidovich doesn't approve. At that, Vladimir Alexandrovich frowns: If Yuri Leonidovich doesn't approve, that's definitely a problem.

Speaking a few words of Russian has intoxicated me, and when the four of us gather that evening at the only restaurant in town still open, I'm eager to forge ahead. The Troika is basically a filthy bar in a cellar patronized by seriously sozzled young people whom we suspect, at least where the male contingent is concerned, of being potentially dangerous. The place serves only *pelmeni*, those Russian tortellini, which I insist on washing down with vodka, and in spite of our bender the previous evening, I get no argument from Alain, a devoted lush, or Sasha, who immediately warms to me. Only Jean-Marie declines with a smile, as he did last night: he never drinks. As for me, I am already high on excitement even before the first glass and decide to test my linguistic prowess on two rather homely girls at a neighboring table who can't wait to socialize. In my kindergarten Russian, I ask them about our Hungarian, their recent local celebrity. I can't guarantee that I caught everything they said but according to one girl, I wrote in my notebook, he didn't want to leave, they had to drag him back to Hungary by force, while according to the other he wasn't nuts at all, he'd pretended to be crazy to avoid getting packed off to Siberia.

I vaguely remember, a little later, asking Sasha whether we could call France from the hotel and his scornful cackle (You'll pay for it with your credit card, right?), and then staggering with him through deserted streets to the post office, which stays open late, a haven for the drunks turned away even by a bar as undiscriminating as the Troika. There one can find a bit of human warmth, enjoy a little light brawling, for which Sasha seems pretty game, and—incidentally—make a phone call. Even while carrying on a conversation that seems fated from the start to turn violent, Sasha rather sullenly helps me place my call. I wait in a wooden booth where someone has recently taken a piss, leaving me to choose between a heaving stomach if I close the door or, if I leave it open, the hubbub of the room, which drowns out the distant ringing on the line. When Sophie finally picks up, my choice is clear: I close the door and immediately begin to describe the phone booth urinal, the post office, the town, the asylum. Which must inevitably remind her of the story about the Trans-Siberian I told her in the Thai restaurant near the place Maubert where we had dinner that first evening, and yet I am euphoric: I tell her that today I began to speak Russian, that I will keep at it, really tackle the language, that it's as important to me as my having met her, and that the swift succession of these two events, by the way, is no accident. I describe my dream on the train, emphasizing somewhat mawkishly the promise of liberation it represents but skimming over Mme Fujimori, because although I've known Sophie for less than two weeks I have already noticed how jealous she is. When I called her I was thinking that it would be late at her end, that perhaps she'd be in bed, naked, ready to touch herself at my request, but I'd been confused by the time difference: it's actually evening in Paris and she's still at the office. When she first heard my voice, she wondered whether I was in some kind of trouble, but now she understands that I'm simply drunk, flying high, even happy, and that the point of the whole thing is—I love her. So then she starts talking to me about my cock, telling me that she really loves cocks, and has known a good number of them, but that mine is the one she prefers above all others and that she would really love for me to stick it in her or—failing that—jerk off. As for her, she has closed the door to her office and slipped her hand up under her skirt, beneath her pantyhose, over her panties. She's stroking the material, lightly, with her fingertips. I envision the marvelous blond hairs compressed by her panties, but I've got to tell her that, at my end, jerking off is impossible at the moment: through the glass panel of the phone booth door I can see Sasha and that guy working patiently to come to blows, they can see me as well, and I'll have to wait till I get back to the hotel. Where there's no heat and the sheets seem too grungy to actually slide between, so I'm already anticipating sleeping fully clothed, piling on whatever I can find in the way of blankets, but I promise to jerk off anyway and that, when I got back, is what I did.

Kotelnich is a hole but an important transportation junction as well, and not ten minutes go by without a train, often very long, rattling the windows of our rooms. I have no trouble sleeping through the racket. Alain does, and this morning, in the hotel's café-restaurant (where two guys are silently downing what are doubtless not their first beers of the day, whereas we have to move heaven and earth for a cup of tea), he is even more wrecked than usual, but in a buoyant mood. To combat his insomnia, he spent the night recording the trains rumbling by, and he plays me back some samples. When I can't easily tell one from the other, he tries to educate my ear, help it distinguish the chug-chug of a freight train from the clack-clack of an express; I nod, saying yes, yes, and he laughs: You'll see; when you're editing, you'll be glad to have all this.

The last one down, Sasha joins us almost walking backward, looking behind him, turning this way and that, and when he finally decides to face us, we see that he's sustained impressive damage. Black eye, swollen cheeks, split lip. Embarrassed, he offers a tangled explanation about how after he brought me back from the post office he set out for a walk to grab a snack in a café that turned out to be a hangout for thugs, where he was trounced by guys who were either cops or robbers—hard to tell from his story—but in any case (and he insists that this has nothing to do with the café), he is not going back to the hospital with us this morning because he has an appointment with a fellow from the Federal Security Bureau about our passports. The FSB is what used to be called the KGB, and a French television crew digging in for a few days in a little town like Kotelnich is sure to attract their attention. So it would be good to distribute a little baksheesh to smooth out the irregularities that will inevitably crop up in our papers. I hand Sasha a hundred dollars; he says that ought to do, for a start.

All day long, we film the hospital. The meals, the routine, the empty lot that serves as a courtyard, where a military railway car from the last war is crumbling into rust. The gate by the rainy highway, and the buses that drive past every now and then, their windows all fogged up. The patients gardening, going about their business, rolling and smoking cigarettes, sitting for hours on benches. The bench András Toma particularly favored because from there he could see a walled farmyard that reminded him of Transylvania. At least that's what Vladimir Alexandrovich says, from what I can gather, since in the absence of Sasha, busy negotiating with the FSB, I'm thrown back on my own linguistic resources. Intoxication galvanizes these skills, but a hangover knocks them sideways. Here's this fellow I was ready to hug yesterday, whose esteem I was so proud to have earned—and today I don't know what to say to him or how to say it, words fail me as I listen to him drone on, monotonously and incomprehensibly, in the carpentry shop where Toma liked to work. Dejected, I punctuate his litany with *da, da,* and sometimes *konechno,* which simply means "of course." My apathy seems to disappoint Vladimir Alexandrovich, who would like to talk more about Chekhov and Russia and France. He dreams of going to France someday, and although his complete lack of French is a problem, he does happen to know a touch of Latin: *De gustibus non est disputandum,* he announces. You should be able to get by on that, exclaims Sasha encouragingly; he has just rejoined us, clearly perked up by his discussions with the FSB. The lieutenant colonel in charge of Kotelnich is also named Sasha, he says, hardly a miraculous coincidence in a country where they use only about thirty first names, tricked out with a battery of diminutives. But it just so happens that both men served in Chechnya during the war, the lieutenant colonel in the Russian army, our Sasha as an interpreter for a French television crew. That creates a bond, which a few drinks have apparently tightened, and Sasha is now raring to help me interview the patients deemed presentable by Vladimir Alexandrovich. Everyone says the same thing about their former companion: a quiet guy, obliging, who never said a word. Did he understand Russian? No one ever found out or seems even to have wondered whether he did or not.

When we leave the hospital at twilight, Vladimir Alexandrovich says *do zavtra,* not *do svidaniya:* "till tomorrow," not "good-bye," and it's with the same casual manner that he hands me—just before I close the car door and he turns swiftly on his heel—a thick manila envelope. I open it in the Zhiguli: it's a copy of our patient's medical file. How about that, says Sasha, laughing, he's really looking out for you!

Tonight we're going to bed early, no drinking; we must be on our toes tomorrow for the hospital's anniversary celebration. Sasha has asked around: there will be a banquet in our hotel dining room. I have high hopes for this banquet: I imagine a total immersion in the colorful Russian heartland, the highlight of which, amid enthusiastic toasts and a whirlwind of dancing, might be an encounter with an elderly retired nurse, a truculent babushka who will tell us all about the Hungarian's arrival in 1947 and hint, with a malicious twinkle in her eye, that even though he never said a word, he had more than one trick up his sleeve, the old slyboots. Meanwhile, since our only alternative eatery seems to be the den of thieves where Sasha received his pounding, we head back to the Troika and its *pelmeni*, examining our loot along the way.

András Toma's patient file contains forty-four pages, in different handwriting, covering the fifty-three years he spent in Kotelnich. The initial entries, which Yuri Leonidovich has already read and explained to us, are by Dr. Kozlova. Rather numerous and precise during those first weeks, the remarks soon grow less frequent, leading us to conclude that doctors are required to record comments on their patients' condition only once every two weeks. These notes, which Sasha begins to translate aloud, do allow us to follow the trajectory of an entire life, however, and the one lived by András Toma, which must have resembled many others, is appalling: an inexorable process of destruction detailed in terse, flat, repetitive sentences. For example:

February 15, 1947: The patient is lying down; he tries to say something but no one understands him. When asked, How are you? he replies, Tomas, Tomas. He will not allow himself to be examined.

March 31, 1947: He is still lying down, with his blanket over his head. He says something angrily in his native language and shows us his feet. He hides food in his pockets. Physically, he is in good health.

May 15, 1947: The patient goes out into the courtyard but talks to no one. He does not speak Russian.

October 30, 1947: The patient does not want to work. If he is made to go outside, he shouts and runs in every direction. He hides his gloves and his bread under his pillow. He wraps himself in rags. He speaks only Hungarian.

October 15, 1948: The patient is exhibiting sexual behavior. He lies on his bed, laughing unpleasantly. He does not obey hospital regulations. He is courting a nurse, Guilichina. The patient Boltus is jealous. He struck Toma.

March 30, 1950: The patient is completely withdrawn. He stays on his bed. He looks out the window.

August 15, 1951: The patient has taken pencils from the nurses. He writes on the walls, the doors, the window frames, in Hungarian.

February 15, 1953: The patient is dirty, angry. He collects garbage. He sleeps in unsuitable places—in hallways, on benches, under his bed. He disturbs his neighbors. He speaks only Hungarian.

October 30, 1954: The patient is feeble and negative. He speaks only Hungarian.

December 15, 1954: No change in the patient's state.

We are on page 6 of the file, with the feeling that the doctors are growing weary, as are Sasha and I. We skim through the rest. Sasha mutters, hums, and soon he's chanting: No-change-in-the-patient's-state-he-speaks-only-Hungarian, no-change-in-the-patient's-state-he-speaks-only-Hungarian . . . Hold on, wait a minute: eight pages further along, we're in 1965 and something happens. The patient has grown attached to the female dentist at the hospital and, to have a reason for seeing her again, he keeps baring his teeth "with a silly smile," notes the dossier. The dentist reexamines him, everything's fine. According to the notes made every two weeks, however, he keeps on displaying his teeth. Through gestures, he explains that he wants the dentist to pull them. It seems the best way he can find to establish a bond with her. She refuses to extract healthy teeth. So he shatters his jaw with a hammer. No luck: he's given medical attention, but not by the dentist he loves. Poor old man, sighs Sasha. Poor old fellow . . . Maybe in all those years, he never fucked, not even once, and maybe he never did in Hungary, either. Maybe he hasn't ever fucked in his whole life . . .

Another twenty pages, another twenty years:

June 11, 1996: The patient complains of pain in his right foot. Diagnosis: inflammation of the arteries. The patient's relatives ought to be consulted about amputation. The patient has no relatives.

June 28, 1996: The patient's leg is amputated, leaving two-thirds of the right thigh. No complications.

July 30, 1996: The patient does not complain. He smokes a great deal. He is beginning to walk with crutches. In the mornings, his pillow is wet with tears.

When we arrive at the hospital the next day, a nurse informs us sternly that Dr. Petukhov wishes to see us. He lets us cool our heels for quite a while. To keep busy, Jean-Marie pans a couple of shots from the gray landscape framed in the windows to the Polynesian lagoon screen saver on the computer. The secretary asks him to stop filming and put away his camera. When she answers the phone a few minutes later, Sasha is outside smoking a cigarette and I have trouble understanding what she's saying, but lowering her voice, she repeats the word *frantsuzki*: Frenchies, and I get the impression that the *frantsuzki* are starting to get on someone's nerves. Finally, Yuri Leonidovich emerges from his office, seeing out an official-looking visitor. Surprised and irritated to find us cluttering up the premises, he briskly sends us on our way. No other brigade—that's the word they use for a crew—stayed for more than a few hours; we've already been here several days, what more do we want? Sasha tries to explain the difference between a two-minute news item and fifty-two minutes of in-depth reportage, but it's useless. Yuri Leonidovich has either made or been informed of his decision. Enough: our presence is disrupting the patients' healing process, and as for that evening's anniversary festivities, we're not welcome there either, it's a private affair, a party for the staff, and has nothing to do with the Hungarian.

But Yuri Leonidovich, our film is trying to show the hospital atmosphere . . .

Sure, and tomorrow you'll want to film me in my bathtub "to show the hospital atmosphere"! I'm sorry, but no.

. . .

Frustrated, at loose ends, we head back. At the entrance to the town, there's a six-foot-tall concrete sculpture of a hammer and sickle beside the road, while on the other side sits a giant cooking pot, a much more ancient emblem of Kotelnich. A stewpot or a cauldron: that's what *kotyol* means in Russian, explains Sasha. A stay inside a *kotyol*, that's like a five-star experience of total and depressing disorientation, and there's every reason to believe that languishing at the bottom of a pot of cold, congealed soup long ago plundered of all its tasty tidbits (that's assuming it ever had any) constitutes daily life for the inhabitants of towns like this one deep in the Russian countryside. No one visits such towns, and no one talks about them. Then one fine day, the world learns of a place in the middle of nowhere called Chernobyl, and that—though on a far more modest scale—is what happened to Kotelnich when the news broke about the last prisoner of the Second World War.

Since the banquet is being held at our hotel, where they can't very well lock us out, Alain has decided to make a last valiant effort to join the party. When the four of us barge into the dining room we find about fifty guests sitting around tables arranged in a U. There isn't a single empty seat, and Petukhov stands facing us at his table, making a toast. He sees us, pretends not to, and ordinarily we would beat a retreat, but when Alain presses on into the room, Jean-Marie and I, unwilling to back down, stride in after him. I recognize a few faces: the nurses assigned to the Hungarian's ward, the official we'd seen that morning leaving Petukhov's office, our friend Vladimir Alexandrovich. Everyone stares at us blankly, dumbstruck. Petukhov has interrupted his toast. Our flying wedge then plays out a burlesque scene, crossing the room with polite little smiles and placating gestures of reassurance intended to mean something like, Don't mind us, we're just passing through, don't get up, pretend we're not here. Our behavior at this moment is so absurd that it disarms all aggressiveness. If this were a film, the heroes would scamper away like rabbits at the moment when, the hypnotic spell broken, the mob leaps up to tear them limb from limb. Luckily, between the two flanking tables and the one presided over by Petukhov (still holding up his glass, mute and openmouthed), there are spaces wide enough to slip through; Alain makes for the closest one, with us on his heels. Our luck holds; there's a door at the far end of the room, allowing us to leave without having to go back the way we came in. Passing through a smelly archway, we find ourselves in the street rejoining Sasha, who had turned back and escaped early in the game. He shakes his head: Are you fucking morons or what? It's dark outside, and cold. Behind the misty windowpanes, the toast resumes, and the hospital staff begin to get sociably bombed. All we can do is head for the Troika.

While downing my bowl of *pelmeni* and watching my companions down theirs, I observe that in the space of three days we've adopted the local table manners. It's probably the disappointment and fatigue, but we each sit with back bent, neck extended for shoveling, one hand clamped on the tin spoon, the other gripping the bread, and both arms stretched in a rampart around the food as if someone might steal it. Above the bar, the television plays a nonstop stream of commercials touting the fairy-tale life led in Moscow or St. Petersburg by beautifully dressed and coiffed young people with predatory

smiles, who emerge from luxury automobiles and use gold
credit cards to pay for restaurant bills that must represent a
few years' salary in Kotelnich. Being hit over the head with
this—how does it affect those who live here? Do the young
toughs slumped at these tables sticky with spilled booze view
this searing exhibition of arrogance and luxury as an insult
or as science fiction taking place in some parallel universe?

Suddenly, at a neighboring table, someone speaks to us in
French. Turning around, I see a young woman of about twenty-
five, with a pointed nose and slightly protruding eyes (but
charming in her own peculiar way), sitting next to a much
older man (three-piece suit, the mug of an alcoholic apparat-
chik), who is holding her rather close. Her name is Anya and
she is beside herself with joy at the chance to speak French
with some real-life French guys. (She actually uses that expression, "beside myself with joy.") Eyes sparkling, she gazes at
us with childish excitement, as if she might start clapping. She
has dreamed of approaching us, without daring to seek us
out. She has known about us since we arrived, in fact everyone knows about us, the town is talking of nothing else, and
all sorts of rumors are circulating. Rumors? Like what? Well,
that we just caused a scandal at the hospital banquet. She
giggles, obviously pleased about the scandal at the hospital
banquet. Plus, she says more seriously, we're filming things
that are not nice. What things? Old women, poor folk, people who drink, it's not nice, it doesn't present a pretty picture
of the town. Also, at the hotel, apparently to avoid making a
bad impression on us, hot water was somehow provided, and
that?—lots of people don't like that at all: almost no one has
hot water in Kotelnich, not since the country collapsed, so
why hot water for us and not for Russians? On this particular
point, we can speak with absolute authority: we're no better

off than everyone else. Anya speaks extempore and at length, in a strange French both hesitant and fastidious, strewn with obsolete slang—"I'm going to smoke a gasper"—but all the same remarkable, if she has as little occasion to practice it as she claims. She learned it at the military interpreters' school in Vyatka, she says, at which point Sasha begins to grill her in a frankly inquisitorial tone: What year? What department? This makes her nervous, so to change the subject she introduces her companion, who, as if he hadn't noticed us, has continued throughout the conversation to paw her and to be, from time to time, distractedly brushed off. Anatoly Ivanovich, a dear friend of hers, the manager of the baking company in Kotelnich. We each shake the wandering hand of Anatoly Ivanovich, who orders vodka, insists that we drink up, immediately refills our glasses, and now that he's one of us, nods energetically at whatever we say, even though it's in French. A rather handsome tall blond guy shows up a little later; Anya introduces him as Sasha, and our Sasha whispers to me that this is his new friend, the lieutenant colonel in the FSB who fought in Chechnya and now fights crime in Kotelnich. As Anya pours out her heart to us, we learn that this Sasha is also her lover, that he even left his wife and child for her, which doesn't keep him from calmly ignoring the liberties taken by her baker friend, or the baker from taking them with an increasingly maudlin insistence. As for us, if we want any girls, some real Russian hotties, FSB Sasha offers to find us some. The whole town has noticed that we are serious guys who return unaccompanied to sleep at our hotel, unlike the Americans at CNN who were here last month. It's good to be serious, but one must be a man as well, and men, they drink and they fuck. He says all this in Russian, of course, and now we have two interpreters, Anya—who blushes, giggles, says,

That, no, she'd rather not translate that, it isn't nice—and
our Sasha, who piles on the raunch. His cordiality rising as
the level of vodka falls in the carafe, FSB Sasha glowers only
when Jean-Marie pulls out his little DV camera, his backup
for just such situations. No way, Sasha warns us: we can't film
him. The others, he doesn't care, but not him. Whether this
taboo springs from personal paranoia or professional obli-
gation, his vigilance is flawless: he may be drunk, but his eyes
never leave the camera, which Jean-Marie—using tried-and-
true tricks to lull subjects into indifference—sends passing
from hand to hand, each of us pointing it at his neighbor
and admiring himself in the little flip-up screen while review-
ing the previous pictures . . . As this impromptu film festival
is going on, the conversation turns to the object of our quest,
and now Anya repeats rumors that leave us flabbergasted.
Everyone in town, as she tells it, knew András Toma perfectly
well. He had friends, protectors, in fact he wasn't crazy at all,
it's a complete cover-up, and she seems willing, shielded by
the French language, to reveal the truth to us. To introduce
us to people who will tell us things quite different from the
hospital's official version: an elderly lady who brought him
honey, the director of the war museum who has archive material about him, and of course Sasha, whose job is to know
everything about what goes on here. Realizing that we're talking about him, Sasha frowns, demanding a translation. He
then harangues us about the Hungarian and although I follow only about a quarter of what he says, it seems to match
exactly what Petukhov fed us. And now Anya surprises me.
She's supposed to be translating for Sasha but she starts shaking her head instead, telling us she's very disappointed: everything her lover is going on about is just bureaucratic flimflam.
Which doesn't surprise her, actually, because the whole affair

is truly explosive. Luckily, we can count on her, it's just that we have to be very careful. She'll come by our hotel to see us tomorrow morning. FSB Sasha nods solemnly as if confirming the translation of his words, Anatoly has collapsed, his head lying among the empty carafes, and we, obviously, are out of our minds with excitement. Later we dance, and I'm so blotto I don't find it strange at all that we're cavorting to the syrupy sixties songs of Adamo: "Vous permettez, monsieur," "Tombe la neige": "Excuse Me, Monsieur," "Snow Falls" . . . Even later, at the post office, I tell Sophie about our evening and explain elatedly that this, this is what journalism is, this is what makes it so thrilling. For three entire days you swallow the baloney they dish out to everyone and then one evening, in a sordid dive, more or less by chance, you run into a girl who tells you a completely different story. By chance? repeats Sophie, who wants to know what the girl looks like. Not bad, but—how can I put it?—a little odd. Which doesn't reassure her, and neither does the news that, given this new development, we'll probably stay on for another few days.

And we seriously consider that possibility while waiting for Anya the following morning. She said ten o'clock, she's still not here at noon, and Sasha thinks that the other Sasha, sobered up, has forbidden her to come. If that's the case, there's no point in postponing our return. It's a letdown, but the truth is that if there is no new direction for our investigation, we have had enough of Kotelnich and its disgusting toilets, the *pelmeni* at the Troika, and banquets at which we aren't welcome. For lack of anything better, we decide to kill time at the war museum Anya mentioned. Sasha points out that it's kind of weird, a war museum in a little dump that hasn't seen any armed conflict since the civil war in 1918, and in fact the museum's collections turn out to be an odd assortment of stuffed animals, posters of Andrey Rublev's famous icon *The Holy Trinity*, agricultural implements of no great age, photos of a local writer named Savkov (one of whose pages is enshrined for eternity in the carriage of his typewriter), and, well, various saucepans and stewpots illustrating the secular totem of the town. Quite willing to talk to us, the director of the museum has nothing to say about András Toma, and neither do the few passersby whom we later question in the streets. Those who bother to answer us know only what they learned on TV: they think it's a strange story, and the strangest part is that, in all those years, he never learned Russian.

Sitting on our luggage, we are waiting until departure time in the hotel lobby, where it's slightly less cold than in our rooms. The door opens, it's Anya. What? We're leaving? Oh, that's too bad! She was planning to take us tomorrow to see the sausage factory where Toma worked for a long time. Sausage factory? The idea occurs to all four of us that if we stay any longer, she'll work a fresh con on us every evening and every morning stand us up like clockwork. To make amends for this morning's no-show, she offers to sing us a song; she has brought her guitar along. In the lobby, at first, and then on the stairs where guests climb up and down lugging plastic bags clinking with empty bottles, she sings patriotic and sentimental songs for a whole hour and what do you know: we are deeply impressed. She sings well but it's more than that. She sings with her soul, gives her whole being to the song. Her rather plain face simply glows. And she's singing for us, really offering us a gift. During the recital, the other Sasha arrives, in a state our Sasha describes as "muddled." Keeping an eagle eye on the camera lens, he starts singing, too, but distinctly less well; then he suggests we all have one for the road, and as a finale accompanies us to the station, so that we leave Kotelnich on the most cordial terms with the FSB. This might be useful, I suggest, if we come back. Not much chance of that, scoffs our Sasha. I put it to him: How do you know?

On the train, Jean-Marie shows me what he filmed at the Troika the previous evening, and watching that tiny flip-up screen, I find the poorly lit, jumpy images surprisingly appealing. They're hardly likely to end up in our film, but they might open the way to a whole other story, a completely different movie. To make that movie, I explain to my companions, we'd have to go back to Kotelnich and stay not four days but a month or two. With no predetermined subject this time, with no other object than to capture such encounters, to spin them out, to untangle the strands of relationships we know nothing about. After all, who are these people? Who does what in this town? Who has power, and over whom? What's going on between this half-pimp FSB guy and this girl who sings like an angel and doubtless dreams of ditching this backwater town for some place where she can really use her painstaking and out-of-date French? Besides, the inhabitants would be amazed to see us return, and even more so if we dug ourselves in. It would be fun to track down and report all the new rumors that would spread about us. Most documentaries are filmed as if the crew members weren't there. We'd do precisely the opposite: our subject would not be the town but our stay in the town, the reactions there to our return. A foreign film crew that spends two months in Kotelnich—that would be something! Let's make that film, it could be wonderful.

I'm getting fired up. I decide to work on my Russian to better tackle the challenge, and my companions, won over by my enthusiasm, aren't far from promising to buy some Berlitz CDs when they get home. We have all gotten along so well, wouldn't it be great to work together again? And to celebrate that, off we go to the dining car to hoist a few vodkas to our future film, *Return to Kotelnich*.

Two weeks later, we film András Toma's return to his native village. This is Hungary, here, see for yourself! says the young psychiatrist who has accompanied him. With his round glasses, the psychiatrist looks like John Lennon, and he is quite gentle, coaxing his patient as if he were a little child. But the old man won't leave the minibus. This is Hungary? He's not at all sure about that. The people taking care of him since his repatriation keep reassuring him, telling him it's true. Back in Russia, his caretakers had told him that Hungary no longer existed. Wiped off the map. So who are these people speaking to him in this vanished language? Who are these strangers acting as though they know him, handing him bouquets of flowers, blowing him kisses? Is it all just a new trap?

Beneath his cap, the old man's face is in ruins. The face of a *zek*, as the prisoners in the gulag used to call themselves, the face of men whose shattered lives were recorded by Solzhenitsyn and Shalamov's *Kolyma Tales*. The young psychiatrist hands Toma his crutches, helps to wedge them under his arms. It takes him a good five minutes to set his only foot on the ground. He has lost all his teeth, too, so he drools and spits a lot. Stumping along, he is guided to the house of his sister and brother-in-law, where he will live. They have prepared a celebratory meal. Everyone drinks to his health. The photographers' flashes frighten him. His brother, who was still a child when Toma went off to war, patiently asks him questions, probably to show the world that he's able to answer them. The brother keeps saying names from long ago, hoping to awaken memories: Sándor Benkö, the schoolteacher ... Smolar, his classmate ... And the old man, still wearing his cap, spits and turns his face away, sometimes sputtering shreds of phrases no one understands, words that don't belong to any language anymore.

It's horribly sad.

During the meal, I talk to Smolar, the former classmate. He says that at eighteen András Toma was quite a handsome boy, that the girls all had a crush on him. But he was hardly the village Casanova: he was delicate, very shy, a perfect gentleman. Smolar was a wild kid, Toma was not. And Smolar thinks he must have gone off to fight without ever having known a woman.

Smolar's version of Toma's departure differs slightly from the official one, which claims that he was conscripted. In the autumn of 1944, when the Red Army entered Hungary and the Wehrmacht was beginning to retreat, there were a few weeks of extreme confusion during which the pro-Nazi Arrow Cross Party, still in power, called for mobilization of eighteen-year-olds. Reporting to the recruiting office, Smolar and Toma were both ready to join up, except that at the last minute, realizing that something more than target practice and marching about the countryside was in the offing, Smolar asked to go to the bathroom and slipped out the window, while the less enterprising and more compliant Toma waited around for his uniform.

In short, did he willingly enlist in the German army? Smolar shrugs. They were peasant kids, ignorant of what was at stake in the war, and since their country had chosen the German camp, that's more or less where their allegiance lay. One went along with it, the other struck out on his own, that was all, politics had nothing to do with it. Whenever they'd had to stay after school, Toma had conscientiously accepted his punishment while Smolar used to go over the wall. That's what saved him, but it's nothing to brag about, in his opinion.

Listening to him, I remember a discussion I had with Sophie before I left. We were talking about *Lacombe, Lucien*, Louis Malle's film. She objects to stories like that because they show how a person can become a collaborationist militiaman—or a Resistance fighter—by chance or through ignorance. She thinks such stories are false and misleading, they repudiate freedom, they're right-wing stuff. Me, I think they are simply right. They tell the truth. She says I believe this because I'm a conservative and that she loves me but it bothers her that I'm a conservative.

Between his departure on October 14, 1944, and his arrival in Kotelnich on January 11, 1947, there is almost no trace of András Toma. After Smolar, I question the young psychiatrist who resembles John Lennon and who, with the help of the Hungarian army, has tried to piece together these two years and three months of his patient's itinerary. He believes that Toma was captured in Poland, interned in a prison camp near Leningrad, then deported to the east, perhaps to Bystryag, to make room for new arrivals as the camp filled up. The story is plausible but supported by no witnesses. And yet, Toma could not have been on his own. He must have had companions, first in combat in Poland, then in the Soviet camp. What amazes me is that no such comrades ever came to his village after the war to bring news of him to his relatives, to keep alive the hope that he might one day return. Even more amazing is that a half century later, when his name, his story, and his picture as a young and old man have been printed in all the papers, not one fellow soldier has come forward to say: I

recognize him, we were in the same battalion, the same barracks . . . one day I was sick, flat on my back, I'd have died if
he hadn't given me a little of his soup . . . another time I was
the one who found him some food, I'd gotten my hands on a
sack of frozen potatoes, and we lay down on it together to
try to thaw them . . . and I remember, as if it were yesterday, the last time I saw him, when we thought we'd be leaving
together, we had no idea where—we never knew where—but
what mattered was sticking together, we Hungarians, we were
sure that together we'd all make it, but at the last moment
they separated us, put us in different freight cars . . . without
even a chance to wish each other luck, and three days later
when I arrived at the other camp, up in the Urals, he wasn't
there. I asked around but no one knew what had happened
to him. I remember I cried that day, I thought I was finished,
I'd never get home, now that we'd been separated, but I got
home. And now, he's home again, too. Well, I'm old, I'm ill, but
I'm happy to have lived long enough to see him again before
I die. The papers say he's gone crazy, he doesn't recognize
anyone, but me—I'm sure he'll recognize me: I'll say András,
he'll say Geza, and he'll remember those frozen potatoes,
he'll remember that last time we saw each other, before we got
into the freight cars, and I'll tell him, You see, it wasn't the
last time after all . . .

It's as if, for all those years, Toma had been utterly alone.

The old man was quickly led away to rest in the room his
sister had prepared for him, but the meal and the conversations went on until nightfall. Back at our hotel, we're a little
drunk, stuffed, and most of all, overwhelmed with sadness.
None of us feels like talking; we go straight to bed. It's not

like in Kotelnich: the rooms are overheated, it's stifling. I toss and turn. Unable to sleep, I leaf through the only reading material at hand, Sasha's written translation of the medical file. And there I discover something I hadn't noticed before.

For almost the first eight years of his confinement, András Toma was a royal pain, violent and rebellious. A sturdy young fellow who fought, spat curses in his jailers' faces, scrawled on the walls the way one tosses messages in bottles into the ocean. A tough case. But around the middle of the fifties, he changed, and his change coincided with something that happened back home, in Hungary, something the young psychiatrist had mentioned to me.

Normal life had picked up again in his village and throughout the entire country. One after another, the prisoners of war had returned. And those who hadn't, well, it was time to declare them dead. It was an act of resignation, distressing but psychically necessary: the missing are phantoms, sources of nameless anguish that can contaminate generations, whereas the dead can be mourned, wept over, forgotten. On October 14, 1954, ten years to the day after his departure, the death certificate of András Toma was delivered to his family. Off where he was, he couldn't have known this, but in some uncanny way it was as if he had found out. For from almost one day to the next, he laid down his arms. He became docile. Still walled up inside himself, having nothing to do with anyone, mumbling in Hungarian, but docile. He was transferred from the special ward for difficult patients to the general ward Vladimir Alexandrovich had shown us, and from then on there was nothing of note in his file until the amputation.

He had been declared dead, and he died.

· 2 ·

While I was editing my Kotelnich film, I turned forty-three, on December 9, 2000. That day my mother said to me, You know, it makes me feel strange to think that you've reached my father's age. She said it the way one says "Christ's age," meaning how old he was when he died. At the time, I hadn't reacted. Later I looked over the notes I'd been collecting for a while about my grandfather. He was born in Tiflis, now Tbilisi, on October 3, 1898; no one knows—or will ever know—when he died, but he disappeared in Bordeaux on September 10, 1944, shortly before his forty-sixth birthday. My mother's accounting error offered a reprieve: I felt I had almost another three years to lay that ghost to rest.

Briefly: my grandfather Georges Zurabichvili was a Georgian émigré who arrived in France at the beginning of the twenties after studying in Germany. His life here was difficult, as was his character, which made things worse. He was a brilliant man, but bitter and gloomy. Married to a young

Russian aristocrat as poor as he was, he practiced various minor professions without ever managing to fit in anywhere. During the last two years of the Occupation, in Bordeaux, he worked as an interpreter for the Germans. After the Liberation, strangers came to his door and took him away. My mother was fifteen, my uncle eight. They never saw him again. His body was never found. He was never declared dead. No tombstone bears his name.

There, I've said it. Once said, it's not so terrible. A tragedy, yes, but an ordinary tragedy, one I'd have no trouble talking about in my personal life. The problem is that my grandfather's fate is not my secret, but my mother's.

When she grew up, the impoverished girl with the unpronounceable name took her husband's—Hélène Carrère d'Encausse—and became an academic, then an author of important and successful books about Imperial, Communist, and post-Communist Russia. She was elected to the Académie française, where she holds the august position of permanent secretary. Her extraordinary integration into a society in which her father lived and disappeared as a pariah was effected through silence and, if not lies, denial.

This silence, this denial are literally vital to her. Shattering these defenses would kill her, or at least so she believes, but for my part I believe that it is critical, for her sake and mine, to throw off the nameless anguish that contaminates our lives. And to do it before she dies and before I myself have reached the age at which my grandfather vanished. Or else I fear that somehow I, too, will have to disappear.

• • •

My grandfather, who would have been more than a hundred years old now, was quite probably killed a few hours, days, or weeks after his disappearance. For years, though, for decades, my mother struggled—or refused, but it's the same thing—to imagine the unimaginable: that he was alive somewhere, perhaps a prisoner, that one day he would return. Even today—and I know this because she has told me so—she sometimes finds herself dreaming about his return.

I've come to realize that I found the story of András Toma so moving because it embodies that dream. He, too, vanished in the autumn of 1944; he, too, went over to the side of the Germans. But fifty-six years later, András Toma returned. He returned from a place called Kotelnich. I went there, and I sense that some day, I will have to go back. Because Kotelnich, for me, is where you can be found when you have disappeared.

To go in search of my grandfather, I'll have to really relearn Russian. I can't say that I spoke it perfectly as a child, but I heard it, I was surrounded by it, and I still have an accent that native speakers agree is excellent. My first sentence in Russian always leads people to believe that I speak fluently. Typically, I start with, *Ya ochen' plokho govoryu po-russki*: I speak Russian very badly, and since my pronunciation is good, what I say seems like false modesty. With my second sentence, however, I prove my point. I took Russian as a lycée student, I was terrible at it, and for twenty years I wanted nothing to do with it. Russia and Russian were my mother's territory, where I preferred not to trespass. A few years ago, however, I convinced myself that learning or relearning Russian would change my life. That speaking or again speaking Russian, I would throw off the shame that always strangles my voice and finally be able to speak truly in the first person. In Russian, the word for speaking fluently is *svobodno*, freely, and that's exactly how I see it: speaking Russian will set me free.

I'd already taken a stab at it, five years earlier. I'd begun a story about a child whose father is a criminal; it took me a year to finally write it, and I spent most of that painful gestation—without understanding why—studying Russian. I wasn't really trying to speak it, or didn't dare to, but I did start reading. Rather quickly, I was able to decipher texts that weren't too difficult. Some stories by Chekhov at first, like "Ward No. 6," then Lermontov's *A Hero of Our Time*, which I took with me into the Karakoram Mountains in the north of Pakistan, where I had gone hiking with my friend Hervé. We slept in little inns for trekkers; there was no electricity, so I read in the evening by candlelight, which fit perfectly with Lermontov's account of a trip through the Caucasus in the early nineteenth century. I remember one sentence in particular, a masterpiece of descriptive economy: the mountains, says the narrator, are so tall that no matter how high you look, you will never see birds silhouetted against the sky.

The book I was carting around contained not only that famous novel but also a selection of poems, and leafing through them, I chanced upon these lines:

Spi mladenets, moy prekrasniy,
Bayushki-bayu . . .

Sleep, my child, my treasure,
Sleep, my boy, sleep . . .

I recognized them immediately. And the melody came back to me as well, because this wasn't simply a poem, it was a lullaby. A Cossack lullaby that every Russian child knows and that someone used to sing to me when I was little. My mother? My *nyanya*? I don't know; all I can say is that even today I feel close to tears when I hear it; actually, not when I hear it (since there is no one now to sing it to me) but when I sing it softly to myself, for myself. I know that what I'm trying to do is to give shape to the emotion that sweeps over me when I hum that lullaby—in other words, when the childhood I don't remember surges back to life in me.

I tried to learn the whole lullaby by heart. I repeated it to myself day after day, fitting my steps to its rhythm as we hiked through the Himalayas, but I failed, even though it's not very long: six verses of six lines each, thirty-six lines whose meaning I understand and that, supported by the melody, ought to pose no problem for the average memory. Mine is excellent, but it turned out that with Russian I couldn't manage it. Something or someone inside of me was rejecting this gift.

And here I am, five years later, with a different woman, emerging from a different library in a different apartment, with the Chekhov, the Lermontov, and the Russian grammar workbooks I haven't touched in years. Having completed all the exercises in pencil at the time, to use the workbook again I must now erase all my answers. I do it lying in bed, page after page, which sometimes crinkle, raining particles of eraser onto the sheets. Sophie observes me with amusement. When she looks at me, I feel alive.

Sophie came to live in the rue Blanche apartment after my return from Hungary. She would have preferred that we find a new apartment together, but I pointed out that mine was very nice, very large, not far from where my sons lived, and not haunted by my past, because I'd lived there alone since leaving the boys' mother. As it turned out, "my place" easily became "our place." Sophie likes to say "our place," "at home." On the list of phone numbers in her cell, where mine is now ours, she has replaced "Emmanuel" with "home." I was afraid I'd have trouble, after thirteen years of marriage, recommitting to a life with someone else, but with her I love it. I love making love with her, as well as falling asleep with her, waking up with her, reading in bed with her, fixing her breakfast, talking with her while she takes her daily bath after work, sitting down with her at a table on the terrace of the café on the rue Lepic. And doing the shopping with her is one of the most intense erotic experiences of my life. Here we are, buying fruits and vegetables together, each of us busy (I'm selecting fruit, she's picking out lettuces), and when I look up, when our eyes meet, I realize that she's been watching me; we smile and she tells me it's as if I were entering her right there in front of everybody. I love the way the shopkeepers and people in the café look at her, at her beauty. She's tall, blond, with a long neck and hair that curls softly at the nape; she has a magnificent bearing and at the same time a quality that's so open, so friendly, that everyone wants to give her flowers or pay her extravagant compliments. She is *radiant*. I love having people envy me because I'm the one she loves. I've never been this lit up by love before, I'm convinced this is *it*.

• • •

And yet, it isn't. It never is with me, it never lasts. If a love affair is possible and happy, that's all it takes: in three months I'll discover how impossible it is. I begin thinking that the woman I love isn't right for me, that I've screwed up, there are better prospects elsewhere, and that by living with her I'm losing out on all the others. So then Sophie feels humiliated. That's an old story with her, humiliation. She might appear regal, but she's socially quite insecure. Her father married her mother long after she was born. At the hospital, her mother was alone when she gave birth, and she cried because she had no one to whom she could show her baby. Sophie feels rejected, illegitimate. It took me some time to understand that and to realize that for her I belong to the enchanted yet odious realm of inheritance. Everything, she says, was given to me at birth: culture, social ease, and the mastery of codes, thanks to which I've been able to choose my life freely and do what I like, as I please. Our lives are different, our friends as well. Most of mine are involved in creative pursuits, and if they don't write books or make movies, if they work in publishing, for example, then they run the company. I'm pals with the boss, while she spends her time with the receptionist. She and her friends are the kind who buy monthly Métro cards, order the daily lunch special, have to schedule their vacations far in advance and at their boss's convenience. I love her but I don't love her friends, I'm not comfortable in her world, the world of tight budgets, of people who say "to him and I" and go on company-organized trips with their office buddies. I'm well aware that my attitude shows me in a bad light. But it's not that I'm ungenerous or unfeeling. I'm capable of being open with others, but

more and more often I dig in my heels, and she resents me
for it.

We're having dinner with some friends of mine, in the fashion-
able Marais neighborhood. Everyone knows everyone else,
they're all more or less in the film business, and more or less at
the same level of success and celebrity. When I walk in with my
new girlfriend, something happens that happens every time
and gives me intense pleasure. It's as if the windows had been
thrown wide open, as if before her entrance the room had been
smaller, darker, more confined. All at once, she's at the center.
Next to her all the other women, even the prettiest, are eclipsed.
I can feel that the men envy me, wondering where the hell I
found her, and the fact that she doesn't exactly fit in—laughing
a touch too loudly, gesturing a bit too broadly—shows how
free I am, how ready to break out of our circle.

But the moment arrives when someone asks Sophie what
she does for a living and she has to reply that she works in
a publishing house that puts out textbooks—well, they're
really more like workbooks. I can tell that it's hard for her to
say that, and like her I wish she could say she was a photographer, a lutenist, or an architect, not necessarily something
chic or prestigious but something chosen, a profession pursued for love. Saying that you work on study guides or as a
secretary is like saying, I didn't get to choose, I have to earn
my living, I'm subject to the laws of necessity. This is true for
the overwhelming majority of people, but not for anyone
else around this table, and as the conversation continues she
feels more and more excluded. She becomes aggressive. And I
depend so cruelly on how others see me that I seem to see her
losing value right before my eyes.

• • •

When we talk about this social mismatch that is poisoning us, I tell her and myself something dishonest. I say that it's not my problem but hers. That personally I love her the way she is, it doesn't bother me if after a dinner party where someone spoke enthusiastically about Saul Bellow, she scribbles a note to herself in her slightly childish handwriting: "Read Solbello." No, the problem is her resentment, her constantly feeling offended. It gets irritating after a while. I'm tired of being cast in the role of the spoiled brat who never had to struggle for anything, while she plays the part of the eternally thwarted proletarian. First off, it isn't true. I've had to struggle, too, and hard, although not in the social arena. Second, Sophie is not working class, she comes from a somewhat unusual but middle-class family: her father is a kind of right-wing anarchist who lives a stubbornly simple life on his 740-something acres in the *département* of Sarthe. And, I add, even if what she claims were true, freedom does exist, everything's not completely predestined, so what's with all this leftist bullshit?

But I'm lying to her and to myself: deep down I don't believe in freedom. I feel as molded by psychological hardship as she does by social hardship, and you can tell me all you want that my burden is purely imaginary, it still weighs on my life just as heavily. And I'm lying again when I say that she's the only one who feels ashamed. Of course she isn't.

One day, she stunned me with this statement: I'm not the sort of woman one marries. And I told myself, Well, I will marry her.

I told myself that, but I didn't tell her. What I did say was something else, and I'm not proud of it. We were at home, hosting an impromptu dinner after leaving a cocktail party. We'd brought back about ten people who were wandering between the living room and the kitchen, where I was preparing some pasta. Somebody opening a bottle behind me remarked that we really made a nice couple, that people felt comfortable in our home, at which point some idiot had to up the ante by asking, So, when are you going to have a baby? I could have let that go but instead, without turning around, I shot back, Oh no, not that, absolutely not. I could understand perfectly why Sophie might want to have a child, but she'd have to have it with someone else. Well, that's clear, said the idiot, rather taken aback. Concluding from my response that Sophie wasn't as well loved as she deserved to be, the next day he began to pursue her, and as the weeks went by, to harass her. He phoned her every day, waited hours for her in the café across from her office. She complained to me about it, and especially about my having indicated so bluntly that she was fair game.

I tell my mother that I'm studying Russian again, that I'm mulling over some sort of project that would focus on my Russian roots. That's nice, she says, but I can tell she's worried. It would indeed be "nice," if what I intended was to write about the Russian ancestors on my mother's own mother's side, who were all princes, counts, grand chamberlains, maids of honor to the empress. Their portraits, dripping with medals and decorations, hung on the walls of the rue Raynouard apartment where I grew up, and now that my parents have moved to their official residence, a grace-and-favor apartment on the quai de Conti, these portraits get along very nicely with those of past members of the Académie française. The Russians' scandals and escapades can be quite picturesque. Strolling through the salons of St. Petersburg, Princess Panine created a sensation by bringing along a few wolves. Count Komarovsky, the one who was vice governor of Vyatka, had a habit of defenestrating people who made him angry, Muslims in particular. Another Count Komarovsky, a hot-tempered man who fought in all the wars—the Transvaal, Manchuria, the Balkans—and whose photographs, generally equestrian, have always made me feel he was a most likable fellow, ended his days tossed down a well by revolutionaries, a tragic but glorious destiny. There is a fabulous historical novel to be written about these colorful characters, who are all in the *Almanach de Gotha*, but my mother strongly suspects that I have no plans to write such a novel because what really interests me are the things that must be passed over in silence.

• • •

I go to see Nicolas, my uncle. What I know about my grandfather may not be the truth, but I think I learned all of it from Nicolas. What my mother has passed on to me is what I *don't* know, what breeds shame and fear and petrifies me when our eyes meet. I'm closer to Nicolas than to anyone else in my family. He was fourteen when his mother died, when he and his sister found themselves alone in the world, and she brought him up. She was his mother as well as his sister, and that makes him my brother as well as my uncle. We have often spoken about Grandfather, the family's secret shame, and my obsessive exploration of evil and the mystery of human identity in the books I write, so he is not surprised that I want to go back over the past. He sets down in front of me the shoe box in which he has collected and organized all he has in the way of family archives, chiefly the *perepiska roditeley*, his parents' letters. I begin to examine these documents. I take notes.

Georges Zurabichvili was born into a cultured bourgeois family in Tiflis. His father, Ivan, was a jurist; his mother, Nino, translated George Sand into Georgian. The family photos show mustaches and some interesting turbans; one can imagine strings of amber beads twined around fingers. There's a whiff of the Orient, but also the gravitas characteristic of intellectuals in colonized countries. Long an object of contention between Turks and Persians, Georgia was part of the Russian empire for more than a century. Controlled by the Mensheviks during the revolution, Georgia proclaimed its independence from the Soviet Union in 1920 and was recognized de jure by the Western democracies. The Zurabichvilis were exultant. Fervent patriots, they were acutely conscious of the responsibilities imposed upon them by independence, first among which was mastery of their national tongue. "To speak a foreign language in a free country would be disgraceful," writes Nino in a letter to the eldest of her three sons, Arshile, who was studying engineering in Grenoble. And in the same letter, she mentions the humiliation of her youngest son, Georges, who knows so little Georgian that he had to resort to Russian while serving as translator at an Anglo-Georgian conference. Actually, it seems that she, not her son Georges, was the one humiliated by this episode. He, for his part, found the language, culture, and patriotism of Georgia deeply provincial. His whole family wrote in Georgian, but he writes in Russian. There is a letter from him addressed to his brother Arshile in which he speaks with affected irony about everything, including that de jure recognition so cherished by his family. At twenty-three, he played the cynical diplomat, the frivolous dandy, the enemy of all forms of sentimentality, and he considered himself "a difficult person, superficial, rarely sincere." Such an attitude naturally shocked his parents. In Nino's letters to her eldest in Grenoble, she constantly repeats how much she trusts her beloved, her adorable Arshiliko, such a serious and reliable boy. (Both mother and father address their son with touching tenderness and a profusion of diminutives.) Georges, on the other hand, she worries about, because of his egotism, his scornful and lazy character. The young man spoken of in such terms by his parents and himself was oddly proud of his bad reputation, saw in it the sign of an exceptional personality: one can sense that he felt superior to his brothers, superior to everyone. Within ten years, his parents' presentiments were fulfilled, and the most brilliant of their three sons was locked into the role of the family failure.

• • •

At the time Georgia proclaimed its independence, the Soviets still believed in world revolution and the emancipation of nations. The bloody defeat of the Spartacists in Germany changed Lenin's mind: since the revolution could now triumph only in a single country, it had better be a big one. Georgia was retaken in 1921 over halfhearted protests by the democracies. The Zurabichvilis went into exile. They spent three years in Constantinople; for his part, Georges went off to Berlin to study—political economy, business, philosophy, it's not very clear, and his correspondence with his mother is less than illuminating on that score. She reproaches him: no one knows anything about what he's doing, whether he's passing his exams or not—and that makes him even more evasive.

Nabokov was also in Berlin at that time, and as I read my grandfather's letters, I feel that although Georges knew nothing of the Russian or his works, Nabokov was exactly the type of person he was trying to be, someone who looks down on everything, a supercilious dandy. But Nabokov was sure of himself and his genius; whatever trials he endured, it's easy to imagine that he woke up every morning thanking God for the privilege of being Vladimir Nabokov, whereas one senses in my grandfather, even as a young man, an uneasiness and a lack of self-confidence that I well recognize: I feel the same way.

Georges rejoined his family in Paris in 1925. His father had found work as a floorwalker in the Bon Marché department store, and the five of them lived the life of poor émigrés in a tiny two-room apartment. The two older sons completed their engineering studies and soon began real careers—one building dams, the other working for Ford. Pillars of the

Georgian community all their lives, the family now became perfectly integrated into French society. All except Georges. I don't really know what degrees he received in Germany, but whatever they were they were not recognized in France, so Georges was limited to menial jobs. His brothers tried to help him, but he was difficult to deal with—too proud, too moody, too thin-skinned.

For a while, he drove a taxi, and that's one of the rare stories my mother likes to tell about him, one of the few things I learned as a child about my grandfather. Being a taxi driver in the twenties in Paris, that was pretty cool, very "Russian prince." In his taxi, my mother says, he spent most of his time reading philosophy books, and when asked if he was free to take a fare, he'd snap back "No!" because he wanted to finish the chapter. He loved ideas, essays rather than novels, and to him reading a book was essentially a discussion with the author, whom he admired or despised, feverishly filling the margins with comments such as, "That's all you could come up with, you pathetic dolt?" When he found a worthy opponent in the flesh, he loved nothing better than to spend the night fiercely discussing politics and philosophy, chain-smoking, and downing gallons of tea: a true Russian intellectual, soaring arrogantly above the realities of daily life.

Under the ancien régime, Georges would never have met, much less married, Nathalie. He was a Georgian, a commoner, while she belonged to the European aristocracy. Her father was Prussian, her mother Russian, and my own father likes nothing so much as tracing and annotating their family trees, littered with glittering names, titles, and vast estates. Baron Victor von Pelken and his wife, née Countess Komarovsky, lived neither in Prussia nor in Russia but in Tuscany, in a lovely home that I visited one day. Despite the birth of Nathalie, their marriage seems to have been unhappy, and when my great-grandmother gave birth to a son fathered by the head gardener, they divorced, which was almost unheard of at the time and in their social circle. Baron von Pelken returned to Berlin, leaving his daughter to grow up rather sadly among an army of servants, an unaffectionate mother, and her half brother, whom her mother preferred. The household lived off the revenue of large estates in Russia, but when the revolution confiscated those estates, drying up their revenue, my great-grandmother fired the servants, sold the house, invested the proceeds unwisely, and within a few years found herself completely ruined. Since there was no love lost among the mother and the two siblings, they went their separate ways, and Nathalie von Pelken—who although she could not be a happy young woman should at least have been wealthy— arrived in Paris in 1925, alone in the world and without a sou. Her trump card was the five languages she knew: Russian, Italian, English, German, and French. As for her other assets, she had mostly studied watercolor painting. One can just imagine this poor but noble Russian girl of delicate health, with her perfectly oval face and her hair parted in the middle, in a boarding house for romantic heroines: "Our Natalia Viktorovna . . ."

Georges wrote her letters of twenty-five, thirty pages. In them he compares their love to a garden where he finds refuge from a deafening and hostile city and a life spent hustling like a crazed animal to eke out a meager living. In that wonderful garden, as he sits beside his Natasha, his soul finds brief moments of repose, but despite such flights of confidence and lyricism, he presents himself to his fiancée as "something rotten beyond remedy," prey to deadly apathy, and subject to terrible waves of grief that flood his being until they blot out the sun, stifling all sound and color, corrupting his life. Nicolas translated and I copied whole pages of these letters, which are difficult to quote because what is important is their hectic and oppressively repetitive rhythm. Here, in any case, is a sample:

My heart has become as cold and hard as steel, and were it not for the touch of your little hand, the only thing it can still feel, it would entirely abandon even the thought of struggling on. If this heart were alive and warm and filled with blood like those of other men, instead of steely hard and cold, it would have broken long ago, spilling its blood into the horrible desert that has strangled it in a cold gray vise. What would become of an ordinary man's heart, living and warm, Natochka, if it were caught in that cold gray vise from which spring only hideous specters, ugly and silent but clear and intelligible through their very silence, their muffled, mocking laughter, their winks, their brazen contempt, these specters of every murdered or mutilated hope, the specters of beliefs forged in the pure soul of my adolescence, the specters of all the deceitful vileness of life—specters that tell me clearly through their mute lips: Well, so, what have you gained? Have you gotten even a single thing you wanted? You never will. Never, you hear, never. Do you understand the word *never*? Why are you shouting, 'Get out, all of you get out, I'm not afraid of anyone, let me see you one by one, face by face'? None of us will leave, and why should we? We're mere nothings, insignificant, we're not proud, we're not looking for a fight, we don't need that to eat you up alive, little falcon. We've polished off tougher creatures than you. One by one? What makes you think we'd agree to that? Why should we? That's not where our strength lies; we walk softly, with tiny steps. We are a multitude, we are legions upon legions, we are the whole world and you—you are alone, do you understand? Wave your arms around all you want; we'll wait, we're in no hurry, we nothings. Shout away, little falcon, shout and wave away; we'll wait, we're not proud, we're not like you, who imagine that the world was created for you to fulfill your dreams. No, our strength lies elsewhere, we go about things quietly, calmly: we send you first one of us, then another, then a third, then a tenth, and suddenly you realize there's a crowd. Well, that's how we're going to land on you, all together, en masse, to crush you. And the entire world will be with us, even those who were closest to you—they'll join our side, too. And who'll be with you, dear heart? No one. Because no one is interested in your grandiose dreams, even if you yourself believe in them. Do you? Do you believe in them? Do you truly think you can make a river flow from the sea to the mountain, make the sun move from west to east? Do you believe that? And if you do, then why are you so sad? And what about the mortal exhaustion of your soul? And that droop of despair at the corner of your mouth? Don't you realize by now that everything you've touched has turned to disaster and misfortune? You still don't understand, little falcon? You are alone, absolutely alone: there is no one by your side. Still waving your arms around? Even though you already know that when your arms give out from weariness we'll come flocking, bright-eyed and bushy-tailed, to crush you with our weight and numbers. And who will defend you? No one, because you trampled on their toes too often with your diabolical arrogance.

You're all alone with your grandiose dreams. Whereas we, we are small, but we are a multitude—what a multitude! And you, little falcon, you wave your arms about . . .

The man who wrote this in a love letter to his fiancée was thirty years old. He already considered himself a failure, an outcast, and not only because of the bad luck that prevented him from finding his proper and worthy place in society. There was also something sick, something rotten in him, what he called "my constitutional defect" or, more familiarly, "the bat in my belfry." A demon pursued him, the world was his enemy, yet he was his own worst enemy—that's what he keeps saying in a tone and cadence I recognize as from Dostoyevsky's *Notes from Underground*, the very voice of anxiety, quibbling madness, and horrendous self-hatred.

Curiously, my grandparents' correspondence continued beyond their engagement. They were married in October 1928, their daughter—Hélène, my mother—was born on July 6, 1929, and less than a year later the letters picked up at an even faster pace. Because Georges and Nathalie separated very quickly, in part for material reasons. They were too poor to rent even a small apartment, and charitable friends often put Nathalie and her daughter up in a cramped room not big enough for all three of them. Georges found his own place, in a hotel or on the couch of other friends, and his wretched jobs took him on long forays into the provinces, which he recounts in detail with bitter irony. And yet the truth of the matter was that he could not stand family life, especially not impoverished family life. Daily existence wounded him, he felt tied hand and foot. Burdened with responsibilities, he had to

renounce his aspirations and trudge through petty, exhaust-
ing days to earn even a pittance.

But what were his aspirations? What were those magnificent dreams doomed by the world's hostility and his own
character? What would he have liked to do, all things being
equal? Literature, politics, journalism? It isn't clear, and I
don't have the impression that circumstances prevented him
from pursuing a particular vocation. His poverty humiliated
him, but he didn't dream of making his fortune. He proudly
wrote interminable letters, but he never—that I know of—
submitted a text to a publisher or even a newspaper. I believe
he would have wanted most of all to be respected. Important. Visible. To exist in the eyes of others. Not to be seen as
a washout, a man fated to live from hand to mouth.

He wrote not only to his wife, and not only in Russian. The
shoe box of the *perepiska roditeley* contains a bundle of letters in French, patiently collected by Nicolas from correspon-
dents who were mostly women: two or three ladies of the
upright French bourgeoisie, whom he addresses sometimes
like a bashful lover, other times in the manner of a despotic
mentor, and often as if he were both. My mother admits indul-
gently that he was a skirt chaser, but he seems to have sought
not so much mistresses as confidantes and bonds of loving
friendship with women who were less subject than he to the
degrading yoke of necessity. He loved their dainty ways, their
apartments that, although not sumptuous, were hardly hov-
els. He had come down in the world, his life weighed on him
horribly, and he threw off this burden in letters that quickly
became as labyrinthine and convoluted in French as they were
in Russian. Long, tortuous, obsessive sentences chase after

his thoughts, break out in dashes and parentheses, and seem
to careen unsteadily until they land on their feet in a burst of
cruel self-mockery.

After the taxicab period, these letters dashed off in pencil
at café tables were mailed from all over France and Belgium.
What business was he conducting? Was he a traveling salesman? Peddler? He mentions stalls that he sets up and takes
down at markets, bosses who exploit him. At first he is determined to consider these painful and ill-paid experiences as
precisely that, experiences, the kind that build character. He
strives to be energetic, Nietzschean, but soon discouragement
sets in. Everything is difficult. When in Paris, he stays in a rat
hole on the rue de Malte, while Nathalie and little Hélène
are with some distant relations in Meudon, but these distant
relations are saying that this can't go on forever, and Georges
fears having to return to family life—which would be, he tells
one of his confidantes, "the most unpleasant solution for
everyone."

What do I know about little Hélène, my mother, at that time?
People called her Poussy, they marveled at her vivaciousness.
There are few photos, a luxury in those days, but in the rare
ones I've seen she is ravishing. Until her fourth year, as she
has told me, she did not speak French. In the émigré society
in which she grew up, they spoke Russian and only Russian.
She even believed that she was living in Russia. Meudon
was pronounced *Medonsk*, and Clamart *Klemar*. One day,
she remembers, her father took her to the Bois de Boulogne,
where they went canoeing with a French lady. The lady spoke
no Russian, the little girl no French: they could only exchange
smiles. Back at home, her father explained to Hélène that

she would soon go off on a holiday with that nice French lady. Hélène was already used to vacations spent in the homes of people she barely knew or even complete strangers, since her parents couldn't afford to take her anywhere, but these various caretakers had usually been Russians. Still, she didn't complain and spent the summer in Brittany surrounded by people speaking a language she did not at first understand. She learned it quickly and well, so well that when she came home in September she had almost forgotten her Russian—but only for a few days.

As a child I loved hearing my mother tell that story, which she readily did. I loved every detail. Today, however, I have trouble believing that she spoke no French before that stay in Brittany and that she truly thought she lived in Russia. How could an intelligent and curious child not notice that in the streets, parks, shops, everywhere, people spoke a different language from the one she used at home?

While Georges set up and took down stalls in obscure provincial towns for a meager living, Nathalie was sad, worried about the future. Her sole joys were her daughter and the church choir in which she sang. "High in my tower," she writes, "I see no one, no one visits me, I visit no one. I grow more and more unsociable and—between us—more and more tired." In 1936, however, she was expecting a second child, and when Nicolas was born Georges returned to live with his family. He found work in Paris as a salesman for Vilmorin, selling plants and seeds on the quai de la Mégisserie. They lived in a small two-room apartment in Vanves, a suburb to the southwest of Paris. Since one of her girlfriends was about to spend a few days' vacation in Nice, where Nathalie's mother lived in a seedy hotel, Nathalie asked her friend to go see her mother, with whom she had not had any contact in years. "Remember, she doesn't know the truth about my life, which would cause her needless sorrow. So, official version: a very happy family."

Official version: a very happy family . . .

On July 18, 1936, Franco's troops rebelled against the Popular Front. The International Brigades were organized to help defend the Spanish government. If Georges had not had "Natasha and the child *to take care of*" (as he wrote in English), he would have dreamed of joining a different brigade: La Bandera, supported by Francoists uniting "the last lovers of hierarchy and order, unselfish devotion, and all that is chivalrous and clean." For several years, Georges had been an admirer of Hitler and Mussolini, and he recommends the works of Béraud, Kérillis, and Bonnard, fellow travelers of French fascism, to his confidantes. He copies out quotations for them, texts full of words like "vermin," "rot," and "decadence," and when he uses the expression "the foul beast," he means the democracies that didn't lift a finger in 1921 when the Bolsheviks invaded his small country. All the themes of fascism crop up in his letters: distaste for parliamentary government, America, materialism, shopkeeping, the petty bourgeoisie, and admiration for strength, authority, will. I note, however, that no matter to whom he writes there is never a trace of anti-Semitism. That would have been, a priori, the ideal outlet for the bitter and obsessive looping of his thoughts. But it seems, and surprisingly so, that he never held the Jews responsible for his misfortunes. Perhaps, as a stateless Georgian, he felt sympathetic to other persecuted people, but he might have gone in the other direction: a man stuck on the lowest rung of the ladder, humiliated by everyone, usually takes comfort in finding someone even more downtrodden to humiliate in turn. But that did not happen.

Politically, he grew increasingly angry toward the end of the thirties and placed all his hopes for the rebirth of Europe—if not for himself, a man already defeated by life—in the dictatorships in Spain, Italy, and especially Germany. At the same time, he was drawn to Christianity as the ultimate recourse for a soul like his. This faith in which he aspired to submerge himself was not that of his wife, a peaceful, resigned, inherited faith expressed through singing in the Orthodox Church choir, Nathalie's only mainstay in the ups and downs of life. His faith, at least the one he dreamed about, was a soaring flight of mysticism, a searing pain more than a soothing balm, and when a good soul quoted Paul Claudel to him on the "reverse election" of the reprobate, on "the saints and the sick, whom God harries without rest," he accused the devoutly Catholic writer in a sarcastic tirade of speaking of such things "from the outside."

> What does he know of true despair, which is like acid poured into your soul drop by drop, penetrating the very marrow of your bones? He writes well about it, very well, for he is a great artist and thus able to imagine the "thing" with extraordinary accuracy and credibility, exactly as he might imagine and describe the state of mind of a man imprisoned in an oubliette for the rest of his days. But what does he really know about it? Let him show me his fingertips. If instead of well-manicured nails I see stumps bloodied from

clawing at solid stone and wrists gnawed to the bone by his
bare teeth, I will believe him, but only then.

When it came to despair, Georges considered himself an
authority, and it was in despair that he attempted to root his
faith. The letter just quoted, along with others that func-
tioned as both defenses and efforts at self-persuasion, sound
all too familiar to me. They remind me of a time when, desperately miserable, I tried to become a Christian, and I see my
experience reflected in his writing: the same desire to believe,
to hitch one's anguish to a certainty; the same paradoxical
argument that submission to a dogma fiercely challenged by
both intelligence and experience is an act of supreme freedom; the same way of giving meaning to an unbearable life
by considering it as a series of God-given trials, a superior
pedagogy of enlightenment through suffering.

Nathalie, his wife, spoke of him this way: "His story is
that of a man into whose life God inserted himself by force
and the wreckage that followed."

Where does this scene come from? My mother, as a child, is
in a Métro car with her father; they're sitting together on the
ordinary seats or on jump seats. He is wearing clothes that
are both shabby and correct: a dark jacket, a tie, a clean if
threadbare shirt, a coarse wool sweater, perhaps with a jac-
quard pattern. This attire makes him look exactly like what
he is, a poor émigré; the phrase *immigrant worker* has not yet
entered the language, but in twenty or thirty years, with his
narrow, careworn face, dull complexion, black hair, eyes, and
mustache, he could easily have been mistaken for an Arab.
His face is dark, too, and his voice hollow. He is talking about

his life to his little girl, with shame and anger. He has succeeded at nothing, he is a failure. Yet he is intelligent, cultured,
he has studied philosophy in German universities, he reads
difficult books, speaks five languages fluently, but all that is
useless to him, only drags him further down. His brothers,
they've managed. They are both engineers, with degrees that
mean something, positions in solid enterprises; they have
no problem supporting their families. They are reasonable,
trustworthy men. Not geniuses, of course. He is different.
The most gifted, the most brilliant, everyone agreed on that,
and in spite of or most likely because of it, he has gotten
nowhere. In French society, he is no one. No one. He does not
exist. A used Métro ticket, a gob of spit on the mica-flecked
floor. He belongs to that mass you see in the Métro: poor,
gray, dead-eyed, with shoulders bowed beneath a life they
never chose, insignificant, negligible human cattle laboring
beneath the yoke . . . The saddest part is that, despite everything, these people have children. This is awful. At least in the
eyes of his children, a man should be strong, smart, respected.
The boy or girl who says "Papa" should know that their Papa
is a hero, a brave champion. A father who cannot stand tall
for his children is not worthy of the name.

The words spring from my imagination, and perhaps the
whole scene does as well, although I have the feeling that my
mother once told me something along these lines. I see her
sitting next to her father in the Métro, listening to this sour,
muttered monologue and blinking back tears. I see her poorly
dressed, wearing shabby shoes with worn-out soles, the stuff
of miserabilist fiction, and I imagine his humiliation at not
being able to buy her new ones, at being forced endlessly to
scrimp, to save up for shoes that will be equally cheap and
ugly because people like him can buy their children only

things that are cheap and ugly. This scene is quite precise in my mind's eye, but I can't remember when my mother—if it was my mother—told me about it. What is certain is that I cannot see a poor man with his child in the Métro without imagining his shame and humiliation, and the child's awareness of that shame and humiliation, and then I feel like crying.

In the early spring, I am invited to Amsterdam to talk about my books. I usually steer clear of such invitations, but this is a chance to spend three romantic days with Sophie. I accept. The day before we are to leave, we have a big fight, as we do more and more often, so I go by myself. Which I regret as soon as I arrive at my charming hotel and sit down on the king-size bed, where it would have been so much fun to make love. Idiot, total idiot, *bedniy durak*!

Immune to shame, I phone Sophie, tell her that I'm unhappy without her, that she can still join me, I'll call to reserve a ticket for her. She listens quietly, then tells me calmly that she loves me but will not live as a hostage to my changing moods. I don't know what I want, I'm constantly swinging between the most all-engulfing desire and the most wounding rejection. She is what she is, with her raucous laughter and her Métro-riding friends, I will not change her, and what she personally can't stand is seeing the charming, brave person with whom she fell in love mutate into a cruel, dried-up, bitter man who in judging her so harshly basically judges and condemns himself. So there.

It's seven o'clock, I have no plans, the conference organizers have nothing scheduled for me until tomorrow, and the disturbing prospect of a solitary evening now looms, one spent lying on my bed while others stroll through the streets, meet up in bars, chat, smile, make out—in short, the usual Saturday night in a big city.

Leaving the hotel, which appropriately fronts a picture-perfect canal, I notice a massage parlor on the ground floor of the neighboring building, and drawing closer I see that

the establishment offers not only massages but "floating sessions" as well, which involve floating motionless, effortlessly,
in a tank of saltwater. Photos in the front window show the
tank, which is the size of a large bathtub but equipped with
a cover that can be tightly closed to keep all sights and sounds
from impeding relaxation. It doesn't take a genius to notice
that the tank looks very like a tomb or to guess that the idea
of spending time in such a tomb cheers me right up. Now I
know how to spend my evening.

Since there is no tank free at the moment, I reserve one for
later and set out for a walk. I have a light dinner in a restaurant where I alone am alone, which bothers me. I call Sophie,
who is not impressed with my plan. What's the point? she says.
To return to your mother's womb? Don't you think you'd be
better off getting out of it?

The tank is in a room reminiscent in equal measure of a
Jacuzzi, a tanning bed, and a funeral parlor. I take a shower,
then enter the tank, shutting the cover over myself.

I float, naked, on the surface of the lukewarm, slightly sticky
water. Complete darkness, complete silence, aside from the
pulsing of blood through arteries. There are buttons for those
who want New Age music and subdued lighting, but I prefer
to do without. Do I like this or not? Hard to tell. The outside
world no longer exists, which I suppose is enriching for people
who spend their days in the constant agitation of stressful
professional lives, businesspeople who dream—from afar—
of serenity and the inner life. *My* problem is precisely the opposite. I don't spend much time in the outside world (real life);
mostly I'm in my inner world, of which I am tired and where

I feel trapped. I dream of breaking out of my prison but can't manage to do it. Why not? Because the idea frightens me and—harder to admit—I actually love my prison.

Sophie is right. I am a forty-three-year-old adult, and yet I live as if I were in my mother's womb. I curl up, huddling, hiding in sleep, exhaustion, immobility. Blissful, and appalled. That's what my life is. And suddenly I can't bear it. Really. I can't take it anymore. I think: The moment to get out has arrived. Just as it does in the Gospels when the cripple who has spent his life lying down, bewailing his fate, is told: Rise and walk, and he rises and walks.

I rise. I lift the tank cover and step out. I take another shower, dress, and when the receptionist is surprised to see me leave so soon, I tell her that no, I didn't really like it, probably just wasn't my day, perhaps some other time.

Perhaps, she says. Good night.

It's raining outside, but I feel full of energy. I remind myself that this is it, I'm free. I have risen, opened the prison gate—thereby noticing that it was never locked—and now I'm striding through the streets with a quick, light step. I tell myself that after lying helpless like a paralytic my whole life, I need to catch up. To walk, straight ahead, without stopping or resting and, above all, without ever turning back. This will be the rule of my new life: forward, wherever my feet take me, no backsliding, no regrets.

Fine, straight ahead, yes, but where? To the outskirts of the city? To the sea? To the harbor? I like the idea of the harbor because of its vague atmosphere of danger. Everyone knows that ports are good places for bad encounters, with drunken sailors prone to whipping out knives, and I'm amazed to realize that I'm almost looking forward to just such an occasion.

Mind you, I'm not the quarrelsome type. I'm scared of physical violence and ten years ago, when I decided to take up a martial art, I picked tai chi chuan, which involves training on your own without an adversary—a kind of martial arts masturbation. But tonight I feel like a fight, and who cares if I hit or get hit. Of course I'd prefer not to get killed or seriously wounded, but I'm definitely okay with getting my face punched in. This isn't about masochism—I sincerely believe that—I'm simply excitedly anticipating something I've avoided all my life: a fight. For the first time, I want to walk full speed into danger.

Well, you'll be glad—or sorry—to hear that nothing happens. I settle for walking around Amsterdam without encountering any adventures or difficulties except the challenge of forging straight ahead in a city where the streets and canals are as convoluted as a snail shell. I try to get lost, but even there I don't get far. My nighttime ramble takes only a few hours, through peaceful neighborhoods, and at dawn I find a taxi to drive me back to the hotel. And then it occurs to me: if it's confrontation I'm after, then Kotelnich is the place to go. Russia in general is considered a dangerous country, and I particularly relish the idea of taking on the tough little town of Kotelnich. After our visit, I'd gotten all revved up with Jean-Marie, Alain, and Sasha over the idea of going back for a longer stay, to make a documentary with no definite subject in mind. It was the kind of idea you play around with before you say good-bye, the way you exchange addresses and promise to keep in touch, and it was hardly likely to survive our boozy train ride home. But six months later, after a midnight stroll around Amsterdam, it's all blindingly clear: of course

I'm going back to Kotelnich. Perhaps to shoot a film, perhaps to write a book—and perhaps to just be there.

I tell Sophie all this when I get back from Amsterdam. The tank, my emergence from the amniotic fluid, the urge to forge straight ahead, to do battle, and then the logical conclusion: Kotelnich. Although the logic might seem far-fetched to anyone else, Sophie finds it as natural as I do. She agrees that it makes sense, it's right. At the same time, it worries her. I'll be going away again, perhaps for a long time, without her. I'll be drawn not just to a language but to a country, a world where she cannot follow me. Not to mention that Russian women are serious rivals. She is jealous. She jokes about her jealousy. I joke about it too. All in all, though, things are a lot better between us after the tank expedition than before.

I'm getting nowhere with my attempt to write something about my grandfather, so it's a relief to drop that for a while. Since I am not ordinarily a hundred percent raring to go except when I pop out of an amniotic tank, I also drop the notion of staying in Kotelnich on my own. I call up Alain and Jean-Marie, the way d'Artagnan drums up the other musketeers in *Twenty Years After*. They are both willing to come, in principle, but we need a framework, a commission, and I quickly realize that it's not easy to sell the idea of a documentary when you haven't got a subject. I meet with TV and film people, show them our footage, explain that I'd like to return to a provincial town called Kotelnich to spend a month filming whatever happens, although there's no guarantee that anything will. They tell me I'll have to refine my approach, find an angle, come up with an actual synopsis of what will be in the film. I reply that I don't know what will be in it, that I don't want to know, that I want to make the film precisely to find out. They sigh. My project is a hard sell.

It's going to take more time than I thought. But that doesn't matter: I'll use the time to improve my Russian, and just as a climber prepares for a serious ascent by training up in the high pastures, I decide to spend August in Moscow, where a friend lends me his apartment. Sophie has, as she says and as I don't like to hear, "put in" for three weeks of "vacation time" starting on July 14, so I announce that we'll spend two weeks together on the small Spanish island of Formentera, after which I'll fly off to Russia, while she (who has told me she'd like to go hiking) should go on a trip I have already taken, in the Queyras mountains. She could go with her girlfriend Valentine. Don't you think, she asks, that you're being a bit bossy? I gaze at her in amazement. I think my plan seems perfect.

One evening in late June, Valentine comes over for dinner. I've bought National Geographic maps at a camping store and a guide to the long-distance hiking trails of France. The six-day loop I'm proposing is one I hiked one June, when no one was there, and it was magnificent. The first week in August will of course be more crowded, but I don't mention that, not wanting to push Sophie's button on the topic of privileged types like me, free to take off whenever we please, while the wretched of the earth are forced like her to vacation all at the same time. I do mention, however, that they will need to reserve spots in the shelters. I have prepared an itinerary, the crowning glory of which is the Agnel pass. There is a hikers' hut there I remember with pleasure. Downing the second bottle of Saint-Véran, I expand on my theme, The Adventures of Sophie and Valentine on the Trails of the Queyras. I imagine them, these two attractive young women, the blonde and the brunette, with their backpacks, their clingy, sweaty T-shirts, and their lovely golden legs bare between the fringed hems of their shorts and the tops of their warm wool socks—I emphasize the thick socks, the best way to prevent blisters. The girls reach the summit of a long slope, beneath a punishing sun, to find a fountain or a watering trough, where they stretch their necks to reach the trickle of water and drink greedily, splashing themselves and laughing with delight amid the faint music of cowbells and the sunshine glinting on the snowy peaks, and now they have but one desire: to lie down in the alpine grass, close their eyes, and drift off in paradise. The girls who hike those trails are usually rather plain, so two such beauties will be a hiker's dream. While Valentine rolls joints, I embroider, conjuring up muscular shepherds, and the hut at Agnel pass takes on a charge of erotic electricity worthy of the Moscow–Kotelnich night train. My riff, the details of which I no longer remember, leaves Sophie and Valentine weeping with laughter. And you, meanwhile, says Sophie, you'll be trolling for Russian models. She says this without acrimony; everything is amusing and good-natured that evening. I love it, she announces, when you take care of me.

At the front of the black notebook I've brought to Moscow to use as my diary, I've glued two photos. On the left page, my grandfather, his face tilted downward: black gaze, furrowed brow. On the right page, Sophie, naked on the terrace of the house in Formentera. It's one of my favorite photos of her. She is open, full of joy. Smiling at me. Facing each other, these photos oppose the light and darkness of my life.

On the next page, I've noted the number of the Agnel pass hut and the date my two hikers will be there. I phone that evening, targeting the dinner hour. When I explain the static by saying I'm calling from Moscow, the caretaker is impressed, and I'm tickled to hear him shout to all and sundry that there's a call from Moscow for Mlle Sophie L. I imagine the communal table, the glances exchanged by Sophie and Valentine, the other hikers watching Sophie as she rises to cross the room, and when she picks up the phone I sense her pride at being the girl who is called at a hut in the Queyras mountains all the way from Moscow by the man in her life. I ask her if everything is how I'd described it, if she and Valentine are cutting a swath. Laughing, she says it's marvelous, that her knees ache ferociously on the descents, that she loves having me call her, and that she loves me.

Notebook in hand, I look at her photo as I talk to her, and suddenly I feel as if my grandfather, on the facing page, is also gazing at her with that hunted yet sardonic look in his glowering eyes. He envies me, wants to hurt me, but at that moment I think there is nothing he can do to us. I love a woman, that woman loves me. I'm not alone anymore.

. . .

I reread the August entries in my diary. For the most part, I'm pleased. The people to whom I have been introduced are neither new Russians nor old Soviets but, rather, professionals and creative types representative of an emerging and vital middle class: thirty-somethings who read the Russian edition of *Elle* and shop at Ikea. Obviously this is a far cry from my vision of run-ins with hooligans in sordid suburbs, but that's fine with me. I join my new friends in cafés that double as bookstores and art galleries; they take me to their dachas on Sundays and, since I'm a writer, to Yasnaya Polyana, Tolstoy's estate. With this routine, I'm making progress in Russian, and that's what is most important to me. I note that the few depressive episodes in my diary are directly linked to plunges in my linguistic confidence. Most of the time, I understand what I hear, manage to express myself, and I can make heartwarming toasts; everyone, especially me, considers me a charming companion, and I see my future as a series of joys and triumphs. With certain interlocutors, however, I am less at ease. I remain silent, smiling to keep up appearances, repeating *konechno*—"of course"—now and then to show that I'm following the conversation, and I start to think I've plateaued or, worse, that I'm regressing, that my former optimism was an illusion, that my life is heading for catastrophe. It's really as simple as this: speaking Russian helps me; botching it hurts me.

According to the guide at Yasnaya Polyana, Tolstoy learned ancient Greek in two months, after which he not only read it and translated Aesop but spoke it fluently. This accomplishment disgusted the poet Fet, who'd been toiling at the same task for ten years. I tend to side with Fet.

I speak Russian as much as I can, however, even when I'm alone. I walk around Moscow repeating words to myself. I go to sleep reading not just Russian texts but the dictionary. I try to identify all the variants formed by adding prefixes to a common root. Which is often discouraging, given the difficulty of establishing a logical mnemonic link grouping, for example, *nakazyvat'*, to punish; *otkazyvat'*, to refuse; *pokazyvat'*, to show; *prikazyvat'*, to order. I keep at it, though, and above all I enjoy it. The words feel comfortable in my mouth, where I roll them around voluptuously. I don't believe I ever had this kind of sensual relationship with French.

Galia is twenty-three. She's a journalist and amateur basketball champion. We often go for walks together; she has taken me to see Chekhov's dacha at Melikhovo. When I kiss her on both cheeks, I lightly squeeze her arm or shoulder and each time I am astonished to feel how firm, how compact her flesh is. One Sunday afternoon, she calls me up and asks what I'm doing. I reply that I'm working at home but if she wants to drop by that would be fine. She says she has work, too, an article that's due in the morning, but that she could come write it at my place. When she arrives, she tells me that she has brought some overnight things. I set her up in the living room, where she plugs in her laptop; I go back to the bedroom, where I'd been reading on the bed. The door is ajar; I can hear her typing away on the keyboard. Later, I go make tea in the kitchen, bring her a cup, and place my hand on that muscular shoulder of hers, but casually. She places her hand on mine for a few moments, casually, before getting back to work. The mood of conjugal peace that reigns in the apartment makes the situation much more erotic than had

we jumped all over each other when she first walked in. We
both know what's going to happen: when she has finished
her article, she'll click to close the file, the laptop will play a
little good-bye jingle, and she'll quietly come join me on the
bed. I wait for her patiently. I open my notebook to continue
my diary. A thought strikes me after only a few lines, however:
I imagine Sophie reading the diary and finding my thoughts
about Galia; I'd never hear the end of it. So I do something
that will seem important to me only in retrospect: I shift into
Russian. I write: *I vot, Galia pishet stat'yu v salone, a ya v kom-
nate eyo zhdu, i my skoro budem zanimat'sya lyubov'yu . . .*
and presto, Galia is writing her article in the living room,
while I wait for her in the bedroom, where we will soon
make love.

Taking her in my arms, I experience what a swimmer feels
entering the Dead Sea for the first time: a change in density.
Her basketball player's body is so incredibly firm that it's as
if I were holding a statue. Except that she is at the same time
warm, alive, very tender. What happens next is delightful, but
most delightful of all, to me, are her words. For the first time
I am making love in Russian, listening to a woman come in
Russian. The sounds she is making astound me. I tell her how
grateful I am, and she's pleased.

   After two days, though, I start feeling guilty. It's just in
my nature. Kissing discreetly, Galia and I are strolling arm in
arm beside the Patriarch's Pond, where the first chapter of
The Master and Margarita takes place. I sit Galia down on a
bench and pour out a virtuous little speech on the fact that I
live with a woman in France and therefore our ever so pleas-

ant and charming interlude has no future . . . She stares at
me as if I've lost my mind. I have a relationship, too, she says,
but he's in the States, your girlfriend's in France, there's no
reason for them to know, it doesn't hurt them in the slightest, and we enjoy it, so where's the problem? While admiring
her down-to-earth attitude, I repeat that it's more complicated than that for me and, like a jerk, I break it off.

I've picked up the habit: I continue to write in Russian. Badly,
but in Russian. What I write remains a diary at first, but soon
I'm mixing in descriptions of dreams, childhood memories,
notes about my grandfather—things from deep down now
rising to the surface, things I don't think I could ever have
written in French.

In Russian, I write not what I want but what I can: my
impoverishment comes to my rescue. I wonder not what to
write but how to do it. Putting together a sentence that holds
up—that's enough of a victory. And I love to write Russian in
the first-person singular: *V pervom litse edinstvennogo chisla*:
in the first face of the single number. I love that expression.
It's thanks to Russian, I feel, that my first face is revealing itself
to me.

My friend Pavel tells me a Jewish joke. Abraham is pleading
with God: Oh Lord, I want nothing more than to win the
lottery! I'm begging you, Lord, imploring you, grant me this,
just this, just once, and I'll never ask you for anything again.
Oh Lord, let me win the lottery.

He's weeping, on his knees, wringing his hands. Finally

God bursts from his cloud bank and says, Abraham, I have
heard your plea and wish to grant it. But please, help me out
here, give me a hand. For once in your life, *buy a ticket*!

I who long and plead to be set free, I tell myself that writing in Russian means buying a ticket, giving God the chance
to save me.

On my first evening back in Paris I proudly show Sophie my
notebooks filled with Cyrillic characters. My fling with Galia,
which within two weeks had faded in importance, is well
camouflaged, and what I want is for Sophie to admire my
accomplishment. I turn the pages, pointing out to her how
much my handwriting has changed in the switch from French
to Russian, becoming bigger, more open. In a year, I will find
myself feverishly skimming a notebook that Sophie used as a
diary, looking for her account of that reunion. I talked only
about myself, she wrote, about what the Russian language
meant in my life and about my plan to write in Russian about
my childhood. It was as if she didn't exist. As for what she'd
done over the summer—I couldn't have cared less. She was
invisible.

But that, that comes later.

Today, October 10, 2001, is the funeral of Martine B., with whom I was so in love during my adolescence. She was a friend of my parents, more precisely the wife of one of their friends. She was younger than her husband, blond, dazzling, and sometimes Sophie reminds me of her. Much later, after their divorce, I had a brief affair with her and when I ended it I felt guilty, as usual. The last time I saw her she was already suffering from the jaw cancer that would kill her, but only after ruining her marvelous beauty. (Before one of the many useless operations that ravaged her face, she told my mother, "I spent forty-five years swanning around as a pretty girl, so that's not half bad, right?") I was ill at ease, she not at all, a woman who was always kind, straightforward, aware, surprised by my awkwardness and certainly forgiving of it. I seem to be idealizing her but I'm convinced that she hadn't one mean bone in her body. She looked at me with affection, interest, indulgence, and I, instead of simply responding in kind, kept telling myself it was my fate to disappoint everyone who loved me, that I was now and forever untrustworthy, a treacherous sneak—in short, my usual song and dance. Forever? If I could pray, I would beg Martine to give me a little of the tenderness, joy, and love she radiated, a love without which, as Saint Paul says, it does not matter what else you are, for you are nothing. I remember the first time I kissed her, in the woods near Pontoise. It was autumn. And I remember her naked in my bed, in the apartment on rue de l'Ancienne-Comédie. But I prefer to remember her much earlier, in Grasse, where she had a house. We had spent a week there, my mother, sisters, and I. She was how old . . . not yet thirty? And I, fourteen, fifteen? We used to listen to Billie Holiday records together and I was on the lookout for every chance to be alone with her. One evening we had all gone to dinner in a little village, and the two of us somehow ended up on our own and walked, by ourselves, through the winding, hilly streets. We stopped beneath the entryway of a house. I looked at her: her face, her smile, her joy. My heart was pounding and so, I'd like to think, was hers. Of course I didn't dare take her in my arms, but I spent the days that followed and, in a way, the rest of my life dreaming that I had, dreaming of her body that was laid to rest today.

While we were waiting for the funeral service to begin, my mother said this: The good thing, you see, is that Philippe was with her throughout that last night.

Philippe is Martine's eldest son. I felt like crying during the whole service, not just because Martine was lying in her coffin a few yards away but because I was thinking about my mother's death and what she had implicitly just asked of me. Not that I'd never thought about it before: I've suspected for some time that despite the distance between us she is counting on me for the moment of her death, and I only hope to be ready when it comes. I write this to prepare myself, to learn to look my mother in the eye, to be less afraid of the love between us.

I speak to Sophie about Martine on the evening of the funeral and tell her what my mother said. Sophie thinks it's terrible, a kind of blackmail. I'm not shocked by my mother's words, however. To be with my mother on her last night . . . I don't know whether I will be able to rise to the occasion, but it would be the right thing to do. It is my place.

The next day, my mother phones to talk about this and that, sounding a little stilted, then suddenly says that she wants me to read a letter from her father. That will be a good start, she adds. Yes, I answer, it will be.

He had written the letter to his mother, Nino, in 1941. It was in French, not their usual Russian, which would have drawn the attention of the German censors during the Occupation. She was in Paris, he in Bordeaux. It's quite a long letter, as most of them were, entirely devoted to explaining why he no longer expected anything more of life. He develops this theme in his repetitive fashion, ad nauseam. Because of the way his character has been molded, he has not yet found and never will find a place for himself in society. He is condemned to a harsh, hopeless, petty life reduced to mere survival. He wishes, by telling her this, not to complain or to hurt his mother but only to set forth, so that she may understand, the sheer naked reality of his existence. No, he is not complaining, he repeats over and over, only stating the truth about a reality from which he has no chance of escape and that nothing can change.

I am sitting across from my mother on a sofa in her luxuriously appointed office on the quai de Conti. I read the letter. She watches me. I have read similar letters, but she thinks this is the first one I've seen and I don't dare tell her otherwise. I've told her nothing about the shoe box Nicolas showed me. She, too, keeps her treasures in a shoe box, which she rediscovered during the move from the rue Raynouard to the Académie. Rediscovered? She really hadn't known where it was? She assures me she hadn't, and that is possible, I suppose. Now she sometimes opens up the box late in the evening, after coming home from one of those grand dinner parties that are everyday affairs in my parents' life, and pulls out a letter or two. Then she cries, and confessing this to me, she has tears in her eyes.

She is thirty years older than her father was when he disappeared. And when she thinks about his life, she thinks: The poor dear . . .

The more years go by, she tells me, the more I resemble her father. It's true. My face has grown gaunt, like his. And I fear that my fate will be like his as well.

I suggest to her that we do this again, that I come once a week to spend a few hours reading the letters with her. We don't discuss what I might do with them afterward, but she cannot be unaware that sooner or later I will write a book about her father. For a long time I thought I would not write it while she was alive, but when I leave the Académie that day I feel more strongly than ever that I should write and publish this book before she dies. I should write it for her. To set *her* free and not only myself.

• • •

I remember this: a few years ago my mother was tempted to enter politics. She agreed to head the right-wing Rally for the Republic Party list for the European parliamentary elections and was seen as a potential French minister of foreign affairs. And then in *Présent*, a small newspaper of the extreme far right, an article appeared that said something to the effect that, with a collaborator father, a victim of the leftist retaliation, she should be one of us, not siding with the hypocritical moderates. No one reads *Présent*, and the thing went no further, but I saw my mother weep like a little girl when she read the article. She considered a lawsuit but realized that would only draw attention to what she wished to leave buried. She gave up her political ambitions, and I think her father's past was the reason. No matter how often she's been told that even if her father had been the worst kind of collaborator, she would be in no way compromised, she still believes that this past, which is not her own, can destroy her.

I think: The poor dear . . .

She was eleven years old, Nicolas four, when the family arrived in Bordeaux in the autumn of 1940. My grandfather worked there, initially, as "an interpreter in a large garage." The first time I saw that job description, in one of Nathalie's letters, I thought it sounded absurd, like nonsense heard in a dream. What could it mean, "an interpreter in a large garage"? In fact, it was quite simple: that garage, the Garage Malleville et Pigeon, worked essentially for the occupying forces—as did most of the garages, actually—and my grandfather was hired to handle the German correspondence. For the first time, his knowledge of languages proved useful. In early 1942, however, he lost his job, and that's when M. Mariaud offered to introduce him to some friends who worked for the German Economic Services.

M. Mariaud was married to one of Nathalie's Russian friends. He was a shady businessman, though pleasant enough, who calmly went about using the Occupation to grow rich in the black market. My mother and Nicolas remember that whenever they visited the Mariauds they were plied with bread and butter, chocolate, and other rare delights. Georges and Nathalie were happy for their children, who usually ate so poorly, but they themselves disapproved of the black market and refused to take advantage of it. German officers frequented the Mariauds', where everyone had a gay old time; when the Liberation came, M. Mariaud ran into trouble, of course, but he was not killed, only sent to prison.

Did my grandfather hesitate before going to work for the Germans? It's possible. His wife and brothers appear to have tried to dissuade him. One did not work for the occupier in one's adoptive country—that was breaking the laws of hospitality. Such principles, however, were appropriate for people who had successfully fit into that country. My grandfather had met with only setbacks and disappointment. And besides, he respected the Germans and despised the Western democracies that had stood idly by when the Bolsheviks invaded his native land. He sincerely believed that Hitler was showing Europe the way to rebirth while avoiding parliamentary corruption and Communist terror. In collaborating, my grandfather was acting from conviction, not opportunism, and what must have displeased him the most was to be in the same camp as speculators like Mariaud, whom he considered the incarnation of every modern vulgarity and who enjoyed, of course, every possible success.

• • •

Unlike his French employers, the Germans showed him some consideration. Not only did he speak German well, but he knew the great German writers and thinkers. The education this cultured man had come to consider a handicap in French society now earned the Germans' respect. Did he become friends with some of them? There is a photograph of a Christmas dinner showing a German officer sitting at the family table in uniform, looking debonair. That must have set the neighbors' tongues wagging. On the ground floor lived a family that for some obscure reason did not like the family on the third floor. The man downstairs seems to have asked my grandfather to arrange to have the upstairs people evicted or, should the occasion arise, arrested. My grandfather refused indignantly and threatened to have him arrested himself if he kept that up. The downstairs neighbor was probably the one who denounced him during the Liberation. None of this has been proven; on the other hand, that version of things certainly seems possible and must have brought some comfort to my mother and grandmother in their misfortune: their father and husband had been denounced not because he had acted badly but because he had refused to denounce an innocent man. (Was the man Jewish? I have no idea.)

What work did my grandfather do? He was an interpreter, and for the Economic Services, not the police. Which excludes, I think, any participation in strong-arm interrogations. But even in a department that wasn't directly involved he must have known what was happening to the Jews whose possessions that department was confiscating. He could not have failed to understand what they were up to, his beloved Germans, the defenders of civilization against the Communist scourge. And at that point, says my mother, he became a ghost. During the last two years of the war, she remembers, he was a broken man who knew he was condemned and for whom the condemnation was the logical conclusion of a life gone wrong, the emblem of his fate.

He could have left, changed sides, joined the Resistance. He did not. Even though he wasn't a scoundrel, and I'm sure of that, he seemed petrified in place, as if he were guilty nevertheless and always had been. As if all he could do was wait for the ax to fall.

The postcard he sent to one of his women friends on June 15, 1944, begins like this: "Since I have reason to believe that by autumn I will no longer be among the living . . ."

This is the last message I have read in my grandfather's handwriting.

The last image my mother has of him is at the beach at Arcachon, where Nathalie and her children were spending the end of their vacation in a rented bungalow. My grandfather had remained in Bordeaux, which had recently been liberated and thus was dangerous for him. One day he came to see his family and embrace them, returning to the city that same afternoon. Did he know he would never see them again? It's impossible to say, but my mother tells me that when he approached her she did not recognize him at first. Looking at him, she felt deeply uneasy, as if he had become a stranger.

Ever since he was twenty, he had worn a mustache; she had never seen him without it. And now he had shaved it off.

I can't prove it, but I am quite certain that this is the first I've heard of the story about the mustache, so I knew nothing about it twenty years ago when I wrote a novel in which the protagonist gradually loses his hold on reality, and finally his mind, after shaving off his mustache. People have often asked me where I got that idea, and I have never known what to tell them.

I look at my mother now. Wait a minute, I ask her, doesn't that remind you of something?

She says no.

I can't believe this. Mama, *The Mustache*! My novel!

Apparently astonished, she shakes her head.

Psychoanalysis has really screwed you up, she says, sighing.

Returning to Bordeaux that afternoon, my grandfather went to the Intelligence Division, where an officer interrogated him about his activities and issued him a laissez-passer but warned him of the risk he ran going about the city in those troubled times. The officer advised him to hole up for a while in some quiet spot, and the best refuge he personally had on offer was a quiet prison cell. My grandfather accepted, it seems, but wanted first to go fetch some things from home. My family heard this story from a friend who was with him and who, fearing that the neighbors had informed on my grandfather, tried to dissuade him from going home, but he went anyway.

Men with machine guns were waiting for him—or were summoned when the informers saw him in the building. The men arrested him, drove him away in their official-looking vehicle, and after that afternoon on September 10, 1944, he was never seen again.

Nicolas, who was eight at the time, vaguely remembers the days that followed. His mother cried and whispered with his sister. Every morning, my grandmother went off to wait outside various offices and departments in the hope of obtaining information about her husband, and she often took the little boy with her. The two of them spent hours in corridors and waiting rooms, where she watched the doors through which busy bureaucrats went briskly back and forth as she tried in vain to catch their eye. Not daring to address them directly, she hoped one of them would notice—and offer to help—the modest lady, sad but with a distinguished look about her, who spent the whole day sitting on a chair with her little boy. When a husband disappears, it's only natural to go to the police; her situation, however, was more complicated. She knew that filing a complaint could be dangerous and would in any case expose her to humiliation. Her husband was not a good Frenchman—indeed, was not even French. Monsieur what? Zurabichvili? What's that? Georgian? Taken away? By whom? Armed men? Partisans? In the Resistance? . . . A collaborator, then.

And the little boy? What was he told? Probably nothing, because at the beginning, at least, there was nothing to tell. No one knew anything, so it would have been cruel at that point to burden him with such terrible uncertainty. The explanation that Papa had gone off on a long trip had not yet been concocted; there was still hope that he was in prison or hiding somewhere and would soon return. During the first days and weeks, the waiting was atrocious but not desperate, so mother and daughter had not yet come up with a coherent story to protect the child. The worst moment came later, when they faced having to go on without ever finding out what had happened.

All around them, throughout Bordeaux and France, there was one truth everyone agreed on: Resistance fighters were heroes, collaborators were scum. In my grandmother's home, how-ever, another truth reigned: Resistance members had abducted and probably killed the head of the family, who had been a collaborator and who they knew for a fact was not scum. He was moody and often angry, but he was an honorable man, upright and generous. Those thoughts could not be voiced outside the home. The family had to remain silent, and ashamed.

After the war, whenever Nicolas was away at scout camp or visiting friends of the family, he wrote a postcard every week to his mother, and at the end he always added the same little scenario:

When Papa comes back, we'll hear: Knock, knock!
"Who's there?"
It's Papa, so happy to come home to Mama, Hélène, and me!

Knock, knock. Knock, knock. For how long did he believe in that?

Our reading sessions have come to an abrupt end; my mother has become withdrawn, and I wonder if my remark about the mustache has something to do with it. Then I decide to go back to Moscow, to spend December there writing and speaking Russian.

Right before I leave, Sophie has an operation on her knee, which had given out during her hike in the Queyras. It's a rather painful, complicated procedure, and requires a month of physical therapy at a rehab center in Brittany. Since I'm not going to stay there with her, I consider this a good time to go off as well, on my own. We'll get back to Paris at the same time, and I'll take care of her during her convalescence at home. Which sounds quite reasonable when you put it like that, but two days after the operation, when I drive her to what turns out to be an especially depressing facility, I can tell she feels really bad. Although she doesn't openly reproach me, she clearly thinks that a man who was truly in love with her would not leave her stranded like this. He might not stay with her the whole time, of course, but he would come to visit two or three days a week, which, unlike most people, I am perfectly free to do. During the whole time I spend with her (and I can't stay more than twenty-four hours because I already have my plane ticket and my visa), I keep asking if she's all right, if everything will be all right, because if things aren't all right, then of course I can change my plans, and she replies that yes, of course things will be all right, in a dreadfully unconvincing tone.

I've brought my file of notes on my grandfather to Moscow and plan to write a kind of report on what I know about his life, to organize facts, dates, conjectures, copy out extracts from his correspondence, and at the same time tell the story of András Tomas, all of this in Russian. But what had seemed like a viable project, a labor of compilation to tame the monster, proves to be anything but. It's impossible. Face to face with the monster, I'm petrified.

What's more, my Russian is regressing. In the evenings, I see French friends or Russians who speak French better than I speak Russian, and I reconfirm what I'd already noticed in August: my mood is directly dependent on my linguistic progress. I read and write in Russian, but I cannot manage to speak it. As soon as I have to actually talk, words fail me.

I call Sophie every day. The conversations are painful. The rehab center depresses her, she's afraid the operation was not fully successful and that her walking is worse than before. She is distant, evasive; I can sense that she's angry at me. I tell myself that I'm a fool for having gone away, that I'm in bad shape, too, without her. I'd be better off leaving and dashing back to her, to take her out for oysters in Douarnenez. But I don't do it.

I stay in bed until the middle of the afternoon, motionless, curled up in anguish and humming my Russian lullaby, very softly, to myself.

A Cossack mother is singing the lullaby to her son. She uses the gentlest, most tender words:

> *Spi, malyutka, bud' spokoen*
> Sleep, my love, hush now.
> *Spi, moy angel, tikho, sladko*
> Sleep in peace, my angel, my darling.

And the most moving words of all, to me: *Spi, ditya moyo rodnoye*. Sleep, child of my womb. The mother cuddles the child close to her breast, as if he belonged to her. He does not belong to her, though, and she knows it. She protects him for as long as he needs her, the way animals protect their young, but she does not possess him, cannot keep him forever by her side. Her wish is that he grow up and become a brave man like his father. She knows that when the time comes for him to be a warrior he will go valiantly into combat and she will weep bitter tears, sleepless with worry, yet she would never want to be spared that anxiety. If there were some way for him to stay with her, safe and warm at home, instead of going off to risk his life in battle, she would reject it immediately, even indignantly. The child she cradles so tightly in her arms must grow up to be a gallant hero, *kazak dushoy*, a true Cossack, like his father.

What the lullaby expresses, and what wrings my heart, is the force of the law, archaic and universal, that governs the family at its core: the father must be a warrior and the mother must want her son to be one as well, or else everything goes wrong. In my case, everything went wrong. I realized early on that my father was no warrior and that my mother wanted me to stay with her rather than go off to battle.

But there was another woman in my childhood besides my mother, someone who must have crooned the words of that ancient law to me, tucking them deeply away in my memory of the Russian language and giving them a kind of life inside me.

This woman was old and ugly, and she loved me.

She joined our household when I was born. Her first

name was Pélagie; my parents called her Polia, and I, Nana, the French version of the Russian *nyanya*, which means governess, but much more as well: a member of the family who wields considerable authority. My parents spoke willingly about her life, or at least what they knew of it, which was the stuff of adventure stories. She came from a famous Hungarian Gypsy family that used to perform in a cabaret frequented before the revolution by the cream of St. Petersburg society. Tolstoy himself went to see them, people say, and applauded their songs and dances. As a young woman she was already ugly, but that didn't prevent her from enjoying enormous success with men. Even in her old age, you felt she was used to that and loved men. In a way, I was the last "man" in her life.

She was eighteen when a Dagestani prince named Nakachidze carried her away from her family and the cabaret. Together they lived an extraordinarily romantic life surrounded by revolutionary upheaval, until the Bolsheviks murdered the prince before her eyes. After that, she somehow managed to emigrate, following almost the same route as the Zurabichvili family: Constantinople, then Paris. While my grandfather struggled to feed his family as a taxi driver, Pélagie earned a distinctly better living the only way she knew how, singing and dancing in cabarets. She called herself Pélagie Nakachidze, perhaps even Princess Nakachidze, although there's some uncertainty as to whether the prince actually married her before he died. Anyway, her papers had been lost, and no one ever tried to find out her real name and age and whether she was the widow of a Dagestani prince or only his ex-mistress: either you believe such stories or you don't, but you don't question them. In Paris Pélagie lived a tumultuous life, which she recounted readily in her old age, with contradictions and confusions that were not necessarily lies. From the fog of those years emerged a friendship with Coco Chanel, who was still alive when old Pélagie worked for us. Sometimes Pélagie would go visit her and return with luxurious evening bags or bottles of perfume she would present to my mother. She lived in the world of haute couture and cabarets, French nightclubbers and Russian émigrés until the end of the war, perhaps a little longer: a career of dancing and love affairs cannot last much beyond the age of fifty. She didn't know how to do anything else, spoke French badly, had no savings to speak of. But she was very pious and even during her years of Parisian revelry had never stopped going to the Russian Orthodox cathedral on the *ryu Daryu*, where she had made faithful friends, including Dr. Sergey Tolstoy, one of the writer's many grandsons. Pélagie went straight from the cabaret to the church, where she found a position as housekeeper to a priest. Unfortunately, the priest was old and sick, and when he died in 1957 she resolved to work not for the elderly again but in a house with children. And not as a housekeeper but as a *nyanya*, which is completely different. And so it was that, recommended by the Tolstoys, she arrived at the *ryu Reynuar*, where my parents had just moved in and I had just been born.

My mother says that Nana frightened her the first time she walked into the apartment. She seemed something like a witch, with her black, piercing eyes, and she radiated an authority that every *nyanya* must have, of course, but only up to a point. She made herself right at home and was clearly unpleasantly surprised when my mother told her that she herself intended, at least for the first month, to stay at home with her little boy. I imagine that while speaking to the old Gypsy my mother held me tight, perhaps as she nursed me. Deep down, she must have been afraid of losing her marvelous child, her tiny boy, so beautiful, so sweet, her Emmanuel whom she loved as she had never loved anyone, except her father, naturally, when she was little. They had taken her father away, but no one would snatch away her boy, no one would ever come between them, ever.

Although Nana had lived in France for thirty years, she spoke French poorly, mixing it with Russian in a colorful pidgin that made people laugh at the Trocadéro park where she took my sisters and me every day. According to my mother, however, she spoke Russian badly as well. Or rather, hers was not a "lovely Russian." My mother is proud of the "lovely Russian" she inherited, the standard by which she eagerly judges others. It was the only treasure her parents were able to pass on to her, and no one could rob them of that treasure, which proved they had lived in palaces. Even today, the highest praise my mother bestows is to say that a person speaks a lovely Russian, meaning a Russian that is neither petty bourgeois nor Soviet: an ancien régime Russian. Without speaking Russian, I speak a lovely Russian. It's my inheritance, and I am proud of it. My accent is admired, and rightly, I believe; moreover, I can easily distinguish between the lovely and the unlovely Russian of others. My uncle Nicolas, for example, speaks a lovely Russian, while neither of the two Sashas does, nor indeed anyone in Kotelnich. Few things entrance me as much as this lovely Russian, and my so far unsuccessful efforts to

learn the language are meant to unblock the beauty, so tanta-
lizingly inaccessible, that I know exists within me.

As my inheritance, this beauty comes to me from my
mother and not Nana. My mother insists on that: she speaks a
lovely Russian; I speak a lovely Russian; Nana spoke a dreadful Russian.

It was Nana who spoke Russian to me, however, not my
mother.

It was Nana who sang me the Cossack lullaby. It is her
voice that leaps to life when I sing it softly to myself, by myself.

It was Nana I killed.

I am eleven years old. There are guests that night. While our
parents entertain them in the salon, my sisters and I are playing in our rooms. Nana, as usual, is fuming because we don't
want to go to bed. She runs after us, becomes exasperated,
and the more she does so the more excited we get, with that
energy that can drive children to do things they would never
ordinarily dare to do, as if they were possessed by little dev-
ils. I remember this moment: Nana stands on the threshold
of my room, her back to the hall, yelling at us. I duck past
her into the hall and I push her from behind. She falls face
down. I don't remember clearly what happened next. I must
have been frightened, called my parents. Everyone came running, including the guests; an ambulance arrived to take Nana
to the hospital, where she died several days later. We children went to see her there several times and were able to talk
to her. The doctors told us she had had a heart attack, and
the question of how or why it had happened was never raised.
As I recall, Nana was particularly kind and gentle with me,

as if I had had nothing to do with her condition. I had not pushed her, she had not fallen, had only fallen ill the way that people her age do sooner or later. Had she forgotten? Or decided to forget, in the hope that I would forget as well and not spend my whole life feeling like a murderer? And my parents? What did they know? What did they guess? Did they decide, knowing the truth, to do their best to hide it—above all, from me? Might my family be hiding a second secret, not about the murdered father but about the murderous son?

Shortly before leaving for Moscow, I invited my parents to dinner and turned the conversation to Nana. They spoke of her with tenderness and emotion, telling story after story. Nothing in their tone suggested any skeleton in the attic. As for the circumstances of her death, here is their version: Nana had been tired since the morning, and my mother had insisted that she rest quietly in her room. That evening, the guests arrived, and while seeing to them, my mother nevertheless went regularly to check on Nana in her little bedroom to see how she was feeling. Worse and worse. A sharp pain in the chest. A doctor was called, who diagnosed a heart attack and arranged for Nana's admission to the hospital, where she remained for a week. My mother visited her there every day. We children were not allowed inside, but we were taken to the garden so that we could wave to Nana and blow her kisses through the window, since she had a ground-floor room. Then she died, peacefully.

I am familiar enough with my mother's expression when a painful subject is broached to be sure my parents are not lying. If their version is correct, and I am certain that it is, mine is false. My memory of the event, however, remains precise, vivid, linked to something real, and the feeling of guilt it awakens has stayed with me all my life. Perhaps I did not kill Nana, but then whom did I kill? What crime did I commit?

Back from Moscow, I pick up Sophie in Brittany and we spend Christmas week in bed, in Paris. Since her leg is still painful, she mostly stays at home; I'm the one who ventures outside to buy food, and I hurry back to slip into bed beside her. We make love, listen to music, talk for hours. Was it very cold that year? Had we said we'd be away for the holidays? I don't remember now, but I have no appointments, the phone doesn't ring much, no one comes to see us, and the days pass by in a warm, clandestine complicity the way I imagine they might in winter up in the Frozen North. The bed becomes a boat, a tent, an igloo, and the trip to the kitchen or the bathroom a minor expedition, even though the apartment is comfortably warm.

One day at the end of this hibernation, we are sitting in the kitchen, for once, when she looks at me with teary eyes and says, There's another man.

That . . . I did not expect. I keep quiet. I wait.

She says: I've wanted to talk to you about this for weeks, for months, and I just couldn't do it. I want you to understand. And she talks, she cries, the words tumbling out. She says she loves me, she knows I love her in my own way, but that it's terrible feeling as if she's in an ejector seat, constantly at the mercy of my moods. She is always afraid of not pleasing me, afraid of the judgmental way I look at her, afraid of feeling unworthy. So, what happened was, well, she met someone last summer, during my first trip to Moscow. His name is Arnaud. He's younger than I am, and younger than she is, too. He fell in love with her. He had never met a woman like her. When she was in rehab, he went to see her every weekend, in Brittany. He knows about me and that I'm a formidable opponent, but he's offering something else. Not an ejector seat from an affair with no future. He wants to marry her, have children with her. He knows she is the woman of his life. He loves her, truly.

I ask: And you, do you love him?

I don't know. You, I know I love you. But I'm afraid you don't love me.

So what do you want? To go with the guy you're sure loves you but you're not sure you love? Or stay with the one you're sure you love but aren't sure loves you?

I don't know . . . It's horrible, the way you put it.

It's you who's putting it like that. But if you want, we'll put it another way. By telling me this, what do you expect me to say? What would you like me to say? Go, or stay?

She thinks it over, eyes brimming with tears, then replies: I'd like you to say, Stay.

I say: Stay.

After that, the subject is closed.

Still, she brings it up again, to tell me this: You haven't even noticed that I'm wearing a man's ring, a heavy ring, on my thumb. I mean, that's hard to miss, a man's ring on a woman's thumb. Arnaud gave it to me. I've been wearing it for three months. In three months, you haven't noticed it.

I bow my head. A little later, gently, I ask her to take it off and give it back to him. I ask her to belong only to me.

She says: That's what I would like, you know. That's really what I would like.

• • •

She is afraid of my trips, my absences, her helpless distress during my absences, and I'm preparing to leave for more than a month. I have found a producer, Anne-Dominique, who is interested in my film project. Together, we present it to the French National Film Commission, which asks for a synopsis. I write three pages, which end like this:

> As I see it, the film will be the diary of our stay in Kotelnich, a portrait of the people we will meet there, and the chronicle of our relationships with them, accompanied by the more personal story of my immersion in the Russian language.
>
> But maybe the film won't turn out to be anything like that.
>
> I think we will appear on-screen, but maybe we won't. I think there will be a voice-over narration, but maybe not. Maybe the film will be about just one resident of the town—or of a neighboring town.
>
> I have no idea, and what I want most of all is not to have one.
>
> Although I don't know if it's possible, I would very much like to maintain that openness all through the shoot. To discover what the film is about only when we edit it, when what will happen to us will become what did happen to us.

Some members of the commission find my approach overly casual, but we get the money, and the production gets under way. Aside from Sasha, always at the ready, it proves impossible to reunite our first crew. Jean-Marie doesn't have a month free and Alain, he tells me, is seriously ill: brain tumor, brief remission, metastases. I telephone Alain to see how he is and, feeling awkward, I say something that still embarrasses me: It seems *you've had* a major health issue . . . He laughs drily and corrects me: Not *had*, exactly, *have*. He jokes, he's fighting it, but he knows perfectly well that he's fucked. I tell him about the *Return to Kotelnich* project. He's sorry he won't be a part of it. Three weeks later, he dies.

I recruit Philippe, a French cameraman who has lived in Russia for ten years. To handle sound, he suggests Lyudmila, with whom he has a good working relationship. The one problem is that she speaks only Russian. Not a problem, I say. On the contrary.

An editor at *Le Monde* calls to invite me to write a short story for their summer series. These are supplements that appear on the weekends and enjoy a significant readership, it seems. Seven or eight thousand words on the subject of travel. My first impulse is to refuse, because I can't come up with an idea, and then I remember that Sophie had once asked me, Why don't you write an erotic story? For me. I'd said: I'll think about it. And I do think about it. In fact, I call the journalist back to say that I'll take him up on his offer after all, but under one condition, which is that I can choose the date of publication. That can be arranged, he says. So, great. It's the end of May, and I want the piece to appear in *Le Monde* as a surprise for Sophie on July 20, when she will be taking the train to join me and my family on the Île de Ré. I polish off the story in three days, just before leaving for Kotelnich. I don't tell Sophie anything about my plan. I have no idea that this story will horribly damage my life, and I don't think I have ever written anything with such ease and delight. I'm not brooding over my grandfather anymore. I'm having fun, laughing out loud, quite pleased with myself.

· 3 ·

At the station newsstand, before getting on the train, you bought *Le Monde*. Today is the day my story is being published, I told you this morning on the phone, adding that it would make excellent reading for your trip. You said three hours was a lot to fill with one story and you'd be taking along a book as well. To avoid making you suspicious, I agreed that yes, that would probably be wise, but now I'll bet that whatever book you chose, you won't be opening it.

You took your seat, watched other people settle in; there are probably quite a few passengers. Someone must be sitting next to you: man or woman, young or old, pleasant or not, I don't know. With plenty of time to kill, you waited until the train pulled out to pick up the newspaper. Graffiti-covered walls along the railroad tracks, the route south, the exit from Paris. You skimmed the first page, and the last one, which has the profile of me. Then you took the special insert section, opened it, refolded it; I hope nothing in the story caught your eye in the meantime . . . And you begin to read.

Strange feeling, no?

What's strange, first of all, is that you know nothing about the story. We were together when I wrote it, but I didn't want to show it to you. I told you evasively that it was more or less science fiction. At first glance, it's rather reminiscent of that novel by Michel Butor, *La Modification*, which takes place on a train and is written in the second person. I suppose that some readers who've reached this point have already thought of that. But you, you're too astonished to think of Michel Butor. You are realizing that instead of a story I have written you a letter that 600,000 people—that's the circulation of *Le Monde*—have been invited to read over your shoulder. You're touched, perhaps a trifle uneasy, too. You wonder what I have in mind.

I have a proposition for you. From this moment on, you will do everything I tell you to do. To the letter. Step by step. If I tell you, Stop reading at the end of this sentence and don't start again for ten minutes, you'll stop reading at the end of this sentence and not start again for ten minutes. That's just an example; it doesn't count. But the general idea—you'll go along with it? You'll trust me?

Well, now I'm telling you: At the end of this sentence, stop reading, close the section, and spend precisely ten minutes asking yourself what I have in mind.

You other readers—gentlemen and ladies (in particular) whom I do not know—I have no right to tell you what to do, but I urge you to play along.

There. Ten minutes have passed.

Everyone else, I don't know about them, but you, you must have figured it out.

• • •

I would now like you to make an effort and concentrate. A modest effort, though, because I'll be asking a lot more of you later on, and easy does it. Simply try to visualize yourself. First, your immediate surroundings, many variables of which escape me. Are you facing forward or backward? Next to the window or aisle? By yourself or facing other passengers (clearly an important detail)? And now you, seated, with the special section open on your lap. Do you want me to describe you, to help you out? Actually no, I don't believe that's necessary, first because I'm not very good at description and also because the idea is not only to make you—*you*—get wet with excitement but to make every other woman reading this get wet as well, and too precise a description of you would put them off. Even just saying a tall blonde with a long neck, slender waist, and ample hips, that's already too much. So I won't say anything like that. Same ambiguity regarding your clothes. I would obviously prefer a summery dress, bare arms and legs, but I was careful not to make any such suggestion, and you may well be wearing pants, practical for traveling—we can handle that. However many layers you've put on—and in this season it's reasonable to hope there is just one—the only sure thing is that underneath you are naked. I remember a novel in which the narrator realizes with a sense of wonder that at all times women are naked under their clothes. I shared, I still share, that wonderment. I would like you to think about that for a while.

Now, the second exercise: to become conscious of the fact that you are naked under your clothes. Focus on, first, those areas of skin in direct contact with the air—face, neck, hands, plus parts of your arms and legs; second, the areas covered with fabric, and here a whole host of nuances comes into play, depending on whether the cloth clings (undergarments, tight jeans) or hangs more or less loosely (blouse, calf-length skirt). There's still a third part, which I've kept for last: all areas of skin in contact with other areas of skin—for example, beneath that same skirt, a pair of crossed thighs, the underside of one resting on top of the other, the upper calf against the side of the knee. Close your eyes and take inventory of all the points of contact: your skin with the air, with fabric, with a different area of skin, or with yet something else (your forearms on the armrests, your ankle against the plastic of the seat in front of you). Review whatever your skin touches, whatever touches your skin. Itemize everything that's happening on the surface of *you*.

Fifteen minutes.

There's a moment that is always delicate—pleasurable, but delicate—during phone sex, and it's the moment when one shifts from normal dialogue to the heart of the matter. Almost invariably, this begins with asking the other person to describe her position in space ("Mmmm, I'm on my bed . . ."), then the clothing in question ("Just a T-shirt, why?"). Next comes the request to slip a finger in somewhere between clothing and skin. Now here, I hesitate. It's like chess or psychoanalysis, where it seems that everything depends on the first move. The classic target would be a breast, to be approached in various ways, depending on whether or not it is encased in a bra. Usually, you wear one. I know most of them, I've bought you several; that's something I like, choosing sexy lingerie. I love to chat with the saleslady, describing the woman for whom the gift is intended; the mixture of legitimate discussion and sexual subtext fosters a kind of complicity that can quickly lead to the question, And if it were for you, which would you choose?

I might ask you to caress one of your breasts, to lightly brush the nipple with your fingertips through the dress and bra, as discreetly as possible. Another thing I love, that we both love to do together: to look at women and imagine their nipples. Their pussies, too, as it happens, but let's not get carried away; for the moment we're dealing with nipples. As I have several times had occasion to explain to lingerie saleswomen, so that they might better advise me, yours are rather special, they look as if they had been put together inside out, with the tip pointing inward, and they pop up, like little animals from their lairs, when aroused. I suppose that's what they're doing right now; you don't even need to touch them. Don't touch them. Interrupt the gesture you had perhaps begun, leave your hand suspended in air, and content yourself with *thinking* about your breasts. Visualize them. As I've already explained, it's an extremely effective yoga technique (although its effectiveness is ordinarily put to other uses): visualizing a part of the body with the utmost precision, then projecting yourself there in thought and sensation. Weight, warmth, the different textures of the aureole and the surrounding skin, the border between the skin and the aureole . . . you are completely present in your breasts. As you read this, someone sitting across from you—but is someone sitting across from you?—should see the tips jutting up beneath the layers of cloth, as if you were wearing a wet T-shirt.

Again, stop. Put the newspaper aside. Think only about your breasts, and about me thinking about them, for fifteen minutes. You may close your eyes or not, as you please.

Was it good?

You thought about my hands on your breasts? That's what I thought about. Actually, my hands not *on* your breasts, but *near* them. You know: the palms cupping and following their curve; a fraction of an inch closer and they would graze your breasts but that's just it, they don't. "Graze" means "to touch lightly"; well, I'm not touching you, I'm getting as close as possible without making contact. The game consists precisely of keeping my distance, a constant distance requiring infinitesimal retractions of the palm in response to the breast as it moves, affected by arousal or simply your breathing. When I say "in response," it's more subtle than that, it's not a question of responding, which would be too late. As in the martial arts, where the object is not to parry a blow but to avoid receiving it, one must learn to anticipate, letting oneself be guided by intuition, bodily warmth, breath, with practice reaching a point where the tip of the breast and the hollow of the palm operate like two galvanic fields. And you and I have had considerable practice. Touché, you lose. This can be done with any part of the body, moreover, and although palms and fingers, lips and tongues, breasts, clitoris, glans, and anus are clearly the time-tested combinations, the ones that within minutes provoke cries that drive the neighbors insane (trying not to cry out isn't bad either), it would be a mistake to stick to the classic erogenous zones, neglecting variations like the scalp/hollow-behind-the-knee combo, chin/sole of the foot, hip bone/armpit (I am a devotee of the armpits and in particular of yours, which were just on the tip of my tongue, so to speak).

That makes you smile because you know how I adore armpits, whereas you, you've got nothing against them but it's not what turns you inside out. My enthusiasm warms your heart more than it heats you up. So: you are smiling. Writing this, two months before you read it—assuming all goes as planned—I try to imagine that smile, the smile of a woman on a train reading a graphic porno letter addressed to her yet read at the same time by thousands of other women and thinking to herself that she's really lucky. It's an unusual situation, which no doubt provokes an unusual smile, and I find that evoking such a smile is an exhilarating literary ambition. I like literature to be effective; ideally, I want it to be performative, in the sense in which linguists define a performative statement, the classic example being the sentence "I declare war," which instantly means war has been declared. One might argue that of all literary genres, pornography is the one that most closely approaches that ideal: reading "You're getting wet" makes you get wet.

That was only an example. I did not say "You're getting wet," so you should not be getting wet now, and if you are, pay no attention to it, concentrate on something other than your panties. There's a story I like, it's about this guy, and a magician promises to grant all his wishes, on one condition: for five minutes he must not think about a pink elephant. Which he would never have thought about, of course, but once it's been mentioned and forbidden, how can he think of anything else? Still, I'll try to help you; we'll think of something else, we'll turn our attention to your armpits. We'll even *do* something else.

• • •

You are now entitled to a little contact. While continuing to hold the paper in your left hand, you will place your right hand on your left hip. Your forearm, which I assume is bare, should be resting on your belly, over your navel. Move your hand up from the hip to the little bulge all women have directly above the waistband of their skirt or pants and gently rub the warm, tender, and elastic flesh there. A soft, relaxing sensation, a base camp where it would be nice to linger. So linger a moment before continuing the ascent toward the ribs and the bottom of your bra. At this stage, the situation might vary a little, depending on whether a second layer of clothing— blouse over T-shirt, light jacket—allows you to operate relatively clandestinely or requires you to advance in the open. In any case, you can always position the hand holding the paper to screen the one now frankly cradling your left breast. There, you have free rein. Take as long as you want and— within the bounds of decency—do everything you wanted to do earlier, when contact was forbidden. But don't forget that our current objective is not the nipple but the armpit toward which your fingers are pointing. There you will surely have access to your bare skin through the armhole of the dress or T-shirt, and if you happen to be wearing a long-sleeved blouse, you'll have to go in through the neckline, which I assume is low-cut. Whatever route you take, from above or below, for the first time since you began reading, you are now touching your skin. Move your left arm a little away from your body; it will look quite natural if you lean your elbow on the arm- rest. With your fingertips, stroke your shoulder, then begin to explore the hollow of your armpit. On a July afternoon, in what I imagine is a crowded train, I'd be surprised if you don't find a few drops of sweat. I would like you, in a few minutes—above all, don't hurry—to bring them to your nose, to smell, then to your lips, to taste. I adore that. Without going to extremes, I'm not crazy about well-scrubbed skin, and you're the same way, you like the smells of sex: dick, pussy, armpit. Your underarms aren't shaved; I love that, too. Not as a general rule, it's not a requirement, more of a case-by-case thing, but in your case, absolutely, I could spend hours—in fact I do spend hours—in that light pelt of blond fur. This, as you've pointed out, is one of the erotic preferences that place me more in the chic-sleazy mode of Jean-François Jonvelle's photos, say, than in the wannabe hardcore spirit of Helmut Newton's. The girl in skimpy panties who massages her breasts with lotion while smiling at you in the bathroom mirror, as opposed to the ambience of spike heels, dog collar, and disdainful pout. But there's more than that in the taste for underarm hair; there is also—how to put it?—a kind of metonymical effect, as when one says "crown" to mean "monarchy," the idea that you walk around with two little extra pussies, two little pussies you're allowed to display in public even though they're irresistibly reminiscent, for me anyway, of the one between your legs. In theory, I disapprove of this sort of thing. Presented with a pussy, I'm for thinking about that pussy, and with an armpit, that armpit. Postulating that everything corresponds to everything else in a system of ineffable echoes and correlations can lead to romanticism, from romanticism to bovarism, and from there to the generalized denial of the real. I am for the real, nothing but the real, and for taking care of one thing at a time, like the Indian guru who, in another of my favorite stories, tirelessly repeats to his disciples: "When you eat, eat. When you read, read. When you walk, walk. When you make love, make love," and so on. Except that one day, during a meditation session, his disciples find him eating his breakfast while reading the newspaper. When they are astonished, the guru replies, "What's the problem? When you eat and read, eat and read." I cite that example when, counter to my philosophical beliefs, I think of your pussy while caressing and having you caress your armpits, and what's more you're thinking of it, too, and I won't mention that passenger over there who's been watching you for five minutes out of the corner of his eye as you lick your fingers.

For the moment, no, I won't mention him.

Another inexhaustible marvel: not only are women naked under their clothes, but they all have that miraculous thing between their legs, and the most unsettling part is that they have it all the time, even without thinking about it. For a long while, I wondered how they managed; in their place, I felt, I'd be masturbating nonstop, or at least considering it. One of the things about you that pleased me right away is the impression that it's on your mind more than it is on the average woman's. Somebody once told you you wore your pussy on your face; you hesitated over how to take that, as a compliment or a vulgarity, and opted in the end for the compliment. I agree. I like it that looking at a woman's face, one can imagine her coming. Some women, it's just about impossible, there's no hint of abandonment, but you, watching you move, smile, talk about something entirely unrelated, one guesses right away that you love to come. One wants immediately to know what you're like when you do and I'm here to say that, well, one is not disappointed. Although it isn't really in the tone of this piece, I'll allow myself a sentimental aside: I have never enjoyed so much seeing someone come, and when I say "seeing," of course, it isn't just seeing. I imagine you reading this: your smile, your pride, the pride of a well-laid woman, equaled only by that of the man who lays a well-laid woman. You can shove your thoughts into your panties now. But wait, don't be in a rush. Try the pink elephant trick. Don't think yet about my dick, or my tongue, or my fingers, or yours; think about your pussy all alone, the way it is now between your legs. It's truly difficult, what I'm asking of you here, but the idea is to think of your pussy as if you were not thinking of it. People who meditate a lot say that the goal—and illumination is strictly a bonus—is to observe one's breathing without changing it in any way. To be there as if one were not there. Try to imagine your pussy from the inside, as if it were simply between your legs and you were thinking about something else, as if you were busy working or reading an article on the new members of the European Community. Try to remain neutral, indifferent, yet consider every sensation. The way the fabric of your panties compresses your pubic hair. The labia majora. The labia minora. The contact of the folds, one against another. Close your eyes.

Ah? You're wet? I suspected that. Very wet? I admit that the exercise was difficult, but, well, wet though you may be, your pussy isn't open. You're sitting on a train, wearing panties, and haven't yet slipped in a finger, so it can't be open. Listen, now we'll see if it's possible to spread those interior labia a little bit, all by themselves. I don't know. I don't think so. You have excellent vaginal muscles but they don't control the opening of the labia; what you can do, on the other hand, is grip and relax, grip and relax, as hard as you can, as if I were inside you.

There, I skipped ahead a bit, I went faster than I intended, but it would be unkind to rewind. You therefore have the right to think about my dick. But without pouncing on it. Take your time. I'm sure all you can think about is thrusting it inside you up to the hilt and masturbating at the same time, but you'll have to be patient, to follow my rhythm, which is basically always to slow down, delay, hold back. I was a premature ejaculator in my youth; it's an awful experience that convinced me that the greatest pleasure is to be always on the verge of pleasure. That's where I love to be, precisely on the verge, and I love to keep pushing back that edge, always sharpening the point a little more. At first you found that a bit disturbing; now, no. Now you love it when, before licking you, I caress your clitoris for a long time with just the warmth of my breath, by breathing close by, drawing out the wait for the first lick. You love it when, before going in all the way, I stay for a long time with the head right at the entrance. You love to tell me, looking straight into my eyes, that you love my dick in your pussy; you love to say it over and over and that's what you'll do now. There, on the train. You'll say, "I want your dick in my pussy," in a very low voice, obviously, but say it, don't just think it, form the sounds with your lips. Pronounce these words as loudly as you can without the other passengers hearing you. Seek the sound threshold and draw as close as you can without crossing it. You've seen someone saying the rosary. Do the same thing, the basic mantra being "I want your dick in my pussy." All variations are welcome and I expect you to give carte blanche to your imagination. Go to it. Until Poitiers, which shouldn't be too far now, if my calculations are correct.

Meanwhile, I'm thinking about your fellow passengers. True, I'm of two minds about these people, whom I'm tempted to put to use but who are dangerously outside my control. I'm aware, also, that this letter seems like both a delightful object of pure pleasure and the disturbing device of a confirmed control freak. If everything has gone as planned, you are reading this page on Saturday, July 20, at around 4:15, the train having just left the station after its stop in Poitiers. In fact, I wrote this page at the end of May, before leaving to shoot my film in Russia. When I asked the people at *Le Monde* early on to fix the publication date, they didn't understand why it was so important to me, so I told them what I told you: that it was a story of anticipation and that to anticipate I needed a precise target. That was true. I knew I'd be with my sons on the Île de Ré in mid-July and that you would arrive there a week later. The special section appears on Saturdays, and I knew you would have to take the train today, on this particular Saturday—but not before 2:00, when *Le Monde* would definitely be on the newsstands. I was careful to reserve your ticket in advance, hoping it would be difficult to change it during the holiday period. So we can say that, like the OCD veteran I am, I stacked the deck in my favor. Which doesn't prevent me from knowing, like every good obsessive, that I'm playing against chance, the unexpected, everything that can foul up the best of plans. An unbearable thought.

Writing this brought me immense pleasure but also agonies of worry—which doubtless heightened the pleasure. I saw time stretching from point A to point B: at A, I send the piece in to *Le Monde*, it's out of my hands, the die is cast— while B is the end of the line, you've finished reading, I'm waiting for you on the station platform, you are wild with desire and gratitude, everything has gone exactly as I'd dreamed. Between A, the end of May, and B, 5:45 on July 20, 2002, anything can happen, and trust me, I've imagined everything, from hapless screwups to hopeless catastrophes. That the trains would go on strike, or the newspapers. That you'd miss the train or it would jump the tracks. That you would no longer love me, or I you, that we'd no longer be together and my lighthearted scheme would become something sad or, even worse, embarrassing.

Only a man immune to superstition could plan his pleasure in such detail without fear of defying the gods. Imagine: you're a god, and a mortal comes along to tell you, Here's the thing—today, Thursday, May 23, I've decided that on Saturday, July 20, on the 2:45 train to La Rochelle, the woman I am in love with will masturbate according to my instructions and reach orgasm between Niort and Surgères. Now, how would you take that? I think you'd think, Well he's got some nerve. Cute, but some nerve. You'd say to yourself that a lesson was in order. Not the lightning bolt that zaps the reckless fool, nor the liver-devouring vulture, but still, a lesson. What kind of lesson? Myself, I believe that in your place— you're a god, remember—I'd try to arrange something along the lines of a Lubitsch film, where the audience always gets what it wants, but never in the way it wanted. And to give this overworked setup the unexpected twist that both foils and fulfills expectations, Lubitsch would call on one of your fellow passengers. Who might be, for example, deaf. Can you imagine an attractive, young deaf woman who for ten minutes has been slyly watching the lips of the woman next to her on the train as she whispers ecstatically, her eyes closed, "I want your dick in my pussy"? To develop the scene, there's a wide range of possibilities, from a light, graceful moment of girlish confusion to the most extravagant sexual encounter. Now, if the idea is to teach me a lesson by nudging your sexual pleasure beyond my control and diverting it toward an unexpected beneficiary, the attractive deaf girl should morph into an attractive deaf *boy*—but that, as you can again imagine, thrills me considerably less. Let's move on, especially since I've thought of another possible scenario.

In real life, writers might sometimes see strangers reading their books in public places, but that doesn't happen often; it's not something you can count on. Quite a few passengers on this train certainly do read *Le Monde*, however. Let's do the math. France has sixty million inhabitants; *Le Monde*'s print run is 600,000 copies; its readers thus represent 1 percent of the population. The proportion of readers on the Paris–La Rochelle high-speed train on a Saturday afternoon in July must be much higher, and I'd be tempted to jump it up to 10 percent. So we get roughly 10 percent of the passengers, most of whom—because today they have the time—will at least take a look at the short-story supplement, just to see. I don't want to seem immodest, but the chances of these just-taking-a-look passengers reading all the way to the end hover in my opinion around 100 percent, for the simple reason that when there's ass involved, people read every last page; that's how it is. So about 10 percent of your fellow passengers are reading, have read, or will read these instructions during the three hours you will all spend on the train. That's a completely different order of probability than that of having a cute deaf woman sitting next to you. There's a one in ten chance—I'm probably exaggerating but not by much—that the person beside you is at this moment reading the same thing you are. And if not the person next to you, someone close by.

Don't you think the moment has come to go to the bar car? Roll up the section, tuck it into your purse, rise, and start making your way through the train. I'll wait for you in the bar. Don't take the story out again until you get there.

• • •

So. You stood in line, ordered a coffee or mineral water. There's a crowd in the bar car. You managed to find a place on a stool, though, and spread the section out in front of you on the gray plastic counter, and now you're reading again. While you were moving through the cars, did the same idea I had occur to you? Someone else on this train is reading this story. He reads, perhaps he smiles while reading, perhaps he thinks, Hey, this is a hoot, what's gotten into those guys at *Le Monde*? And then he does a double take on the 2:45 Paris–La Rochelle high-speed train on Saturday, July 20. Eyebrows raised, he looks up from his paper, has a little moment of . . . vertigo would be too strong, but confusion, let's say. He rereads the sentence and thinks: Wait a minute, that's my train! And a moment later: Then the girl, the one he wrote this for, she's here, too, on this train! Put yourself in this passenger's place, man or woman. Wouldn't you find that exciting? Wouldn't you try to find her, this girl? You have very little physical description, I was careful about that, but you do have a clue, and quite a precise one: you know that between Poitiers and Niort, i.e., between 4:15 and 4:45, she should be in the bar car. So what do you do? You go there. Me, anyway, I'd go. Ladies, gentlemen, be my guests. Don't sit around twiddling your thumbs: take your copy of *Le Monde* to show you're playing along and head for the bar.

I don't know if you've shown up here fully aware of the implications or whether you're realizing them only now, and I don't know what you think about this whole situation personally, but I love it. What I like is that unlike the scene with the cute deaf woman, it has nothing to do with chance but proceeds automatically from the mechanism already set in motion. If the story has been published on the appointed day, if the train is indeed running that day, if the bar car is not closed, then it's certain—or I give up—that a few of the men and, I hope, women on the train will turn up on time, meaning *now*, hoping to identify you. They are there, around you. I don't know them, but I summoned them two months ago and here they are. How's that for performative literature!

Even though you are something of an exhibitionist, I imagine that you have now buried your nose in the paper and don't dare look up. Look up a little. You are facing the window. If it were nighttime or if the train were streaking through a tunnel, the car interior would be reflected in the window and you could see *them* without turning around, but there is no tunnel, no reflection, only the dreary landscape of the Vendée, water towers, low houses, towpaths, beneath a sun still high in the sky.

And *them*, behind you.

Come on. No use keeping your head in the sand.

Take a deep breath, then turn around.

Innocently, casually.

Go on.

They are all here.

Men, women. They're trying to look innocent, too, but several are holding *Le Monde*.

Are they looking at you?

I'm sure they're looking at you. I'm sure they've been looking at you for several minutes; didn't you feel their eyes on your back? They were waiting for you to turn around, and now you're facing them, it's as if you were naked in front of them.

Do you think this has gone too far? That things are beginning to resemble a scene in a horror movie? The heroine believes she has taken refuge in a safe place, a crowded bar, when a seemingly harmless detail suddenly reveals that the people around her, also seemingly harmless, are all part of the conspiracy. Spies, zombies, alien invaders, it doesn't matter—they all read *Le Monde*, that's what identifies them, and now they surround her, closing in . . .

Do you feel caught in a trap?

Just joking. That's not where this story is going. Think about it. First off, you are not the only suspect. I'm sure that other women in the bar are carrying prominently displayed copies of *Le Monde*. How many? One, four, eleven? Three or more I'll consider a real success. Not only did I ask these women to come here—as many of them as possible and preferably alone, so as not to cede the terrain to a horde of men—I also asked for something else. Well, I'm asking them now, actually, but I strongly suspect that, unlike you, they have not strictly followed the story's instructions, so they have reached this paragraph ahead of you. This is what I ask of them: if you have read this letter and found it arousing, even just a little, then play the game; during the last hour of the trip, between Niort and La Rochelle, behave as if you were the intended recipient. The role is simple: read *Le Monde* while drinking coffee or mineral water in the bar car and pay attention to what is happening around you. Simple, yes, but it can be extremely sexy. I'm counting on your help.

There, everything is ready. I'll go over the rules again. In the bar car, a certain number of men and women have read this story and are, with various motives, all essentially sexual, trying to identify the heroine. That heroine is you, but only you know this, and the other women are pretending to be you. The heroine has been achingly wet now for two hours, and the other women are following suit, but unlike the heroine they have read the whole story and therefore know what happens next.

I do love this situation. I love it that thanks to *Le Monde* it *really* exists, but I no longer see how to control it. Too many characters, too many variables. So I'm no longer in charge. I throw up my hands. I continue to imagine things, of course: a ballet of glances, discreet smiles, a wink among "us women"; a stifled giggle, perhaps a peal of laughter, possibly some extreme acting out or maybe a scandal, why not? Someone who says loud and clear that this is disgusting—and that he doesn't buy Hubert Beuve-Méry's paper to read such garbage; perhaps a sharp, sophisticated exchange along the lines of I-know-that-you-know-that-I-know or maybe two strangers who come to the bar and then leave together. I wonder what the passengers who haven't read *Le Monde* are noticing. Anything? Do they sense that something is going on without knowing what? I wonder, I imagine, but I no longer decide: now I let everyone improvise his or her individual role, and I'm awaiting your arrival in an hour so you can tell me all about it in bed and later over a big platter of seafood, or maybe the other way around. You see, I'm not *that* bossy.

There are forty-five minutes left to the trip, and about a thousand words left for my story. Eight thousand is my limit. The other female readers of *Le Monde* already know what can still happen, outside of everything beyond my control, and you, naturally, have your suspicions. You saw one woman get up a few minutes ago, watched her leave, and noticed others were watching her, too. They all know what it means and she knows they know. It means: I am going to go get myself off.

So the woman leaves the bar, heading for the closest restroom. Occupied. She waits a minute. Thinking she hears the sound of panting despite the racket of the train, she glues her ear to the door and smiles. A man standing nearby in the corridor looks at her in some surprise; he's holding a different newspaper, and she thinks, Poor guy, he has no idea what he's missing. Finally the restroom door opens; a woman emerges with *Le Monde* sticking out of her purse. The two women exchange a look; the one leaving the restroom has come hard, the woman waiting sees it in her face and that excites her, so much that she boldly asks, "Was it good?" The first replies, very convincingly, "Yes, it was," leaving the guy who doesn't have *Le Monde*, poor fellow, to think that something really strange is going on on this train. The waiting woman goes in, locks the door. She looks at herself in the large mirror on the wall behind the sink, which allows her, when she lifts up her dress—or pulls down her pants—to get a good view of what she is about to do. She takes off her wet panties, raises one leg, and places a foot on the edge of the sink; with one hand she grips the grab bar for balance and begins touching her pussy with the other. She goes for it, fingers in, too late for dainty refinements, she wants it too much and has been ready for at least an hour now. She uses two fingers right away, shoves them in, it's dripping wet and gets wetter as she watches her hand go at her pussy in the mirror, fingers working away. Or perhaps she goes about it differently, starts with her clitoris: each woman has her own technique. I love that she's showing hers to me, and here I'm projecting yours on her; that

doesn't matter. Maybe this is the first time she has mastur-
bated standing in a train restroom, and it's certainly the first
time she's done it knowing that people outside the door
know what she's doing. It's as if she were doing it in front of
everyone; she looks at her pussy in the mirror as if everybody
were looking at it, as if they were watching her fingers slid-
ing between her wet labia; it's incredibly exciting. She thinks
about you, whom she hasn't identified for certain; still, she
has someone in mind: the tall blonde with the long neck, slender waist, and ample hips, the one mentioned early in the story.
Perhaps that was to put people off the scent, but maybe not,
and there was one girl who really looked the part. The woman
thinks that, given what time it is, you are probably in a restroom yourself, in another car, doing the same thing; she
imagines your fingers thrusting through your blond bush and
even though she's not particularly interested in girls, at this
point she'd go for that, really enjoy it. She's seeing her own
fingers in her pussy, and yours in yours, and the fingers of
other women in their pussies, all getting themselves off at the
same time on the same train, all dripping wet, all closing
in now on their clitorises—and all because some guy, two
months earlier, decided to take advantage of a commission
from *Le Monde* to whip himself up a little erotic scenario
with his girlfriend. Now she's there, her fingers are on her clitoris, she spreads the labia to get at it, to see it better in the
mirror over the sink, and let's say she does it the way you do
at this point, fingertips, index and middle fingers, rubbing
harder and harder; she'd love to caress a nipple with the other
hand, but she has to keep hold of the bar to steady herself. She
looks at her face—it's rare to see oneself about to come—she
wants to cry out, it's building fast, she knows there is someone
outside the door, she knows she's breathing hard, making

noise while someone's listening, but she's so close now, she wants to shout, she wants to say yes, she wants to shout yes!— she holds back from shouting yes when she comes but you hear her anyway, you are outside the door, you say yes, too, yes, the train's pulling in to Surgères now, at last it's your turn.

Back in your seat, just before the train arrives in La Rochelle, you read the last paragraph, in which I invite all the men and women who made the trip, on the train or elsewhere, to tell me about their experiences. Perhaps that will lead to a sequel, which will be not only performative but interactive. What could be better than that? I even give them my e-mail address: emmanuelcarrere@yahoo.fr. You think I've got some nerve. You're right, I've got some nerve. I'm waiting for you on the platform.

· 4 ·

All the same, says Anne-Dominique on the eve of our departure for Kotelnich, it would be nice if . . . not that you knew in advance what you want to do—I know you like not knowing—but if you could settle just one thing: Are you going to be in the film? When the train pulls in to Kotelnich station, is Philippe supposed to get off first with the camera and film your arrival, or do you want the camera to be your eyes?

I didn't know what to say. It's strange: ever since I thought up this project, I've talked a lot about the film, usually with enthusiasm, and I've jotted down ideas, found the money, put together a crew, all without addressing that simple question. And now, on the night train from Moscow, the question begins to bother me. Like the man with the beard who's asked whether he sleeps with it over or under the covers, I toss and turn in my berth, uneasy about the film, taking little comfort from the phrases I've been trotting out: Don't anticipate events. Just be alert. Let things happen.

What if nothing happens?

What if I can't put a film together? Clearly, that will

depend on my ability to speak Russian, and that's the only thing that really worries me. I've spent two months in Moscow this year, doing grammar exercises every day, reading Russian, and even keeping a kind of diary in Russian, yet— despite my excellent ear—I'm getting nowhere. I can just about read and write but can barely speak at all. I'm counting on a breakthrough, however: one day, suddenly, something will click and everything I've patiently filed away but can't find when I need it will become accessible. I will speak Russian. Maybe this will happen in Kotelnich. And then, yes, of course I'll be in the film.

Half-asleep, I think back to my first trip, on the same train, and remember the dream I had, which seemed so portentous, and Sophie's face blurs into Mme Fujimori's. Russian words sneak into my Paris–La Rochelle short story. I imagine Sophie reading *Le Monde* in exactly six weeks on another train, which I will meet when it arrives. I imagine our joy, her pride. Yesterday, while I was finishing my packing, a journalist from *Le Monde* came to see me for an interview to accompany the story. He was amazed to find me setting out so blithely, given that I was leaving behind, as he put it, "a ticking time bomb." I thought he was a real prude, easily shocked. Do I truly feel so nonchalant? For the moment, yes.

Just like the first time, when we reach Kotelnich there's only one car at the station available for hire. It's the same Zhiguli as before, driven by the same Vitaly, who doesn't seem particularly surprised to see us again and drives us to the same Hotel Vyatka, then on to the Troika, where we have lunch and make plans. As a practical consideration, Sasha recommends that we register with the authorities right away, a necessary

formality in a Russian city—my failure to do so, at the beginning of my stay in Moscow that winter, led to my arrest in the
metro and two hours in a pen, until the police, deciding I was
sufficiently intimidated, offered to fix everything in return for
a hundred rubles, the equivalent of a few dollars. On the artis-
tic front, Philippe would like to know what kind of people
I'm hoping to meet. In the back of my mind I think: Anya with
her French, and Sasha, the FSB guy. But with evasive confidence I reply that I have no preconceived notions, that chance
will provide our cast of characters. All we need to do is be
ready, when a door opens, to film whoever walks through.

Speaking of which, the door promptly opens to admit a
trio of bums and now the Troika's clientele this morning is
complete. We go over to their table to strike up a conversation and to film said conversation. The first move falls to Sasha,
who certainly has his faults, notably the personality of a pig,
but who is without peer when it comes to chewing the fat à
la Russe, complete with chummy sarcasm and melodramatic
sighs. One of the bums launches into a long monologue, which
Sasha punctuates, like a psychoanalyst or sociologist, with
brief interpolations designed to goose along a tirade in no
need of extra prodding. Now and then, Sasha leans over to
give me a recap, but I'm way ahead of him: the guy is pissed
off and has every reason to be, because life is hard and God
knows it wasn't good before, but now it sucks. What I'm having trouble with are the details getting swamped by his gummy
diction, but I can't very well ask Sasha for a simultaneous
translation, which would destroy all spontaneity and, worse,
force me to admit—even to myself—that despite my best efforts
I'm pretty much lost. Irritated, I go sit by myself off to the side.
The waitress, an old woman with a sad face, comes over to
ask me why we're filming these people, who aren't a pretty

sight. She is my first customer for the speech I subsequently perfected and served up, I believe, to everyone I talked to: No, they're not a pretty sight, but this is reality, which is what we've come to film, and yes, there certainly are pretty sights in Kotelnich (although what they might be I can't imagine) and we will film those, too. When she learns that we're French, the waitress looks even sadder: Why come all the way from France to film . . . that? I invite her to sit down; I introduce myself. And she is? Tamara. What she says, once she starts talking, is basically no different from the bum's tirade, but I can understand her a bit better and so try to transform the monologue into a dialogue, taking every opportunity to insert, like Sasha, words of approval or understanding. Tamara reads the Bible but draws no comfort from God's almighty power. She prefers the wisdom of Ecclesiastes: life's a vale of tears, then you die, and plainly she has experienced more than her fair share of this cruel truth. In the spirit of tackling a difficult homework assignment, rather than from any hope of sparking her interest, I tell her that I recently participated in a new translation of the Bible into French, but she doesn't seem to care. Frankly, I'm not surprised.

When we visit the mayor's office, I speak French and Sasha translates, which lends the meeting a more official tone. I present our project in a resolutely positive light, in impeccable officialese that appears to be persuasive, because the mayor tells his assistant, Galina, to secure all the necessary permits and even to find us an apartment.

But to the surprise of my companions, I'm not pleased by that last part. The search for an apartment is essential to my project. I figured that the Hotel Vyatka was okay for a week, but a month is a long time, so we'd have to find something better, and we'd rent a place. For a few hundred dollars lots of people would probably be ready to move in with some cousins for a month and let us have their apartment. Or maybe not; we'd see. I was sure, though, that a French film crew trying to rent an apartment would be an unprecedented event in the history of Kotelnich and might give rise to encounters, negotiations, screwups—all sorts of situations worth recording. It wasn't that I expected an apartment to bump up our comfort level but rather that the hunt might work as a unifying theme in our chronicle. That's why I am now a little annoyed to see the problem resolved so quickly. And Galina doesn't waste time. That very day, a Volga from the mayor's fleet picks us up for a drive out to the electric power station, a complex of brick buildings surrounded by barbed wire and wasteland. No less cordial than the mayor, the station director listens with gentle amusement to our description of the Vyatka; no, no, distinguished guests like ourselves must not be allowed to languish in that dump, and he shows us around a little house at the entrance to the complex, where visiting engineers stay and which he is happy to place at our disposal. It's clean, almost cozy, with a kitchen, a shower, and three rooms where burgundy carpet covers even the walls; in short it's just what we're looking for, except that I would have liked us to find it for ourselves after an eventful search instead of having it dropped in our laps by an obliging mayor. So I ask for some time before we decide, and that afternoon we explore other leads, that is, we question passersby who shake their heads, and we buy the local paper, where the few real estate ads offer only the odd room for rent in someone else's apartment. Conscious of giving up rather quickly yet concerned for my crew, I agree to the little house, but only for the moment: the power station will be our temporary base, but we'll try to find something better. Well, not better, but different, something more picturesque, more *deserved*—in any case, we're going to keep looking.

Naturally, that was the end of that.

The news of our return has spread swiftly through town, and by our second evening I'm expecting Anya to drop in with her guitar to welcome us back. But no, no news of her or of Sasha. He must know we're here, though. Why doesn't he or Anya show up? I'm puzzled.

Tomorrow is the Kotelnich town fair, which we're counting on to jump-start our project. Philippe thinks we should prepare carefully by choosing one or two people to follow throughout the day, so we send Sasha out to gather information. The highlight of the festivities, according to Galina, Sasha's chief informant, will be a ceremony honoring two model citizens, the director of the gasworks (a snappy dresser, Galina says) and the foreman of the local masons' guild. What we should do, according to Philippe, is catch one of these men just getting out of bed—show him eating breakfast with his family, the proud wife knotting the worthy's tie—and then stick with him all day. Alas, the mason's mother-in-law died the previous evening, so he won't be in any mood to strut before our cameras and might even miss his own celebration. And the dandified gasman, whom Galina has tried to phone, is nowhere to be found.

Frustrated, we straggle around town, and since there's nothing to see but the incessant train traffic, we decide to go film that. On the metal bridge crossing the tracks, Philippe sets up his camera tripod, Lyudmila arranges her microphones, and with the small DV camera I film them filming the trains. The one thing we can count on here are vistas of railroad tracks; if all else fails, we'll use them as a running gag: the intrepid filmmakers, having nothing better to do, go up on the bridge to film interminable freight trains. A good ten or so have gone through when a security guard politely asks us to stop filming and follow him to the railroad police office. The chief of security, who receives us equally politely, is a blond young man with very blue eyes whose face radiates the humble, beatific innocence one associates with the Christlike fools of Holy Mother Russia and finds in certain characters in Tarkovsky's films. This officer confirms that without explicit authorization we may not film the station, trains, tracks, or the bridges over the tracks. For reasons of national security? Philippe asks, with knowing irony, to which the officer, who would clearly like to accommodate us, responds with a kind smile and a resigned shrug: It's rather ridiculous, of course, but that's how it is. And this authorization, who can give it to us? Well, the FSB. I ask if the local FSB officer is still one Sasha, whose girlfriend speaks French. The blond young man doesn't know about the girlfriend, but yes, Sasha Kamorkin, he's the one. And can he be reached by phone? Obligingly, the blond young man calls the number, without success. He advises us to just go see him and provides the address. We linger a little in the soft, golden late-afternoon light that fills the dusty office and steeps us all in a restful torpor. Our host is in no hurry to see us go and we're in no hurry to leave, so we chat casually about France, which the young man would like to visit one day even though he knows he has little chance of ever getting there, and about Kotelnich, our interest in which he has a hard time understanding. And our desire to make a film here leaves him wistful but not hostile, and with his kind smile he suggests a title to us as we say good-bye: *Tut Zhit' Nel'zya, Poka Zhivut*: We Can't Live Here, and Yet We Do.

Philippe is an easygoing guy, but on the morning of the town fair he's feeling testy. He has filmed many documentaries, in Russia and elsewhere, he knows what he's doing, and we've already agreed with him that the only way to recount the day is to follow one particular person from the start of the fair to the end. But we have nothing. Nobody. No angle. We're reduced to wandering around the municipal park filming sausages and shish kebab sputtering on grills and young women setting out heaps of cakes on tables covered with paper cloths. Sasha pretends to scout for information while I sit in the bleachers on the soccer field, jotting things down in my notebook, which already records my growing discouragement. I have a worrying tendency to distance myself from my crew, to just let them work on their own. I do of course see details I'd like to point out to Philippe, but I really can't tap him on the shoulder when he's got his eye to the viewfinder and tell him to film things outside his field of vision— those flies on that cake—because by the time he gets the cake in the frame, the flies will be gone. Anyway, who cares about some flies on a cake? Who cares about the Kotelnich fair? This morning, day four, I envision the film as a montage of images in which I will not appear, with an introspective voice-over drawn from my diary describing what I was thinking when the images were being filmed. It's a depressing idea, this narcissistic contrivance, so I'm pinning my hopes on the sudden appearance of something that will knock it for a loop. Something, or rather—someone.

Someone, as it happens, comes up to us: it's the photographer-reporter from the local daily, the *Kotelnichnyi Vestnik*, recognizable by his multipocket vest. Great, I think, we'll follow him, show him at work, and along the way he'll fill us in on the town gossip. The problem is that today his work consists of interviewing *us*. When I take advantage of the interview to sound him out on the scuttlebutt, he explains that his paper (circulation 8,000) tries to look on the bright side, reporting, for example, on the huge fish recently caught in the Vyatka River or on the construction of a boat by an upstanding citizen who uses it to take his family for Sunday outings. I ask about Sasha Kamorkin and Anya, but he claims those names mean nothing to him. That a local reporter would not know or would pretend not to know the local FSB officer is astonishing. As is the fact that Sasha himself has not yet made an appearance, which adds a vague hint of menace to the mystery surrounding him.

The ceremony for the town's honorees begins at noon, in the soccer club hall where all the leading citizens are gathered. Hardly have we begun filming the toasts, however, when—without even offering us a drink—the locals ask us to buzz off. Clearly, the audience distrusts us, and rightly so. They know that if a French film crew has come to Kotelnich, it's to show how shabby and sad their lives are, and anyone claiming the contrary is just plain lying. We keep hearing the same question: Why our town? Along with the variant: What do you think of Kotelnich? If I say I'm favorably impressed they'll peg me for a fake, so I try out a new approach, testing it on the reporter with the multipocket vest: The town is certainly dirty and life hard, the conditions difficult, but the people, well, they're good folks, courageous, and it's the people who interest me . . . But no one believes me and of course they're right again.

Outside, on a small wooden stage, a show is in progress: singing, dancing, and comic interludes presented by the town's schoolchildren, among whom Philippe singles out a possible lead character. Kristina—that's her name—warbles (with no great talent but much fervor) a Britney Spears song and says, when questioned, that she'd like to be a professional singer. Short and a tad chubby, she's seventeen but looks fourteen, has a pretty, open, laughing face, prattles away freely, and says she's thrilled that we're filming her. I'd imagined a different type of leading lady, one of those ravishing tall blondes who frequent Moscow nightclubs, the mistresses of the New Russians, wearing fur coats over very short, expensive dresses, driving around in Mercedes with tinted windows, choosing their companions for the caliber of their credit cards, fixing the world with a gaze as cold as steel. Many of those girls must come from the backwaters of the Russian heartland, from families earning six hundred rubles a month—about twenty dollars—and living off nothing but potatoes. One day, determined to escape their parents' fate, they get on the train and, armed only with their beauty, their heads stuffed with the commercials broadcast in loops before the slack-jawed drunks of the Troika, they sign up for more or less high-class prostitution; a recent poll revealed that two-thirds of young Russian women have no scruples whatsoever about prostitution as a way to grab a place in the sun. I would have liked to find one of these girls before she left Kotelnich, to learn what was going on in her head, but I don't see Kristina in that role. On the other hand, she does dream of leaving, of one day exploring broader horizons, being applauded on a real stage. Philippe is right: she might become an engaging character.

At the edge of the park is a café called the Rubin, which Sasha points out with obvious uneasiness as the dive where he was beaten up on our first visit. This evening, because of the fair, the whole town is crowding into the Rubin, along with the thugs from the café's hard-core clientele. There is a bad guy in residence, though, and as we soon learn, he's the boss bad guy, Andrey Gonchar, an enormous bare-chested man with tattoos all over, a shaved head, and a potbelly. As I pass by his table, he challenges me, the Frenchy (half aggressively, half in jest), to an arm wrestling match. I decline, saying it's not worth it, he's obviously the stronger man. A few minutes later, I regret my prudent reaction: he would have hurt my arm a little, but we'd have laughed about it, struck up a relationship, and it might have been good to be on friendly terms with the local gang leader. Sasha, however, disagrees: No, not good, dangerous.

Later, everyone dances in a kind of open-air enclosure. Little Kristina wiggles and giggles like crazy; boys with shaved heads are torn between their longing to be filmed and their desire to swipe the camera. Philippe captures whatever he can and the next day, looking at the footage, I'll notice a funny, ravishing blonde who might very well have been the lead character I'd been hoping for. Too bad, we won't find her again; perhaps she wasn't from Kotelnich. At one point, Philippe filmed me answering that perennial question, Why come here to film us?, with my ready-made one-two on how hard life is and the courage required to face it, but I'm talking to a tall guy in his forties who's got twenty-five years in the army under his belt—Tartarstan, Chechnya, Mongolia—and he just squints at me like someone who can't be conned. He knows perfectly well what interests us: it isn't Kotelnich, there's nothing interesting about Kotelnich, but Morodikovo . . . Morodikovo? Yes, thirty miles away, a factory that until recently produced chemical weapons. It was dismantled but no one really knows what they did with the toxic materials used there. On our first visit, there'd been some vague mention of Morodikovo, which I'd thought was a lot farther away, and suddenly I see the town's earlier suspicions about us in a new light: filming Kotelnich could only be a cover for trying to reach the forbidden zone. So people must be thinking that we're seriously devious—not only do we not actually go to Morodikovo, but we don't even mention it, we wait for others to bring it up. I ask the veteran if he'd be willing to talk about the factory and about his life in general, but no, he doesn't want to be filmed. As for me, I'm cold and I've had enough. At three in the morning, the sun that never sets is beginning to rise—we're on the same latitude as St. Petersburg, with the white nights of June—and the café is closing. The fair is over. Nothing happened.

The FSB is on the corner of Karl Marx and October streets, in the same building as the *Kotelnichnyi Vestnik* newspaper, and when I run into the reporter with the multipocket vest, I see him flinch a little, since he had said that he didn't know Sasha Kamorkin, on whom we're now dropping in. In an office decorated with a large portrait of Felix Dzerzhinsky, founder of the Cheka, Sasha shows no sign of surprise as he welcomes us cordially, but he makes sure that the camera lens is capped. I introduce him to Philippe and Lyudmila and tell him about the death of Alain, news he seems truly sad to hear. In a year and a half, he has aged considerably. He still holds himself like a hero of the Soviet Union, but his face is puffier, his eyes bloodshot. He assumes the calculating, superior air of someone who sits tight and waits for people to come to him, but I sense that our return intrigues him. He, more than anyone—it is his job after all—must suspect we have some hidden agenda, one connected with Morodikovo. Following what he surely sees as a particularly convoluted strategy, I don't mention the place, I simply ask him for permission to film the railway station and the trains—he'll see what he can do—and take the opportunity to ask about his friend Anya, the one who spoke French. Not having seen her around, I wonder whether she's left town, found work somewhere as an interpreter, but no: they are still together, they have a child, she's currently with her mother in Vyatka but will return soon when their new apartment is ready. At the end of the meeting, which is brief, he asks to speak in private to Sasha, who rejoins us in the street and gleefully informs us of the new rule governing relations with our friend in the

FSB: the new rule is—that there is no FSB. Our friend now works for the protection of the environment. Voilà.

But that's absurd.

Absurd, cackles Sasha, but that's how it is.

Since we now have a house with a kitchen, we head for the market to stock up. As soon as Philippe aims his camera at the vendors and customers, most of them indicate that they don't want to be filmed. A butcher leaves his stall, buzzing with flies, to flat out threaten us. One old guy with enormous hands who used to work at the local sawmill before it closed is afraid of being arrested if he appears on TV and won't listen when we tell him that people aren't arrested for that anymore and besides, our film will be seen only in France, not in Russia. It's the same old story: We live like dogs while you, you live in paradise, you're real bastards to come film us. We beat a hasty retreat.

Over dinner, prepared by Lyudmila, we draw up a list of possible characters for our project. Philippe is rooting for Kristina, whose parents he has already contacted about filming her at home. Myself, I have high hopes for the Kamorkin couple. We remain divided over Andrey Gonchar, the interesting albeit dangerous gang leader, but agree that there's no question of seriously investigating the connection between the police and crime or the rackets in Kotelnich. That isn't our subject. But what *is* our subject? I'm hard put to say.

As we attack the tough, stringy meat bought from the churlish butcher, Lyudmila points out that there are no knives in this town, either in the restaurant or in our kitchen drawers—only tin forks and spoons. She thinks it's to avoid tempting the devil, more specifically the drunks, and I delightedly propose a new title for our film: *Gorod Bez Nozhey*: The Town without Knives. If I am delighted, it's mostly because during dinner in our kitchen I've spoken only Russian, first with Lyudmila but also with the others, and I'm not doing badly. Another bit of good news, doubtless the only notable change since our previous stay, is that cell phones now work here, so there's no more need to go to the post office. In bed early, I spend a half hour with Sophie, telling her about the doubts I'm suffering. She's not having such a good time either. Her job is a drag, as is the prospect of looking for another one. I try to console her; I love her, and she loves me. We wind up making love on the phone and glory be, it's not bad, not bad at all.

Kristina's parents, whom we visit laden with cakes, chocolate, vodka, and *shampanskoye*, live on the outskirts of town in a small communal house, where they have two very well-kept rooms with shelves full of knickknacks, family photos, and books in gold-tooled bindings. Initially nervous, the family warms up to us—with no help from me, I must admit. Kristina has eyes only for Philippe, whose graciousness works wonders. The gentle and self-effacing father is thirty-two and looks forty-five; he's a soldier but plans to retire soon. It seems to be the mother who lays down the law in this household. She would like to leave Kotelnich, she says; Morodikovo worries her as it does everyone else: many people are ill, young people, with cancers, but where can they go? For herself and her husband, it's already too late; her hopes for a better life are now for her children. Although I get the gist of this, I have trouble joining the conversation. I keep thinking about the pretty blonde discovered too late in the town fair footage and feel almost as if this Kristina and her nice family have been forced on me—but I took no initiative myself and ought to be grateful to Philippe for doing what it takes to keep things moving along.

And it's thanks to him that the next day we come up with a new character. This one just couldn't be more upbeat; he's perfect for reassuring the mayor's assistant, who is quietly unnerved by our tendency to film passed-out drunks in the town's dilapidated public squares. Vladimir Petrov is the personal trainer at the bodybuilding club. Thirtyish, with a forthright handshake and a handsome, open smile, he came in tenth in the 2001 Community of Independent States Championships and was offered a position in St. Petersburg, which he turned down, unwilling to leave his club and the young men he trains there. He feels responsible for them, many of whom are former delinquents who, thanks to his influence, no longer smoke, drink, or wander the streets and have returned to the straight and narrow by lifting weights. Not content with supervising their physical redemption, he encourages their professional rehabilitation, giving them jobs as night watchmen in the factory where he's in charge of security. In short, here's one guy in this crumbling town who hasn't thrown up his hands. Filming his group workout, we imagine clever plot twists: that Vladimir's regulars might include some of Andrey Gonchar's henchmen; that one of the boys snatched from delinquency might have a less lucky pal locked up in the juvenile detention center mentioned by the mayor's assistant, who offered, to our astonishment, to take us there; that Kristina might come work out at the club, fall in love with the barbell enthusiast with the luckless pal, and go with him to visit his friend at the center. All these stories would link up before our cameras, and to put the finishing touch on this series of fortunate encounters, I imagine a grand banquet to which we'll invite everyone when the shoot is over. This is a day when I have faith in the film, and I even think of suggesting to Sophie that she take a week's vacation to join us at the triumphant wrap party. I consider it, but I don't call her. What course might our lives have taken if I had?

FSB Sasha, whom we now call Sasha the ecologist, summons our Sasha for one of their private chats, on the nature of which the latter remains evasive but which seem mostly to provide a pretext for getting plastered. In fact, when we catch up with them at the end of the evening at the Zodiac, a restaurant that passes for the town's latest hot spot, they are both bombed. Which has no effect on the ecologist's obsessive fear of being filmed. I am a nice person, he declares, but if someone tries to trap me I can turn nasty. It's Saturday night, however, the place is crowded, and he can't prevent Philippe from filming the scene on the dance floor. This turns into a game as Philippe, whirling around the dancers, attempts to steal a picture of Sasha while I sit with our quarry at a dimly lighted table trying to distract him. Insisting that I drink to the beauty of women, he delivers increasingly slurred speeches on culture, France, his skills as a psychologist, his expertise at judging people, and by prancing around us while pretending to film something else, Philippe finally captures a shot of him in three-quarter profile. When we get back to the house, we rejoice over this meager booty like hunters who have bagged some particularly rare game, and it's only the next day that I feel somewhat ashamed. After ten days in Kotelnich, our chief success turns out to be catching a furtive shot of a man whose job prohibits him from being photographed. An unhappy man, a sentimental, vindictive alcoholic whom I have decided must be in our film—simply because he doesn't want to—along with his wife, because I think she will tell me things in French she won't say in front of him in Russian. Based on nothing but a few minutes of film shot a year and a half ago at the Troika, in which one can hardly see or hear anything, I have constructed a whole novel around this couple whom I now propose to entrap. As if in punishment, my Russian suddenly seems to regress.

When Philippe asks me at breakfast each morning what we'll be doing that day, more and more often I say that I don't know. He could sit around waiting for me to decide, but that's not his way, so he decides for himself and generally that means going to film Kristina, her family, her girlfriends, her exams. While he's doing that, I sit on a bench in the sun and on a good day write things in my notebook, but mostly I take short naps. Theoretically, I am in charge of our crew; in reality, I decide nothing and just tag along, a dead weight in every encounter, occasionally smiling or adding, *Da, da, konechno*, to show that not everything being said escapes me.

I was expecting this return visit to be the trigger that would finally get me speaking Russian and thus help me develop some warm relationships here, yet I hardly talk to anyone and each day I withdraw further into myself. The familiar language that surrounds me is intimate and maternal, yet barely comprehensible, and I let myself be soothed by its sound and sense. But the problem isn't simply that I don't understand half of what I hear, it's mostly that I honestly don't care. Is it really true that half the meaning escapes me or would it be closer to say

a third or a quarter? How does one evaluate the skill of someone who can keep a diary in Russian for two months and
carry on conversations in Moscow bristling with mistakes and
stop-gap English yet fluid and alive, but who now, in Kotelnich, seems stricken with aphasia? When I tell my companions
that despite my efforts I can't break through my psychological block with the Russian language, they shrug: Why use the
word "block" for the classic difficulty in shifting from pas-
sive to active practice in a foreign language? And yet, *I know*
that it really is a block, that something or someone inside me
dreads and rejects this return to my mother's language, and I
know there's a mystery here, one that this project—which
began with the story of the Hungarian András Toma, continued with my use of Russian to recover childhood memories,
and is now failing in Kotelnich—will bring to light. If I am
in Kotelnich, if I decided to make this film in Kotelnich, it
was to find the key to that mystery.

Still, why Kotelnich? The short answer—that I'm looking for
my roots—it is a load of crap. I have no roots in Kotelnich,
or even in Russia, when you get right down to it. That great-
granduncle who was vice governor of Vyatka for six months
and defenestrated Muslims always makes a big impression
on the locals when I mention him. Sasha the ecologist offered
to try chasing him down in the archives; I accepted enthusiastically but the truth is I don't give a damn. My grandfather
was Georgian, my grandmother grew up in Italy, I couldn't
care less about my great-grandparents' vast estates. This country means nothing to me, beyond its language. And my mother
learned Russian not here but in Paris, and that's where I heard
it as a child. So why come to Russia, why return to Kotelnich,

if not because it's where the Hungarian soldier washed up, which lets me draw closer, in a roundabout way, to my grandfather's fate?

Sometimes I tell myself this: it's all about a journey in which point A is the Hungarian's story, point Z is Georges Zurabichvili's story, but I have no idea what comes in between. The wager, a true leap of faith, is that I will find out in Kotelnich. I could have gone to Georgia and followed my grandfather's emigration—Tbilisi, Istanbul, Berlin, Paris, Bordeaux—all the way to a place I imagine strangely burned by the sun: to the building housing the German Intelligence Division. But no, I'm in Kotelnich.

I've brought along the file containing the photocopies of my grandfather's letters and sometimes, while the others are off filming, I stay at the house to decipher them. In French as well as in Russian, he developed a language truly his own, but it's so much his own that it winds up having little to do with ordinary speech: it's a private idiom that, however cultured and alive, strongly resembles that of András Toma, who for fifty-six long years muttered to himself in a language so shredded by time that no one can understand it anymore. To chew over his obsessions, his bitterness, his megalomania, and his self-hatred, my grandfather forged himself a language that is almost *too* personal, and as I read his letters an idea occurs to me, and I am afraid: these are the letters of a madman.

• • •

Now that we have our permit, we film trains passing beneath the bridges, but we quickly tire of that. We film the barbell boys at their exertions and follow Vladimir's musclemen on their security round in the factory. We film little Kristina's final exams, her fit of tears because she didn't know any of the answers (really, not a one), and her smiling relief because she managed to get a B anyway. We film her classmates, and I find one of them, Lyudmila, entrancing. We film their teacher, Igor Pavlovich, a lazy bear of twenty-eight who looks forty, whom we propose to interview about his vocation and the noble selflessness it represents, but he tells us straight out that he doesn't like teaching at all, it's just a way to avoid military service. Next year he'll have reached the age limit for enlisting and will quit. While waiting for his well-earned retirement, he teaches four hours a week for six hundred rubles a month—about twenty dollars—and doesn't want more. He divides his time between his parents' place in the countryside and Kotelnich, where he stays with his brother, a student. It's a good-enough life; why work harder? This relaxed Oblomovism makes me like him. At least he's not as boring as Kristina's wholesome family, whom we join after her exams to toast her success. She's touching, though, this young girl who dreams of becoming a singer like Britney Spears or Celine Dion but probably already suspects that without a great voice or looks she has little chance of achieving much more than her poor parents. I watch her leaf through the family photos: Kristina as a baby, as a child, onstage for the first time, with her big smile and chubby cheeks. I'm not too keen on Philippe's big idea of following her through a succession of school award days and singing contests; I could just say no and suggest something else, but my inclination is to go along with everyone else and I've decided to make this my policy. We'll see where this leads; no doubt Igor Pavlovich would applaud the idea.

I've been saying all along that making this film is an experiment, which implies that it might not succeed, and strange as it may seem for someone who's usually so anxious, I behave as if that were okay, as if there were nothing so terrible about the possibility of failure, or as if failure might have some significance that would only later become clear. One month from now, my short story will appear in *Le Monde*; other things are bound to happen and, well, Sophie loves me. All this helps enormously to give me some peace of mind.

One morning, I get a call from Anya. She's in Kotelnich for a few hours; we arrange to meet at the Zodiac. She hasn't changed much: not pretty but lively, wired, always changing her mind, slightly awkward, and that's why I'm more interested in her than in our other dramatis personae. That long-ago first evening in the Troika—and the tart commentary she delivered instead of faithfully translating her lover's words—gave me the impression that unlike Sasha, who even when drunk keeps himself on a short leash, Anya speaks freely, sometimes wildly, without second thoughts. True to form, hardly has she sat down when she starts talking, talking, her eyes sparkling, as if this were the first chance she'd had to open her mouth since our last visit, which she remembers, she says, as "a fairy tale" or "the arrival of the Three Magi." That we've come from someplace else, a different world, makes many people here distrust us, but to her it's dazzling. And now our return proves that miracles do happen. Until work on the apartment Sasha mentioned is finished, she is living at her mother's place in Vyatka with her four-month-old son, little Lev (whom she calls Léon, in French, when she's with us), but she'll be back in Kotelnich in a few days and is looking forward to seeing us often. Back for good? She makes a face. The idea of a definitive return to Kotelnich is painful. But Sasha's work is here, this is his world, his life, so it will also be Anya's world and life since she seems to have agreed to bury herself here for love. Because Kotelnich, she says with naïve conviction, is *la ville de l'amour*. Love isn't easy here, however, not when people scowl at you for being an outsider and living unmarried with a man who not only left his wife for you but must serve the state by dealing discreetly with tricky situations.

Oh? Tricky situations? She claps her hand over her mouth, like a child who fears she's said too much, but she keeps right on prattling about Sasha and his work in a way he certainly wouldn't like. Either he hasn't told her what she can and cannot say (which is unlikely) or she's new to this business of keeping secrets—and careless about it, as well. She proves it again when we drive her to Sasha's office, meaning the FSB, so that she can pick up her suitcase. When I offer to go in with her to help with her bag, she says yes but then opens her eyes wide, brings her hand to her mouth, and says no, Emmanuel, no, I'd better go alone. A little later, at the station, she explains that this is where the town comes to buy hashish, that more and more people are smoking it (we won't see anyone smoking it, and no one ever offers us any), and that it's part of Sasha's job to keep an eye on them. Oh really? Isn't he busy protecting nature? Exaggerated astonishment: He told you that? She laughs.

Anya turns out to be a bit of a letdown when she returns to Kotelnich. I am expecting the Mata Hari of Kotelnich and find myself with a fairly ordinary young mother. I don't quite know what to say to her. Yet ever since that first intoxicated night at the Troika, I've continued to feel there's a mystery, or at least a romantic aura, surrounding Anya and Sasha. Little Kristina, Vladimir the bodybuilder, lazy Igor Pavlovich, and even the prettiest of his students—basically, I couldn't care less about them, but those two, I really want them in the film.

Then I have an idea. I suggest to Anya that she help us out as a backup translator. My stratagem wouldn't fool anyone, I clearly don't need two interpreters, and even though I explain my ploy to our Sasha he sulks a bit about it, as if I were announcing that his work was no good. By hiring Anya, however, I'm counting on hearing her frank, spontaneous commentary on our subjects and on having our "assistant" become a bona fide character in the film. In any case, my offer thrills her. It's good for you and good for me, she says, but even better for me, she adds, with a mix of coquettishness and shrewd modesty that at that moment makes her irresistible. I'd expected Anya's enthusiasm, but what surprises me is that the next day her Sasha goes along with the plan. He negotiates the fee, fifty dollars a day, with our Sasha, and I wonder how he manages to explain his own replacement without losing face. It's a done deal, anyway: Anya is working for us.

Officially, this change frees our Sasha to attend to other, more urgent business. What business? We're vague about that, but his first move when he's off the hook is to go bend elbows with the other Sasha, which ought to expose our ruse, but no, not at all, everyone goes along with it.

Proud of her salary, proud of doing real work for us, Anya has prepared for our visit to the juvenile detention center the way a student preps for an important exam. She looks forward to surprising the director, Sergey Viktorovich, when he sees her walk in with us; he's a good friend of Sasha's, she says, and one of the few people who welcomed her after Sasha left his wife. But Anya's the one who gets a surprise when we go into the office. Sergey Viktorovich, a dumpy little man in fatigues, greets her briskly, wasting no time on chitchat, and launches directly into a speech. That's when Anya's disappointment must have begun. I cannot remember what happened in that office; my memories come mostly from viewing the footage a few months later with my editor, Camille, who was in stitches watching my polite despair as I listen to Sergey Viktorovich's harangue about the prison system and the various stages of the inmates' rehabilitation. The film shows me having one of those bad days when nothing and no one interests me, when my whole mind is focused bitterly on my boredom. Chin in hand, I keep nodding, stifling yawns, and at the end of every sentence Anya, pad and pencil in hand, begins to translate with a zeal that oppresses me even more. There's an hour and a half of that, after which Sergey Viktorovich takes us on a tour. Receiving permission to visit the place had surprised me, but the tour explains everything: the facilities are rather well maintained. The dormitories are clean, the classrooms look like classrooms, with children's drawings tacked up on the walls, and the incarcerated adolescents we encounter wearing uniforms in the halls seem like students at a fairly strict boarding school. I'm angry at myself for being there, angry that I'd been excited at the prospect of visiting a juvenile center I'd hoped to find Dantesque, angry at being disappointed that it's not at all Dantesque, and angry at Anya for her irritating eagerness and for the dutiful way she leans in to translate Sergey Viktorovich's endless blather. Curtly, I tell her that it's okay, I understand, and since I've always been very nice to her, this brusque change of tone upsets her. On the return trip, she watches me uneasily, as if I were a Dr. Jekyll who'd suddenly become Mr. Hyde. She can't figure out what she did to annoy me. Even I'd be hard put to explain it, but she does get on my nerves. Everything that has gone wrong with this trip that I can't blame on anyone else, well, now I dump it on Anya. I could almost curse my own blindness: I was all worked up about this romantic figure, when really she's just a poor bewildered girl who tries too hard, whose voice grates on me and whose expressions exasperate me,

like her way of using the definite article, saying, for example, I have to buy *the* tube of toothpaste, not *a* tube or *some*
toothpaste—and suddenly that minor slip, from the lips of
someone who speaks French a hundred times better than I
speak Russian, becomes the focus of all the exasperation I feel
about this trip and indeed my whole life. We drive her home;
she timidly asks when we might need her again, and I say that
I don't know, we'll see. I know I'm being cruel, I'm angry at
myself and her as well. I hate remembering that day.

Kristina and her pals have passed their final high school exams,
and to celebrate their entry into adult life there is a party for
parents, teachers, and students in the local cake factory's caf-
eteria. Led by a pinched little man who claims to have seen
our films about Kotelnich and "knows what we're up to," a
group of blustering parents tries at first to turn us away, but
Kristina will be singing in the program and her mother and
father want us to film her, so we are finally allowed inside and
attempt to mingle, which in my case means that I get method-
ically blotto. Kristina performs her Britney Spears numbers
and the lovely Lyudmila, who clearly takes her patriotism
seriously, sings songs to the glory of the Russian army in
Chechnya. I, too, have a contribution from my repertoire,
that Cossack lullaby with its cruel Chechen as the enemy,
and although I don't know all the words, I achieve modest
success at my end of the table by singing the first few verses
and everyone around me takes them up, praising my efforts.
As best I can, I tell the story of my Russian roots, my mother,
my *nyanya*, the vice governor who defenestrated Muslims,
and soon I find myself engaged in a rambling but affection-
ate exchange with a mustachioed guy named Leonid, who

an hour earlier was one of the parents trying to keep us from attending the party. At one point, I make Leonid a promise: I will try to make a film I can show to the people of Kotelnich with pride. Because of course I'll be showing it to them; in six months, a year, we'll be back and invite everyone in the film to a huge screening. And they'll like it—that's what I'm promising. Or at least (because perhaps I was promising too much) they won't feel ashamed. That's what struck me about the parents' initial refusal to let us film their banquet and their later effusions of anxious sentimentality: they're not only suspicious but also ashamed—ashamed of being poor, pathetic, drunk, and afraid of being shown like that. They are horribly afraid of being sneered at, and as I talk to Leonid, keeping my promise and not betraying their confidence seems to me like the most important thing in the world.

The party lasted a long time, and 4:00 a.m. found everyone down by the riverside. The sun was already up: it was June 21, the shortest night of the year, a night that had lasted only an hour or two. Toads were croaking. Holding up the hems of their long dresses and clutching their shoes, the girls walked barefoot in the water, their shoulder straps hanging down on their arms. People poured streams of vodka or beer straight into their mouths; some revelers were still singing, but increasingly off-key. Me, I was dead drunk, lying in a heap in the backseat of the car, and to evoke this jaunt to the riverbank, I'm relying less on memory than on the images captured by Philippe: they have the grace of the dawns and waning revels in the films of Emir Kusturica.

I learn the Cossack lullaby all the way through. I find it incredibly moving and feel like crying when I murmur the last

verse to myself. But the enthusiasm that had me speaking
Russian to Leonid and the girls at the party quickly melts
away. It doesn't matter whom I talk to—they hardly interest
me. Unless I've had one drink too many, I can't think of anything to say and fall right back into my aphasia. I'm not so
much directing the shoot as tagging along with it. Sasha asks
questions, Philippe films, Lyudmila records, and I'm off in
my corner. I sit on benches and take scattered notes, more
about what's going through my head than about what's happening in front of me. I think about András Toma, who lived
here for fifty-three years without speaking Russian or com-
municating with anyone. I think about my vanished grandfather, about the madness that flickers through his letters,
about my mother who is so afraid that I might write about
him one day, about my own fear of doing just that and my
conviction that it's that I must do, since for both of us it's a
question of life or death. I think about the detective in I can't
remember what crime novel who manages to solve mysteries
in his sleep while everyone else is busy running around. Sinking into fitful drowsiness and the occasional nightmare, I wonder what mystery I have come here to solve.

We visit Vladimir Petrov, the bodybuilder. We've filmed him
at work and now the idea is to show him at home with his
wife and little boy. What you're going to do, Philippe patiently
explains to them, is behave as if we weren't here: fix dinner,
play with the child, talk to one another about what your
day was like. I can't take it, I feel in the way, and using the
cramped apartment (where I'm constantly at risk of winding
up in the shot) as an excuse, I go out to wait on the landing.
Then I keep on going down the concrete stairs and outside

the building. Facing me is another apartment building, an empty lot where cows are grazing, and in the far distance, the cake factory. The sun is beating down on everything. I film this view, out of sheer idleness, with the little DV camera. In counterpoint to the scenes Philippe is filming in Vladimir's apartment—scenes I must have reviewed later on while editing the film but can't recall—these overexposed images appear bathed in a raw light and permeated, for me, with a strange, unspeakable sadness. In this film in which I had hoped to appear, directing my crew, speaking fluently in Russian, these images mark the moment when I, too, allowed myself to disappear.

Anya invites us to go on a boat ride organized by her Sasha: the boat belongs to a friend of his and this outing is meant as a kind of gift, yet Sasha himself prefers not to join us. It's all the more peculiar since according to Anya, who as usual says whatever comes into her head, there has been a lot of tension between her and Sasha over the last few days, for which we are partly to blame. The "ecologist" suspects us of trying to worm secrets out of her—in particular, I suppose, about Morodikovo—and he suspects her of being only too happy to oblige. Why, in that case, send us out boating together and not come along himself? One more mystery, which I will never solve.

Captained by Sasha's friend, the little vessel motors gently up the Vyatka River, passes beneath the railway bridge, and heads for a graveyard of rusty boats that turns out to be our destination. Anya acts as our tour guide, but her commentary on the local points of interest quickly turns personal. When we pass a bare hillock, she tells us that people call it the Summit of Love, explaining that it's a favorite with lovers. Sasha took her there the first time they met and a few days later left his wife and daughter to move in with her. Together they braved the mean-spirited gossip in a town where Sasha, being with the FSB, was already not too popular and where Anya, a girl from the big city, wasn't all that welcome either. People didn't like Sasha but they feared him, so they aimed their nasty looks and wounding remarks at her. She'd laughed them off, and even felt proud, because she was with Sasha and they loved each other. She describes him as a romantic man, wounded, shrouded in mystery, and speaks of those early days of love with a kind of intoxication, but after dropping hints that those days are over, she finally admits that things have gone wrong between them. She tries to speak lightheartedly because she thinks we expect her to be lighthearted, and shrugging with affected carelessness, she blurts out that he wants to leave her and little Léon. For another woman? No, not particularly, even if he does have mistresses. It's just that the first flush of love has passed and what he, too, had found romantic and mysterious in their affair now irritates him. Once he adored her speaking French; now he finds it louche and vaguely disquieting, perhaps even compromising for him in his position. And she feels that her French is fading, like a gift one might lose, a precious eccentricity dulled by the gray oppression of ordinary existence. I find her story sad, yet at the same time I understand the disenchantment because I feel it as well. On that first evening at the Troika, I, too, had found this couple romantic and mysterious. I'd fallen a little in love with them, but now what do I see? A nice, naïve, sentimental girl who wants to live in her fantasies, and a guy who's sentimental, too, but weak and paranoid. Their love blazed for a few months and is now dying, smothered by the boredom of a provincial life many dream of leaving but never will. I was cruel to Anya during our visit to the detention center, but now I try to be kind and pretend to sympathize. The truth is that I'm fed up—with Anya and her Sasha, Kotelnich, and myself in Kotelnich. I wish it were three weeks from now, when I'll be with Sophie and my short story comes out, or even just ten days from now because then my crew and I will be out of here. Suddenly that feels like a very long time, ten days, and I think: It's up to me. Why wait?

Do I want to film the detention center again? Good-natured Vladimir and his bodybuilders? Kristina's singing aspirations, Tamara's waitressing, and Anya's commentary on Kotelnich, *la ville de l'amour*? Do I feel like filming anything at all? No. Having anticipated this moment of discouragement, however, I had already decided that the important thing was to complete the experiment, even if it seemed boring and fruitless at the time. There was always the chance of a last-minute miracle, just when you've given up. The same evening, though, I announce that after much thought I think we should cut the trip short. We can wrap up in three or four days, so why sit around an extra week? This makes sense, but everyone feels that ending our stay early is an admission of failure. Sasha, Lyudmila, and Philippe are sad and a little angry.

The next morning, when I wake up, my stomach is in knots from the anxiety that has been my lifelong companion, although, curiously, it had been leaving me alone during this visit to Kotelnich, where I've felt apathetic and assailed by doubts but not truly anguished. I also feel, at the tip of my foreskin, the swelling that heralds a bout of herpes—and, while brooding on that, I'm abruptly certain of having made, at a crucial moment, the wrong decision. Why hadn't I kept believing in our film and held out one more week?

The previous evening, wanting to talk things over with Sophie, I'd called her at midnight—ten o'clock in Paris—but she hadn't been home. I'd left a message that I would probably be returning in a few days. It's early in the morning when I try again; she's still not home. This surprises me, but I figure she probably spent the evening with a girlfriend and stayed over. I leave another message, and one on her cell phone. My tone is more insistent because I feel uneasy; my decision to leave Russia bothers me, I need to discuss it with her. At eleven my time, nine o'clock there, she calls back, saying she just got out of the Métro and heard my message on the cell. She doesn't mention not sleeping at home last night. I can tell that she's nervous, confused, which worries me. You didn't get my message last night? Last night? Well, no, I got back rather late, I guess I didn't check the answering machine . . . And this morning? I called at seven this morning. I mean, you weren't out at seven, right? She seems rattled, says she must have been in the shower when the phone rang. I sense that she's lying to me. If she is, what does that mean? That she spent the night somewhere else, but not with a girlfriend? With another man? I don't say this straight out but immediately become quite chilly, and she picks up on that. What's wrong, Emmanuel, why are you angry with me? For not having been there when you needed to talk? I'm here now, I'm happy that you're coming back early. I miss you. Coolly, I cut the conversation short.

• • •

One of the things I wanted to do before leaving was try an experiment: instead of running around after vaguely picturesque characters, we would simply spend a day on a bench, in the public square across from the railway station. We'd sit down, stay there, and film what happens—or doesn't. I suspect that for Philippe, who's the impatient type, this might be torture, but I lay down the rules: filming the square from every possible angle is out; we stick with the point of view of the bench. The camera must be at eye level and can only pivot in place, just as if Philippe were turning his head. Right, he says, and sits down stoically, with Lyudmila and her mike on one side and me on the other, taking notes.

Noon. Aside from us, there are three people in the square, seated on two benches. An elderly couple and a young man. They have no luggage and don't seem to be waiting for a train, merely resting for a moment. Soon it will be lunchtime, but they don't bring out any sandwiches. They don't talk and don't seem to notice us filming. True, we aren't moving or talking either. The woman fans herself with a newspaper. Sparrows chirp. Several trains pass, including the express on its way to St. Petersburg.

One thirty. The couple have left. The solitary young man has fallen asleep, head tipped back, snoring gently. Another man has arrived to sit by himself with a bag of sunflower seeds bought from the pushcart lady in front of the station. The man cracks and eats them one after the other in a perfectly even rhythm. He keeps at it until the bag is empty. Then he rises and leaves.

FSB Sasha shows up and plops down next to us. When

we explain what we're doing, he laughs. What's the point? Philippe laughs in reply. It's one of his whims, don't even try to understand. Sasha has just been at the station buying his daughter's ticket for St. Petersburg. She's going there to study. To study, well, whore around, more likely. He's joking, but we can tell there's more to it than that: his voice betrays both belligerence and admiration. His daughter's name is also Kristina, and she is also seventeen and fresh out of school, but the resemblance to our Kristina ends there. As soon as Sasha shows us her passport picture, I decide that had I seen the photo earlier, our documentary would have taken a different turn: she's exactly the kind of girl I wanted to follow on her journey from a backwater like Kotelnich to the nightclubs of St. Petersburg, Moscow, or New York, where her beauty and strangely innocent cynicism will get her noticed in a big way. Pretty little whore, hey? says Sasha again, before reciting her vital statistics. We're a bit embarrassed, but not Sasha: he's a pimp at heart, that's just his way of being proud of his daughter.

A half hour after Sasha leaves, Anya—whom he no doubt alerted—arrives to sit with us. She's brought her son along in a baby carrier. This is the first time we have seen little Léon. He'll soon be five months old. He's asleep. She gazes at him adoringly, showing him off with a tenderness eclipsing everything else that sometimes makes her seem unattractive. She becomes touching, graceful. Our relations with Sasha and Anya have had their complications, God knows, but today things are simple. They've both learned that we're spending the day parked on a bench near the station; it's peaceful and not unpleasant but a little boring, and they have come to keep us company, to chat for a moment. It's funny, but today I think of them as friends, not intimates, but pals, people with whom I have shared things, and I enjoy our lazy, aimless conversation.

I haven't forgotten Sophie, however. Do I really believe that she cheated on me last night and lied to me this morning? If true, is that so serious? Is that really making me suffer? Or am I just worried that a fight between us now will spoil the publication of my short story? I realize, of course, that the prospect of soon seeing my story in print is what's taking the edge off my disappointment in our Kotelnich visit. But what if failure creeps into the rest of my life? What if this moment of love and glory that I've planned for Sophie and me collapses as well? What if she falls in love with someone else? What if she leaves me?

I've resolved not to call her, but she calls me on my cell phone. I remain cold, distant, although I know I can't keep it up. She really doesn't seem to be getting ready to leave me. So either I stubbornly persist in thinking that she's lying and torment myself until it becomes intolerable or I choose to believe that she was in fact in the shower when I called and that she completely forgot about the answering machine she normally checks a thousand times a day. Her story's pretty flimsy; on the other hand, her loving protestations sound so sincere they could only mean . . . what? That she's a good liar? I know she's a good liar, she already lied to me about Arnaud and then reproached me for not having sensed it intuitively. Because she couldn't lie so well if she didn't love me, whereas my cluelessness meant that I don't love her enough. So, now let's say that she slept with someone last night. If she's anxious to hide it, that's because I'm the one she loves. So I tell her that my intuition about last night means that I love her, too—more than before, better than before. She laughs.

You're really twisted, she says. I still have my suspicions, but I can tell that we have begun to make peace, and I'd rather have that.

All other activity in the public square has dropped to zero, so I relax our rule, permitting Philippe to move around and film Anya and baby Léon. Anya is delighted because, she explains, Sasha is so wary of photos or films that she has practically no pictures of their son. He's a child who is never photographed. Then, without changing her tone, as if speaking incidentally, she repeats what she said on the boat, that Sasha is preparing to leave her, and she sadly sings a French song, "Plaisir d'Amour": The joys of love are but a moment strong; the pain of love endures a whole life long. I tell her no, both last no more than a moment. On that note, Léon wakes up and begins to cry. Anya sings him a lovely lullaby that I don't understand too well but that has something to do with a cricket. Then, at her request, I take the baby in my arms and in a low voice, I sing him my childhood lullaby.

> Sleep, my child, my treasure,
> Sleep, my boy, sleep.
> Bright moonbeams
> Watch over your cradle.
> I will tell you tales,
> I will sing for you.
> Close your eyes, fall asleep, dream,
> Sleep, my boy, sleep.
>
> The torrent rushes over stones,
> The frothy water tumbles.
> The cruel Chechen lies in wait for you,
> Sharpening his dagger.

But your father is a valiant hero
Who has fought in many battles.
Sleep, my love, hush now,
Sleep, my boy, sleep.

One day, you know, the hour will come
To join the warrior's life.
You will mount your horse,
You will take up your weapons.
With gold threads will I
Embroider your saddlecloth.
Sleep, child of my womb,
Sleep, my boy, sleep.

You will have the pride of a hero,
And the soul of a Cossack.
I will come to see you leave,
You will bid me adieu.
Alone, how many bitter tears
Will I shed that night.
Sleep in peace, my angel, my darling,
Sleep, my boy, sleep.

There will be times of anguish,
Of endless waiting,
Of portents and prayers,
Of sleepless nights.
I will fear that you are sad,
Far, far away from me.
Sleep before the evil comes,
Sleep, my boy, sleep.

For your journey I will give you
An icon blessed and holy.
Place it on your breast
When you pray to God.
When the hour of battle arrives,
Remember your mother.
Sleep, my child, my treasure,
Sleep, my boy, sleep.

· 5 ·

On the page proofs from *Le Monde*, I make one last correction. "The woman I am in love with" becomes "the woman I love."

I leave for the Île de Ré, where my sons are waiting for me. You, the woman I love—you're staying in Paris another week for work and should be taking the train to join me the following Saturday, the day of the short story about which you as yet know nothing. You seem tense and uneasy when I leave you. As I give you a kiss, in the doorway, I tell you, Trust me.

I have never said that to you before. I never say it to anyone. I'm afraid to have people trust me, because I'm afraid I'll prove unworthy and betray them. But that morning, remember this: I said it to you.

I find having to be both father and son at the same time difficult, and I prefer to avoid long visits with my parents and my children together. But this week, all goes well. I cook outside on the grill, I accompany my mother to the market, I take groups of children to the beach. No one recognizes me. One afternoon, helped by my nephew Thibaud, I clean out the shed, pump up the bike tires, rustproof the frames, sort through the bike locks, and throw out the ones missing keys. While we're at it, Thibaud suggests tossing a tricycle as well; no one will be using it, since neither my sisters nor I will be having any more children.

I say, You're forgetting Sophie and me.

You're thinking about it?

Why not?

I run and swim for hours on the Plage des Baleines, Whale Beach. While I'm running and swimming, I review what will happen in five, four, three more days—a mildly intoxicating countdown, a mix of elation and apprehension, with the first feeling distinctly outweighing the second. I think back to the journalist who came to interview me and found me so non-chalant, despite my ticking time bomb . . . Time bomb . . . Poor guy . . . I wonder what glitch could possibly spoil our triumph. A lovers' quarrel? My family? I know my parents are straitlaced, but I've been careful to warn them, using one of their pet phrases: I've written a short story for *Le Monde* that's a bit *olé-olé*. Rather than be shocked, they'll decide to approach it as a good joke. Anyway, my previous books, in particular the last one, were a lot more shocking than this lewd but happy story. My first happy story: they can't fail to see that. I'm done with madness, loss, deception—finally I've moved on to some-thing else, I'm telling a woman that I love her, the story is a declaration of love. After a night in La Rochelle, where I've reserved the most beautiful room in a wonderful hotel, the two of us will join everyone for breakfast on Sunday and they will all burst into delighted laughter. The following week, we'll give a party at the house. Many of our friends are staying on the Île de Ré this summer; they'll tease us, congratulate us, we'll be a dazzling and slightly scandalous couple, the toast of the town. I just know the story will be a huge success because once word gets around, even people who don't read *Le Monde* will be scrambling for a copy all over France, and I'm also sure that this is only the beginning, that there will be a sequel. What kind, I don't know—perhaps an article using the thousands of e-mails I'll receive or perhaps something completely different—and I'm glad not to know, to simply see what life brings without trying to anticipate it, but I anticipate it anyway, of course, I can't help myself. I imagine a short book, sexy, playful, that will also be hugely successful and might be called *L'Histoire porno du Monde et sa suite*. I like the way the title translates into English even better: *The Porn Story of the World and What Came Next*, which works perfectly because the book is obviously destined to be an international best seller. I'm bubbling with laughter, alone on the beach.

Thursday, two days before the story is to appear, you call me, distraught. You've just gotten a message from Denis asking you to call him, and he sounded as if he were speaking "from beyond the grave." Denis and Véro, your best friend, are splitting up. You've been talking about this for a while but I haven't paid much attention because I don't really like them. You're afraid to call him back because you have this awful feeling that Véro is dead, she's killed herself or died in a car accident. I try to calm you down: It's one thing that there's trouble between them, but to jump to the conclusion that she's dead . . . Just call Denis.

I'm going to, I know I have to, but I'm scared, I'm sure she's dead, and then, you know, it's horrible to say this, but if they bury her this weekend I won't be able to come to the Île de Ré and I want so much to come, to be with you, that I think I'd rather not find out.

You're sobbing and I'm really worried, not because Véro's dead, which I don't believe for a second, but because you seem to be a nervous wreck, obviously under great stress, which I'd sensed during your calls earlier in the week and had put down to problems at work. I want you to take the train on Saturday happy and relaxed, which isn't looking very likely at the moment. I sleep badly.

I've rented a boat, and on Friday I take my father, sons, and nephews to the Île d'Aix. Blue sky; sea ranging from calm to a slight chop; breezing along, the hull slaps the waves. I let the children take turns at the wheel, and when I'm at the helm I handle the boat with bold confidence. The day before, my father had remarked that my driving was faster and more decisive. You've really changed lately, he says.

When we reach the island, I call you. I don't know what Denis's voice sounded like yesterday, but yours truly does seem to be coming from beyond the grave. Véro isn't dead, no, but she's in a bad way, seriously bad, she might do something stupid, you absolutely have to stay with her this weekend.

At that, the world caves in. On the dock, out in the sun, while the children are hosing down the boat and the rental agent checks the propeller, I explain that for two months I've been preparing a surprise for you, a surprise that no one else has ever given you or ever will, that few men have ever given a woman, and that this surprise has to be tomorrow, it cannot be on any other day.

But what is it?

I can't tell you anything more, except that you just can't not come!

Emmanuel, I just can't leave Véro on her own either.

Bring her along.

Not when's she's like this.

Then I'll come back to Paris. I want to spend tomorrow night with you.

No, no, don't do that, I have to stay with her, so what's the point?

That evening, I invite myself to dinner with my friends Valérie and Olivier, who have rented a house in a nearby village. In the garden picturesquely overgrown with weeds, I drink heavily, and even though Sophie and I stopped smoking a year ago, I chain-smoke bummed cigarettes and forget to eat. I'm angry and I explain why, sounding sometimes like a patiently rational adult and sometimes like a child throwing a tantrum because someone has broken his toy. I'd been wondering what punishment the gods reserve for those who defy them, and— bingo! But it could be worse; your distraught friend will feel better, you'll come tomorrow or the day after, and we'll both drink to the irony of fate. The little I've said about my story intrigues my hosts, who can't wait to read it. At eleven, after I've left you two messages, you call back. You can barely speak: the situation is awful. So awful, apparently, that I ask you whether it wouldn't make more sense to get Véro some psychological help, take her to the emergency room.

No, no, it's not *that* dire, what she needs most of all is to talk. What we're thinking of doing tomorrow is taking her car and getting out of here, spending the weekend in the country.

Listen, judging from what you've told me, she's on the verge of jumping out a window, and you don't seem in much better shape yourself, so I think that's a really bad idea.

Don't worry, I can handle it.

But when are you coming?

I don't know, in two days, maybe . . .

Two days?

Emmanuel, please, you've got to understand.

I understand, I reply coldly, I've got no choice, but I'm horribly upset.

Please don't make me feel guilty, it's hard enough as it is.

I'm not making you feel guilty, I'm just saying that tomorrow you're going to be as miserable as I am now. Something's been ruined between us, broken, that's it, there's nothing we can do, so let's not talk about it. What are you doing this evening? Where are you?

I had dinner with Véro, she came home with me, we'll probably go sleep at her place in Montreuil, and we'll hit the road tomorrow morning.

That's ridiculous, you're both exhausted, totally strung out—at least stay home, sleep there.

Listen, we'll see. I'll call you later.

The next morning, I've bounced back. I'm going to be flexible, adapt to the new situation, turn every obstacle to my advan-

tage. I study the timetable. It's too late for a round-trip, but
there's a La Rochelle–Paris train (2:45–5:45) that arrives in
Poitiers ten minutes ahead of the Paris–La Rochelle (2:45–
5:45). Since you won't be making the journey, I will get on at
Poitiers and sit in the seat I reserved for you. I'll observe the
trip from your point of view. I'll study the passengers you
would have sat with, I'll imagine how you would have looked
at them, how they would have looked at you when you murmured "I want your dick in my pussy." I'll go see what's happening in the bar car.

I call you on my cell. You're in Montreuil; Véro had insisted
on sleeping there. I apologize for my coldness the previous
evening; I was disappointed, of course, but I understand—this
is an emergency, you shouldn't feel guilty. I never say specifically that I don't want any bad feelings to spoil the moment
when you read my story, but I do ask you to buy *Le Monde*
when you have a free moment to think of me.

You don't quite see why it's so important that you buy *Le
Monde* today, but you promise to do it.

When are you leaving?

This afternoon, probably for the Île de Ré.

Don't do anything rash. I'm worried, you know. You'll
call me along the way?

Yes, yes, my love . . . Hang on, the connection's breaking
up . . .

Cut off.

Poitiers, 4:19. I'd made a note of your seat number on the
Paris–La Rochelle train; no one is sitting there, so I take it.
Walking through the car, I can see already that this train was
a bad bet: almost no single women and none of them pretty,

lots of families, retirees, all busy with the comics or cross-word puzzles. Difficult, with this bunch, to imagine the promised orgy of knowing looks and double entendres.

At Niort, I go to the bar car. No one is watching, no one has *Le Monde* tucked under his or her arm. Complete failure. While I'm sitting at a table by a window, nursing a mineral water and thinking ruefully that I can't even turn this disaster into a funny story, a plump, pleasant young woman comes up to introduce herself: Émilie Grangeray of *Le Monde*. Sitting down, she adds: Special correspondent on the 2:45 Paris–La Rochelle. I am aghast. *Le Monde* has sent a reporter to witness my defeat. Impulsively, I begin babbling that I'm very disappointed because my fiancée was unable to take this train, there was an emergency . . . Smiling, Émilie Grangeray records what I say in a notebook. I watch her write "disappointed," "annoyed," "upset," and I'd like to correct her, project an image of witty detachment, but instead I feel a shame I thought I'd long left behind, the shame of a shy adolescent who invented girlfriends and then realized that no one believed him.

And now, this fiancée prevented by some emergency from taking the train—Émilie Grangeray doesn't look as if she's buying that. She tells me that back at *Le Monde*, leaving aside the question of whether or not to publish the story (which sparked a stormy debate), opinion was divided: some people believed everything in it was true, others were convinced it was fiction, and she herself leaned toward the fiction camp. Strangely enough, that last possibility had never occurred to me, and what's even stranger is that appearances do seem to be on Émilie Grangeray's side. I tell her this; she nods, and I can see I've made my position worse.

Shortly before we arrive in La Rochelle, I check my voice mail. Three messages from friends who've read the story: A marvelous love letter, you must both be so happy, there's no point in wishing you a good night! Then a message from you: We're about to set out but we decided to shut off our cell phones because Denis keeps calling and it's driving Véro batty. Here, I'll put her on.

Véro: Yes, Emmanuel, I'm taking off with your Soso, who's my Soso, too, you have to understand that this happens when someone has a friend who's in deep shit. Kisses.

Véro's way of ending messages with "Kisses" or, even worse, "Kiss-kiss," has always rubbed me the wrong way and today I'm even less forgiving than usual. And anyway, she doesn't seem so distraught, this friend who's in deep shit. Is everything okay? asks Émilie Grangeray. Everything's fine, yes. We have some more mineral water. Sad, bleak sunlight on the plains of the Vendée; dead midges on the train window.

Since there is no way to pass between the front and rear sections of this train, *Le Monde* has sent not one journalist but two, and we join up with the second one on our arrival in La Rochelle. He doesn't look too surprised to see me and tells us things weren't any livelier at his end. He didn't much believe in the existence of my girlfriend, either, or rather he did but imagined the story was something along the lines of payback for being dumped by her. I laugh: No, I mean really, that's not it at all. And instead of dumping the two of them, I decide to be friendly in the hope that their article will be less cruel. Having a drink with them down at the waterfront, I act like a guy who's rising above his disappointment, wax eloquent about the pleasure principle running smack into the reality principle, and with a final flourish announce that since I haven't canceled my fabulous hotel room, I prefer to sleep there tonight instead of returning to the Île de Ré. Maybe we can have dinner together.

Seafood, grilled striped bass, white wine. Frankly, I joke, it wasn't you two I was hoping to spend the evening with, but I like you anyway. It's true. Fralon, who usually works on the foreign desk, talks entertainingly about his assignments, and Émilie is just as comical, recalling the different jobs she held before landing at *Le Monde*: trapeze artist, ever-smiling coordinator for Club Med. She describes the Russian vacationers who take over the resort villages and the havoc they wreak; in short, our dinner is pretty jolly, but my phone is silent. They have stopped talking about my story—I assume they don't want to make me feel bad—but I bring the subject up again anyway. It turns out that Émilie had thought of calling a mutual acquaintance to see if you actually exist and correspond to the description in the story, while Fralon had considered recruiting a girl who fits the bill to take the train and add to the confusion. A tall blonde with a long neck, slender waist, and ample hips; he likes that part, the ample hips, but I get the impression that he thinks it's a nice way of saying a big ass. When I admit I still feel truly sad, they do their best to console me: I'm going to get hundreds of e-mails, maybe thousands, and there will be so many people who weren't on the train but wish they had been that they'll form their own online club. I'm sure, says Fralon kindly, that the story isn't over, that there's more to come. I agree, but it's almost midnight and my phone still hasn't rung.

• • •

At the hotel, where I've stretched out fully clothed on the bed, I leave you a somewhat curt message: I would have liked to hear from you, I still would; you were supposed to call when you got there, and what's all this business about turning off your phone? Then, lying there, I think about my story again. Is it possible that you read it and were so shocked that you don't want to talk to me anymore? No, I can't believe that. If I wrote the story for you, that was because I knew you'd read it as a declaration of love and would be excited by the exhibitionism. Anger fades into worry. I'm afraid there's been an accident, I should have gone back to Paris, should never have let you drive in such a state.

I finally drop off; the phone wakes me up. But it isn't you, it's my friend Philippe, who says: You know, reading this, I felt that Jean-Claude Romand was truly dead.* I want to tell him that I'm not so sure, but instead I just say that at the moment I am busy dealing with a serious problem. Philippe seems stunned by the idea that, today of all days, I might have a problem.

There are other phone calls during the day, which I spend shut up in the hotel room chain-smoking, leaving you increasingly frantic messages, calling hospitals, the police, the highway patrol, your friends . . . The people who call expect to find me flying high, sated with love and self-satisfaction, but the man who answers is a zombie who tonelessly repeats what he'd said to Philippe: There's a problem, I'll call you back.

---

* Jean-Claude Romand, who killed his wife, children, and parents in 1993, is the subject of Carrère's *The Adversary: A True Story of Monstrous Deception.*

I cannot tell anyone, even those closest to me, what the problem is. I'm not even sure myself. All I know is that it's one of two things: either you're in the hospital, hovering between life and death, or for some reason I can't imagine, you're having fun torturing me. There's a notebook in your purse with my phone number, in case of an emergency; if you were in the hospital someone would have been in touch. And even if you did turn off your cell phone, you must have checked your messages in the past twenty-four hours, since you check them all the time, and you also call me three times a day to say that you love me and are thinking of me.

So what's going on?

I didn't let the maid clean the room, where I'll be staying and chain-smoking until I find you. I won't allow myself to phone you more than once an hour. There's a church not far from the hotel, I can hear its bells ringing: four peals—it's already four in the afternoon. I call you for the tenth time today, exasperated in advance by the tenth encounter with your recorded message.

But this time, a miracle, you answer.

Emmanuel, darling, I just listened to your messages, what's going on? What's happening to you?

I shout: What do you mean, what's going on? And what do you mean by turning off your cell phone? Where the hell are you, why haven't you called me?

But I was going to call you. And I left you a message to let you know that I was turning off the cell, I told you, Véro's in a terrible state, I'm taking care of her—you're crazy to get all worked up like this, my love! What's going on?

Where are you?

We're in Saint-Valéry-en-Caux, we've been talking, she's really distraught, you know.

She's there with you now?

A pause. Then: Yes, she's with me.

Put her on.

She's not here in the room at the moment.

Wait a minute. She's so messed up you can't leave her for a second, you can't even take the time to phone and reassure me—then she can't be very far. Go get her.

Another pause. Then: Fine, I will.

I hear you call: Véro! Véro! . . . Véro, Emmanuel wants to talk to you. (Silence. No voice, no reply, not even a faint one.)

You're back: She doesn't want to speak to you.

She doesn't want to speak to me? And why not?

I don't know, she just doesn't. She's mad because you were angry about me going away with her.

First off, I wasn't angry, I only said I was sad, plus even if she's mad at me that doesn't mean she can't talk to me.

Now you start shouting and sobbing: I'm telling you, she doesn't want to! . . . Véro, please, talk to him . . . She won't. Emmanuel, there's nothing I can do, she doesn't want to.

Sophie, you are not with Véro. I don't know whom you're with, but you are not with Véro.

Who else could I be with? Listen, it's horrible, what you're doing to me. I'm exhausted, a nervous wreck, for two whole days I've been trying to keep her from coming apart and now you throw this completely insane fit. You have to get a grip.

You want me to get a grip? Easy. Put Véro on the phone to say, "Hi, here I am." She can even say, "Here I am you fuck-ing bastard," but have her say it. I simply want to hear her voice. She can talk to you instead of me—all I want to know is that she's there.

I told you she doesn't want to, can't you understand that?

No, I can't, and if Véro doesn't say anything that can mean only one thing, and that means we're through.

You're crazy.

Maybe I'm crazy but why can't Véro talk to me?

I didn't say she couldn't, I said she wouldn't. She hates you.

I don't understand why, but even if she hates me, she doesn't hate you, so you're going to explain to her that our future depends on her being kind enough to get close enough to the phone so that I can hear her voice. She can't very well refuse you that, can she? You say she's your best friend, so if she won't do that it's because she's your worst enemy.

Listen, Emmanuel, you've gone insane. Véro's in *such* bad shape and what you're doing is really despicable. So step back and think about what you're saying and we'll talk again when you've calmed down.

Cut off.

I call right back. Voice mail.

Sophie, it's ten minutes after four. If you are with Véro, which I find hard to believe, you have twenty minutes to convince her that our life together is in her hands. If you're with a man, you might as well tell me: anything would be better than these idiotic lies. So if you haven't called back by four thirty, with or without Véro, you'll have one week to collect your things and get out of the apartment. That's it. I'll leave my phone on until four thirty.

Of course I left it on longer than that. But no call by four thirty, no call by five o'clock. I can't take it anymore. I don't see myself returning wretchedly to the Île de Ré to face my appalled family. I decide to go back to Paris.

I'm waiting in the station café, a terrace laid out under the glass roof covering the platforms. I have cigarettes but no lighter, so every five minutes I ask a guy sitting near me for his, which he hands over with silent courtesy. Two elderly ladies and their little dog arrive and, finding all the tables occupied, turn to me: May we sit down, are you by yourself? I am, I reply, and I would like to stay that way. Outraged retreat, laughter from a table of young people. I wait there for two hours, going over everything that has just happened with the idea that perhaps through disappointment, lack of sleep, worry over not being able to reach you, I have somehow managed repeatedly to misinterpret what will turn out to be a perfectly ordinary chain of events. But I get nowhere. Point by point, things refuse to make sense. I think about my novel *The Mustache*, about my hero, tormented by impossible hypotheses, and I remember that line Michel Simon delivers in the movie *Bizarre, Bizarre*: "If you write enough horrible things, the horrible things will finally happen." And the worst of it is that they are happening just when I thought I had escaped them at last.

One minute before the train leaves and almost three hours after my ultimatum, you call me back.

Emmanuel, where are you?

At the station.

I'm putting Véro on.

No, it's too late.

I hang up. I laugh bitterly. It took you three hours to get hold of her: you're not only a liar, you're a fool. The phone rings again. I turn off the ringer and get on the train. The messages pile up; in the end, I listen to them.

Hi, it's Véro. Listen, I just don't get you and I even think you suck. I mean, fuck, sometimes you've wound up in deep shit yourself, so you should be able to understand that it happens to other people, too, and that there's more to life than you and your stupid moods. So you see, I *am* with Soso, everything's fine, not to worry. I was pissed off before, you can understand that, can't you?

No "Kisses." Her hip-proletarian lingo has always annoyed me but I've made an effort because of you, telling myself that she's had a hard life, she's a generous girl, really, and full of spirit. I detest her, now, but not as much as I hate you. After all, she's just giving you an alibi.

Next message, Véro again, identifying herself as Public Enemy Number One—her idea of an attempt at humor. For a woman on the verge of suicide, incapable of speaking to me three hours ago, she's become curiously talkative. Then you, pleading with me to call you back, to tell you when my train arrives, you'll come get me, I don't understand, what's happening my love, it's awful. This becomes as repetitive as my own calls over the past twenty-four hours.

I leave my seat to smoke a few cigarettes. Outside, the evening light is heartrending. Lots of people are reading *Le Monde*, some of them deeply absorbed in my story, including three pretty women traveling alone. They must all be thinking, Too bad, I took the wrong train, and most of the e-mails I will receive begin by expressing that regret. The bar car is packed; I wait on line for twenty minutes to get a mineral water. Although the only bartender is swamped, she behaves with unbelievable kindness and good humor, with a funny remark for everyone. Despite the wait no one gets impatient, all these pretty women could play out my scenario in the restrooms and emerge smiling at the next woman in line, it's really an enchanted train. As I return to my car, I encounter an elegant woman of a certain age with a handsome, open face, who asks if I am Emmanuel Carrère. When I reply no, she smiles and says, Bravo anyway!

The first thing I do, back home, is change the message on the answering machine. You had recorded it right after moving in with me; I remember how you loved saying, "You have reached the home of Sophie and Emmanuel," and how much I loved hearing it. After his wife left him, one of my friends kept the message with her voice and both their names for more than a year. I'm not going to be like that, and when I've changed your message I feel proud. Proud of the cold, unalterable hatred that has replaced anguished uncertainty. You no longer exist for me, you are nothing to me now. But somehow that does not stop me from hoping that you'll call so I can revel in your distress and my steadfastness. Since you're taking your time about it, I'm tempted to call you, but I begin checking my e-mails instead. Eighty-five messages. That's a start. Aside from a few gripes, they are enthusiastic: What a love letter! How I would have enjoyed being on that train! I'd really like to know what happened, I hope we'll be able to read the sequel soon. She must be one lucky woman, your fiancée. Every woman dreams that her man will send her a letter like that, you must both be so happy. . .

Poor souls, if you only knew.

You call around midnight, on my cell.

Emmanuel, where are you?

At my place.

At *your* place?

Yes, and I have just one thing to say to you and then I'm not answering any more of your calls: you can come tomorrow anytime after noon to start packing your things. Good night.

There follows, on the apartment answering machine, a series of pleas, to which I don't respond. Begging, tears, then anger. You are particularly enraged by the new phone message. So I don't exist anymore? Our love really means nothing to you? You want to destroy everything because I turned off my cell phone, because Véro was in a bad way? Emmanuel, please pick up, talk to me, I beg you, I know you're there . . .

I smile wickedly: payback is fair play.

You show up at eleven in the morning, while I'm going through the hundreds of e-mails that arrived during the night. You use your key to get in. Without looking up from the computer, without a glance at you, I say curtly, I told you noon, and all this week I would like you to respect that request and to ring the doorbell, this is no longer your home.

Emmanuel, until further notice I live here.

Not anymore, and let me remind you that I'm the one who pays the rent.

Emmanuel, we have to talk.

About what? You have an explanation for me? I mean something that makes sense, not that crap from your girl-friend?

But I mean—she called you! You wanted her to talk to you, she didn't want to, I spent the whole trip back fighting with her and she called you!

I sneer. Your expression of wronged innocence is inde-scribable; no one has ever looked so honest and true. You're wearing a black dress with a plunging neckline, no bra; I take in your shoulders, your arms, and try to persuade myself that I'll never miss all that. You park yourself on the living room sofa and light up a cigarette. So, you've started smoking again, too.

Emmanuel, I don't know what's in your story, I haven't read it yet, but I didn't understand how important it was for you.

It was important for you, too. For us.

Okay, it was important, but *you* have to understand that you're not the only person in the world, your wishes aren't the only ones that matter, and people don't necessarily take the train when you want them to. You bought me that ticket, you told me you'd prepared a surprise for me, and of course that pleased me, I wanted to come, but then Véro fell apart. She's like my sister, and whenever I've had trouble she's always been there for me, so I could not let you pressure me like that.

I did not pressure you, I did not ask you to abandon Véro, I only said that your not coming made me sad and was going to make you sad as well. Other than that, I asked you to call me to tell me how things were going, which was the least you could do, after all.

But I told you that I could handle the situation, that things would be fine.

Sophie, this discussion makes no sense and you know that. It would make some sense if you could prove to me that you were with Véro this weekend. At four o'clock yesterday that was simple; now it's definitely more complicated. So yes, I was upset, I was disappointed, I wasn't thinking clearly, but I'm thinking clearly now and this business with Véro not talking to me at four but then bombarding me with apologies at seven thirty? Excuse me, but there's only one possible explanation.

Which is what? Say it. I was with a man?

Well, I don't think you were with your mother.

Do you hear what you're saying? You actually imagine I would be with a man when Véro was in all that trouble?

I stand up, depressed by her evasions yet knowing I won't have the strength to really break things off. You look at me as if I were a madman; I would have liked to take you in my arms. I sit down in the gray armchair, across from you, and start again, more gently: Sophie, I want only one thing, and that's to believe you and ask you to forgive me. If only I could blame jealousy and paranoia—but I'm not like that. For four months you cheated on me and I never suspected a thing—you even reproached me for that. Well, now anybody in my position would have doubts, and I can't live with them, so we have to figure a way out of this. We have to find some way to reassure me definitively, some proof.

You raise your head, with a flicker of hope: What kind of proof would you need?

I don't know. Where did you sleep?

I told you, in Saint-Valéry-en-Caux.

At a hotel? What was the name of it?

The Eden. It was crummy, but there were no vacancies anywhere else.

Who paid?

After hesitating, you say: Véro. Which surprises me, since one of the reasons Véro is in such dire straits, aside from harassment from Denis, is that she's broke.

How did she pay?

I expect you to say in cash, but you can't think that quickly: By credit card, I guess, or a check . . .

Then we're saved. There's a record. She kept the receipt, and even if she didn't all she has to do is give me a copy of her credit card bill or the canceled check. Hotel Eden, July 20, it's quite simple.

But not for you, apparently. You think about it for a moment, with your head in your hands, then say: She won't do it. She won't give you that.

Why not?

Because a guy who asks for proof, she won't put up with that.

At that instant, your cell phone rings. Yes, Véro dear, you reply in a soft voice. I can't talk to you right now, I'm with

Emmanuel, he's raving again, it's a nightmare . . . I'll call you back.

You put down your cell. I'm stunned.

Sophie, unless you're lying, Véro is deliberately destroying us as a couple. You should be begging her to stop this nonsense and give you the receipt right away or you'll tear her eyes out—but no, you talk to her sweetly without even asking about it. This is insane.

It's insane to you because you've never been able to see anything except your own point of view. You don't know Véro.

Why the fuck would I want to know Véro! I just want her to give you that piece of paper.

You sigh. Then, looking me straight in the eye: You know what's going to happen? I'll tell you what's going to happen. I'll do as you say, I'll collect my stuff, move out, and Friday I'll drop off the key in an envelope, and in that envelope there'll also be the proof you want. Then you'll see.

I'm silent, suddenly shaken.

All right, I say finally, and then I will feel atrociously unhappy. But a minute ago we couldn't get past Véro's stubbornness and now you tell me that you already *have* the proof. So why put us through all this? Give me the proof now, I'll throw myself at your feet, you'll forgive me or not, but we'll end this madness. What's your proof?

Now *you* say nothing. Tears fill your eyes. Then, very softly but distinctly, you say: A pregnancy test.

Thunderbolt.

You're pregnant?

You nod. The tears spill down your cheeks.

• • •

You're on the sofa, eyes closed, head thrown back, and I see a vein throbbing in your neck. For the past hour we've been smoking nonstop. You've kept the lighter clenched in your hand, and when I ask you for it, with either a word or a gesture, I am careful not to touch you when I take it, careful never to touch you again, like a reformed alcoholic who won't even look at a brandied peach. Now I get up and very delicately remove the cigarette burning down between your fingers, stub it out in the ashtray, and tell you: No more of that, now. Then I take the pack and the full ashtray, which I empty in the kitchen. I stay there a moment, alone. I feel that you'll need some time to forgive me but that you will forgive me. You'll read my story, you'll see my love for you there, you'll understand my fit of insanity. So . . . There was an explanation after all. A simple one—one that I never thought of. Even though I'd told you you could trust me, you'd been afraid I wouldn't really want this child, that I'd accept it, if at all, more from necessity than from desire. You had wanted to go off alone to think; you turned off your cell because you couldn't talk to me. If you had, you couldn't have kept yourself from telling me about the baby, and you didn't dare tell me yet. There are still some things that aren't clear—that business with Véro, Véro who you fear is dead, Véro who's falling apart, Véro who won't speak to me—but right now all I'm thinking about is you being pregnant, about us having a child. Only a few weeks ago I would have said it was too soon, we'd have to think it over, wait, but I was wrong: what I believed I did not yet want, I already unconsciously desired. I even find it extraordinary that this should happen the moment my story is published; there's a stunning logic in this, and also (I can't help thinking ahead) the ideal ending for the book I will write.

I return to the living room. Moving around the coffee table, I cross the five feet that separate me from the couch and sit down beside you, without touching you. You are huddled up, arms crossed, have almost turned your back to me. My hand brushes yours; I don't know if you're going to give me your hand, but you do. I hold it. It seems lifeless. With my fingers around yours, I count to nine: it will be in April. You must have understood. You squeeze my hand, you guide it; you place it on your belly. You say, My breasts have already grown twice as big, it's incredible.

You lean your head on my shoulder. You say, Emmanuel, my love, what is this obsession you have with lying? Who has lied to you?

We go into the bedroom. We lie down on the bed. We aren't going to get undressed, though, not so fast, but we're in each other's arms and I caress your breasts, saying, My love, my love, and you cry softly.

You fall asleep. I don't. Everything that has happened in the past two days whirls in my head. No matter how I approach it, there's something that doesn't quite add up, but I lay all the blame on Véro. Any other reasonable friend, hearing you explain the situation, would have encouraged you to join me. You'd have taken the train, read my story, and that evening, in the restaurant, you'd have told me with shining eyes that you had a surprise for me, too. The celebration we might have shared never happened because that nasty shrew put I don't know what idiotic ideas into your head—that I might take the news the wrong way, that you had to talk it over woman-to-woman—I mean, what kind of crap did she tell you, and why? She hates men and probably hates you. Jealous, she hopes more or less consciously to destroy us because I'm not the type she thinks you need, meaning some pretentious hippie loser, someone who'd drag you down to his pathetic level. That poor girl, poor crazy witch, you really have to stop seeing her. Aggressive, not getting laid enough—girlfriends like that, they get together for little dinners where they bitch about their husbands, they're like cigarettes, a bad habit. As for me, I've been smoking like a chimney these last three days, but I'm going to stop tomorrow. We'll both stop tomorrow.

In the meantime, I go down to buy another pack, as well as *Le Monde*, which I skim while sitting in a café. The article by Grangeray and Fralon is on the last page: not too mean, even if I do inevitably come off as a pouting, disappointed child. What do I care—I know how the story ends.

You're still sleeping when I get home. I lie down for a moment beside you; we fit together like two spoons, but your breathing doesn't reassure me. It doesn't seem peaceful. Your face seems to grimace with pain; you shift as if in the throes of a bad dream. I get up and turn on the computer: 220 e-mails at this point, most quite favorable. A few sexual propositions, some of them charming. A few insults are just stupid, but I'm hardly impartial. There are already reactions to Grangeray and Fralon's article. Touched by my disappointment, many readers try to console me: the story is the important thing, it doesn't matter whether the woman exists or not. But she does, I feel like shouting, she does exist! And among the most recent messages, there is this:

May I start reading?

Not yet. Wait until the train leaves. You have to follow

the instructions in the text exactly. When the train starts to move, you begin. Not before. Another ten minutes.

Tell me the first sentence.

No, we said we weren't going to cheat.

Please, just the first sentence.

Okay, but that's all. It begins with: "At the station news-stand, before getting on the train, you bought *Le Monde*."

He himself had bought the paper an hour earlier. He hadn't planned on taking the train that day, hadn't intended to accompany her all the way to La Rochelle. It was the husband's story that changed his mind. The strange piece published that day. Of course she'd told him about the story, about its appearing in *Le Monde*, but she hadn't said any-thing about what was in it. After reading the last line, he'd put down the paper, paid for his coffee, and dashed to the station in a taxi. When he'd joined her quietly in her com-partment, she hadn't seemed surprised. Sitting across from her, he'd issued his own set of instructions. The lover's instruc-tions. Actually, she was to do nothing other than scrupu-lously follow the directions in the story. But with one big difference: he would be there. They would read the story together, and together they would deceive the husband—he, by watching her face throughout the trip, noticing the slightest quiver of her skin, envisioning her naked under her clothes, following her finger as it slipped into her armpit, divining the words on her lips: I want your dick in my pussy. Yes, but *his* dick, his enormous dick that makes her scream. Because the lover, he's no pussyfoot who takes his time com-ing, no sexual aesthete. The lover, he takes her like the bitch she is, with great ramming thrusts, her back up against a wall off in the corner of a parking garage. He penetrates her until she chokes, he plows her, and when she collapses, exhausted, trembling all over and drowning in brutal waves of pleasure that take her breath away, he knows that she's much more than his bitch, more than his pet. That she is part of him. Because his huge tool has reshaped her cunt and molded her to him. Because his sharp, pungent sweat, the sweat of a hot-blooded man from the south of France, has left a clinging film on her, has left his traces and their nourishing secrets running deep beneath her skin. And because when the sheen of sweat finally dries, when her womb unclenches and the pleasure fades, her hunger for him seizes her again.

But today, none of that. He looks at her, that's all. In fact, he watches from a distance as she makes love with her husband on a train. He is careful not to change the original plan. For as she reads the story, her desire will grow along with his. And becoming excited by her husband's words, under her lover's gaze, will bring her a new and powerful pleasure. At the end they will masturbate together in the restroom. She facing the mirror, he behind her. He'll be careful not to ejaculate on her, make sure to empty himself slowly on the floor without spattering her. They'll have to struggle not to touch each other—and she not to take into her mouth that enormous cock she loves: its shape and smell, the squat, round tip, the swollen vein wrapped around the shaft like a vine, which she loves to stroke and trace with her fingertip, and his ivory sperm, so plentiful, which she smears on her face. When they have time, she likes him to come in her blond hair. Then he massages her skull for a long while, telling her he's working all his seed, all those tiny living creatures, into her head.

But this time, no touching. It will be exactly as written in the story. As a finale, the e-mail sent off as soon as they reach the station. He has his laptop with him. When he gets off the train, he'll look for a cybercafé to send the message. This is what excites them the most. That the husband will know but be kept in doubt, trapped in his own game. *Le Monde*, circulation 600,000; probably quite a few e-mails. It will be so hard to untangle the true from the false in this spiderWeb: the usual reactions from readers, the clumsy sequels sent by amateurs, propositions of all kinds, and then this. At first, it will make him smile. He'll think: Not bad. It's got the right tone, it's amusing. And then, doubt will creep in. The lovers have agreed that however this works out, she will deny everything. And even between them, they will never mention the trip again. Not a word, not a sign, nothing.

So, Emmanuel. My story is over. I am the lover. There's your performative statement. I declare war on you. With my enormous dick. Before casually sending this e-mail, just a few last words to really let the doubt take hold and trouble you: at night, what she likes is to sleep together like spoons, on her side, back curved and you (or me) tight against her.

Philippe, from Nice.
La Rochelle, July 20, 2002, 6:00 p.m.

Not a single typo or grammatical error. Sheer cruelty. There's not enough here to make me believe this guy really is or has been your lover (the physical details would have been more precise), but enough to hurt me. You and I sleeping like spoons. You sleeping like that with someone else, making love with someone else. I tell myself he's a pervert, Philippe from Nice.

But my story, isn't that perverse as well? No. No, I don't believe so. Naïve perhaps, immature, but perverse, no. I turn off the computer and, sitting in front of it, start thinking about this pregnancy business, and the more I think the more it's clear that it doesn't make sense. I rewind the whole film one more time. I left for Russia at the end of May and came back with a bout of herpes that forced us to make love with condoms right up until the day before I left for the Île de Ré, when, for the first time in a month and a half, I came inside you. That was a Friday and one week later you learn that you're pregnant and your breasts are swollen. Isn't that a bit quick, one week? I wish I could wake you up to ask you. I go back into the bedroom, watch you sleep. You seem to be suffering so! I shut myself up in my office with the phone book; speaking softly, I call up several neighborhood gynecologists. A Dr. Weitzmann, rue de Maubeuge, can see me at six o'clock. I promise myself not to question you until I've seen him.

You get up at five. Worn out, you run yourself a bath. You don't seem well at all. I make some tea, which I bring you in the bathroom. I sit down beside the tub and, forgetting my promise, say that I'd like to ask you one question, only one.

No, Emmanuel, stop it, I'm not up to answering your questions right now, you've hurt me enough as it is.

Listen, my question, it's just—this pregnancy test, you had it when?

I'm not sure, this weekend . . .

What do you mean, I'm not sure? That's not the kind of thing you forget.

Actually, it is. I'm completely out of it, I'm forgetting

everything, dates, places, I don't have your memory, okay? Stop torturing me, what do you want? You want this child inside me to die?

What about your gynecologist? Don't you have to see her?

I have an appointment tomorrow morning.

I'll go with you.

No, no, I'd rather you didn't. This is about me.

Oh, and me, I have nothing to do with it?

The more we talk, the more I'm sure, and I cruelly enjoy watching you dig yourself in deeper and deeper, but I don't want to finish you off without official confirmation. Then you tell me that it would be better if we separated for a few days, you need to be alone, and then there are my kids, they must be worried, I ought to go back to the Île de Ré . . .

Just what am I supposed to do on the Île de Ré? No one has any idea why you never showed up or why I took off, and since I still don't understand what's going on either, what could I possibly say to everyone?

I'm telling you I need to be alone, it's a female thing, can't you understand that?

No, I can't. Unless, obviously, the child isn't mine.

There, I've said it. You stare at me in horror.

Did you hear what you just said? You tell me you love me and then you say something like that?

I say, I can't take this anymore, I'm going out for a walk.

Dr. Weitzmann, bound by the professional code of confidentiality, can't reveal what we discussed, but I can, so I'll report that I found him most satisfactory. Fifty, friendly, frank. The period between conception and a positive test is two weeks;

it can be a bit less, of course, especially with women who don't run like clockwork—but you, you do. He says: Friday the twelfth, Sunday the twenty-first, I'm sorry but the chances are slim that it's yours. A sonogram would show how far along she is, and she'll need to have one in any case if she plans on keeping the child. If there's a confession to make, there's no point in putting it off. And that astonishes me, too, that you persist in lying when you have no chance of being believed.

Walking me to the door, Dr. Weitzmann, who has read my story, asks, Is it her?

Yes.

That's too bad.

I sit in the gray armchair and wait for you to come sit on the sofa, across from me. It's as if these were our assigned places; the range of gestures and pathways in the apartment has become grotesquely restricted in the last twenty-four hours. Going from the bathroom to the bedroom, the bedroom to the living room used to be simple; now it's a trap.

Calmly, I tell you about my visit to Dr. Weitzmann. I repeat everything: the dates, the waiting period, and you listen to me as if you don't understand. Me, I'm wearing that awful smile you later tell me that you hate, like "a chess player sure of his checkmate" and taking his time.

So, what you're saying is, you think the child isn't yours?

A sonogram will tell us how far along you are. Why don't you get one tomorrow? You'll have to have one sooner or later anyway.

You detest me, is that it?

That's it, yes.

You stand up, take your purse, and leave without telling me where you're going.

You don't slam the door, you don't close it softly, either. If there is a neutral way of closing a door, that's how you do it.

Four in the morning. I've just written down everything that has happened in the last two days. Recording the words we said as precisely as possible is the only way for me to get through what has happened to us and is going to happen in the coming days. (Much later, I will make a few adjustments, a few cuts, but most of the preceding narrative was written that night.)

Never tempt the devil, my mother always says. Did I tempt the devil? Is it my fate to tempt him, no matter what I do?

I would like to think not. I would like to think that my short story was an act of love that happened to coincide with an act of betrayal, which it in no way provoked. I would like to believe I am not guilty of anything.

But I can't.

Strange, that I care so little about finding out who the other man is. Or whether he wants to keep the child, whether he wants to live with you. And you, what do you want?

There are moments when I tell myself that you're a monster, a pathological liar. Then I think that I'm the one who's out of control. A quick fling, an unwanted pregnancy, it's an accident, a domestic crisis, but not truly monstrous. If it hadn't coincided with the publication of my story, I'd be able to deal with it without going so crazy. But there's my disappointment—and even more, my wounded pride and humiliation, the anticipated triumph turned to ridicule. That's what I can't bear, what makes me torture you, and what forces you deeper into ever more incoherent lies.

At dawn, at the end of my rope, I call your cell phone. Your voice is flat; we speak quietly, as if there were people nearby we didn't want to awaken.

I say: I'm afraid for you.

Yes.

Where are you?

I don't have to answer your questions. I never loved anyone the way I loved you.

I know. Me, too, I never loved anyone the way I loved you. But I can't not ask you these questions. It's too serious.

What's serious? That I didn't get on a train? That I didn't do what you wanted, like some character in a novel?

No. That you're pregnant by another man and you tried to make me believe the child was mine.

I did not try to make you believe it was yours.

So it isn't mine?

I don't want to answer you.

Fine.

You don't know the truth. You don't know anything.

But that's all I want, the truth. I want you to talk to me.

Give me some time. I need to sleep now. It's good that you called.

. . .

When you say that you never loved anyone the way you loved me, never desired anyone the way you desired me, I know it's true, with all due respect to Philippe from Nice and his enormous dick.

And when I say the same thing back, you know it's true as well.

I want to say those words again: my love. For at least a year, I've said them often, alone, in a low voice: my love.

I loved you so much.

Three hundred thirty-nine e-mails. I'm beginning to find them repetitious. Always the same praise, the same questions. But in the heap of messages there is one as touching as Philippe from Nice was hurtful. Here it is:

This is to say thank you.

The Saturday, July 20, edition of *Le Monde* came my way by accident—some friends passing through forgot the paper at my house. I left it lying around until this afternoon.

The house is calm. It's a lovely day, very hot.

Siesta time, you understand?

So I read, and used, *Le Monde*.

And that brought me pleasure.

The man who once brought me such pleasure is no longer in a position to do so, at least not in the simple, direct way. But he knows that, with me, words work wonderfully. And so he went through you, I think, and he used your words, and it's only right that I thank you for having passed on his message.

The man who once brought me pleasure died almost five years ago.

Since then, I haven't taken a siesta.

I am seventy years old.

Thanks again.

You've come back to talk to me?

Yes, I've come back to talk to you.

Well then, first, listen to me. I love you so much it's killing me. There might be a chance for us to pull out of this, but today you have to tell me everything. No lies. If you lie to me, I'll find out, not because I'll hire detectives but because of this bizarre connection between us that means I call you at dawn from Kotelnich on the day you slept somewhere else, then you learn you're pregnant by someone else on the day I'm telling the whole world I love you. If I learn, and I will, that you lied to me today, we're dead.

I won't lie. But I don't want to tell you only about what's been going on this past week or so. I want to tell you about us from the beginning.

You remember our first dinner, at the Thai restaurant near Maubert?

Of course I remember.

You arrived late. I showed you papers about a job I'd been offered in my firm. I didn't know whether I should take the job or not. It was important to me, I wanted to talk to you about it, and you listened for a few minutes, pretending to be interested, but you quickly moved on to talking about the documentary you were going to make in Russia, and you told me the story of your Hungarian man. Well, I wasn't pretending, I really was interested. But that sets up the pattern for everything that came after. Your concerns interest us both, mine interest only me. You find them insignificant. At first I wasn't bothered by it. I was falling in love. And you were, too, I know, I don't doubt that for a minute. I'd gone out to dinner with the idea that we might wind up in the same bed, and when I woke up there the next morning, I knew we were going to see each other again that night, and the following one, and that you wanted this, too, and that's what happened. It seemed obvious, and a little miraculous.

When you asked me to come live here on the rue Blanche, I was happy but also afraid, because I could tell you were afraid. You didn't say so, but I realized that you'd have liked me to bring over a few suitcases but not give up my apartment, in case we didn't work out. I remember, when you showed up with the van, everyone laughed because you'd picked the smallest kind and then seemed dismayed by how much stuff I had. There wasn't really all that much, but even so, there was too much for you. I felt uncomfortable introducing you to the friends who'd come to help me move. You did your best to be pleasant, but I could tell you didn't like them. You were older, richer, in a more prestigious profession, and you looked down on them in a way that hurt me. My friends are important to me, I love them, and I did not want to give them up for you.

I interrupt: But Sophie, I never asked you to. We saw your friends as much as we saw mine, we gave parties where everyone mixed together. What bothers me, as I listen to you, is that you talk as if you've never been happy with me.

Not true. I *was* happy. Deeply happy. Happier than I've ever been with anyone. I loved living with you, making love with you, having breakfast with you. But I've never felt safe. You were proud of me and at the same time a little ashamed. As if I weren't worthy of you, as if I were just a pleasant stage in your life while you waited for the right woman to come along. If something I said sounded commonplace or I used one of those nicknames that annoy you so much, from one minute to the next your loving face would turn hard and distant, you looked like an enemy. I loved you, I knew you loved me, but the whole time I was afraid you would leave me. Of course we know that nothing lasts forever, that couples break up, but usually it's just a vague possibility. With you, though, it was a permanent threat. You kept telling me that I shouldn't trust you, this was just a trial run and always would be, that we were in love but weren't building anything together. You remember the evening when you said in front of everyone, in the kitchen, that if I wanted to have a child, too bad, it wouldn't be with you? You remember the guy who started bombarding me with e-mails, sending me flowers and books at the office? When I told you about him, you didn't take it seriously, as if no one could threaten you. I felt that you were too sure of my love, too sure that if one of us left, it would be you. I resented you for that, terribly.

Later, there were your trips to Russia. I dreamed, at the beginning, that you would invite me to go with you, to at least join you there for a week, to share this thing you kept telling me was so important. But I bet that never occurred to you. It's not just that you wanted to keep the experience to yourself— every time you left you hinted that something might happen over there, that your life might go in a completely new direction. I thought about Russian women, of course, and was jealous. And I had the feeling you were searching for something I could never give you. I felt sidelined, with nothing to do but wait, and without even being sure you'd come back to me.

You remember the dinner with Valentine, just before you left for Moscow last summer? You remember the stories you made up about the hikers who were going to hit on us in the Agnel pass while you were off chatting up Russian models? I laughed, but actually I didn't find them so funny, your stories.

I felt you were trying to tell me, You're free, go live your life, because I'm going to do as I like and so should you. And you know what happened? I didn't tell you, because deep down I sensed you didn't give a damn, but the hut at the Agnel pass, that's where I met Arnaud. The evening you called from Moscow. He was hiking, too, with some friends. We talked. I think he was impressed that you called me from Moscow, he asked what you were doing there while I was in the Queyras, and he said that in your place he'd have taken me to Moscow or come on the hike, but in any case he'd have stayed with me, wouldn't have let me out of his sight for a minute. He was afraid to try picking me up, but I could see he liked me and that felt good. And I felt available, although I wasn't happy about it. I figured it was you, with your stories, who had pushed me into his arms, that you'd seen it coming and it was what you really wanted, in the end. You know what happened next. We saw each other in Paris, exchanged e-mails.

You slept together.

Yes, but for Arnaud that wasn't the most important thing, that we sleep together. He wanted to get married and have children. And spend our lives together. He really believed it was possible, and I wanted to believe it, too. It was good to be loved that way. Simple, straightforward, with a future. He knew I loved you, naturally, but he said that you weren't making me happy and he was ready to wait until I understood that, too. And he did, he waited. He was miserable and so was I; you were the only one who wasn't, because you never noticed a thing. Not even the ring. Finally I told you about him. You asked me to stay and I did. I told Arnaud about my decision that same day. I broke up with him.

For good?

For good, yes, and what's so terrible is that you and I

never spoke of it again. For you, it was over and done with, two days later you'd forgotten all about it. I had met a man who truly loved me, asked me to marry him and have children with him. I was torn apart, but you never took it seriously for one second.

Yes I did, I took it seriously. I realized that if I wanted to keep living with you we would have to have a child. I asked only that you wait a year, so we could be sure.

Yes, you asked me to wait a year. But once again, it was you who made the decision, you who marked the calendar. I had nothing to say about it.

No, don't you remember, at that dinner at Jean-Philippe's, we drank to the child we'd have someday and I surprised everyone by making the toast?

That's true, and you told me that the idea of me pregnant was very erotic. I loved you saying that, I thought it was a gift, to me and the child.

You sob and repeat softly: That's true . . .

When you went back to shoot your film in Kotelnich, I don't really know what happened but it was as if I were drowning. I felt alone, abandoned, I was afraid, I thought my life was coming apart at the seams. I spent a night with a man.

One?

One, the night you tried to call me to say you were coming back early.

I knew it. I knew you were lying to me.

I lied because it wasn't important.

Who was it?

I told you, it's not important.

Do I know him?

No.

And you fucked without a condom?

Silence.

When did you realize you were pregnant?

Last Thursday. A few days earlier, you'd said, Trust me. It was the first time you'd ever said that. It's the first time I've been pregnant. I've never had an abortion before.

You bow your head. You weep.

I don't dare touch you. I ask softly, You've decided to have an abortion?

I wanted a child with you, Emmanuel, not anyone else. I wanted to get it done as fast as possible, to join you Saturday with the whole thing over, but there's a required waiting period, it wasn't possible before Monday. That's why there was no way I could come to the Île de Ré. I didn't want to see you until it was done. And then everything got mixed up with this business of your story. I don't know what's in it, I haven't the heart to read it right now, all I understood was that you wanted me to join you at any price, you were ready to come back to Paris, and that—that was impossible. Every phone call was an ordeal—that's why I finally turned off my cell phone. I thought, I'll explain later. Either you'd understand or you wouldn't, but what I needed right then was to cut off communication between us.

You were with the other man, that's it? The one who got you pregnant?

I couldn't bear the burden alone, Emmanuel.

And what did he say? What did he want?

To keep the child.

Sophie, I don't get this. You sleep with a man just once, you tell me it's not important—and he wants to keep the baby?

You murmur: He loves me.

After a pause, I ask: Is it Arnaud?

You lower your eyes. Then, after a long silence, you tell me that you took the first abortion pill on Monday, you have to take the second one tonight, the gynecologist has warned you to expect a night of pain and bleeding. You need to be alone and would like me to leave you the apartment for a few days.

Okay, I'll leave tomorrow for the Île de Ré.

Then I'll come back tomorrow.

What about tonight?

I'll sleep somewhere else tonight. This thing is my business, I don't want to go through it with you.

Then with him? You're going to stay with him?

I don't have to tell you.

We call a truce. I come over to the sofa, where you lie down in my arms. Caressing your face, my lips brushing against your hair, I murmur, My love, my love . . . But the shadow lengthens. I think of Arnaud, this young man whom I don't know and who loves you, who is waiting for you, waiting for you to understand that being with me will lead nowhere, waiting for you to choose him. I think about his misery, wonder if he loves you as you claim he does; I believe he does, since you felt the need to tell him about the pregnancy and that you've decided not to have the child. I think about the moment when you had me touch your swollen breasts. The way you would have if you'd really been pregnant by me.

You've gone, I'm here alone. I look at my e-mail. Someone—a devotee of mantras and Transcendental Meditation, I suspect, given his fondness for Capitals—writes in English:

You say in your story that you love the Real but it exalts the Evil and the Unreal. I hope that when you met her the woman slapped you for degrading her in that way. I hope she left you. You deserve it. You deserve to have your heart broken.

Do I deserve to have my heart broken? Do I deserve to have you leave me? Slap me? You didn't slap me, you did worse, but it's because I made you suffer. I failed to love you, to see you. You lied to me, you betrayed me, but when you discovered that you were carrying another man's child you didn't hesitate to abort it. Because you want to have a child with me.

Will we ever have a child, one day?

Before setting out in the car, I skim through *Le Monde* at the café. The ombudsman, who comments once a week on letters to the editor, devotes his column to my story and makes an act of contrition on behalf of the newspaper. He quotes only from indignant letters that include threats of canceled subscriptions and then concludes that *Le Monde* has stumbled badly by publishing a story that is both scandalous and mediocre. If I had the courage, I'd send my own letter, reminding the ombudsman of this elementary rule of journalism: happy readers write to the author; angry readers write to the editor. In the past five days I've received more than eight hundred messages, 90 percent of which are enthusiastic. The ombudsman knew that I had included my e-mail address in the piece; he could easily have asked me for a few of the messages I'd been sent. The most wounding aspect of his article, obviously, isn't his indignation but the dismissive way he treats my story, as a childish provocation that falls flat, something vaguely ridiculous and embarrassing. In my modest and so-far unblemished career, this is the first time I've been snidely trashed, and one of the first things I learn when I reach the Île de Ré is that the acerbic critic Philippe Sollers has followed the ombudsman's lead, mocking my story in *Le Journal du Dimanche*, wondering why *Le Monde* published this bit of prepubescent porn, and winding up with a joke about what the permanent secretary of the Académie must think about it all.

What she thinks of it is clear, but she'd rather be torn to pieces by wild horses than even mention it, so she sticks to

other topics—the neighbors, the weather, errands to run—
without alluding in any way to the story, your absence, or
my erratic comings and goings. As for my father, he seems to
have been struck by a dart tipped with *rajaijah*, the poison in
the Tintin books that drives victims insane: whenever I appear,
he begins to pace about, gazing into the distance. In the living
room, I ask him where Jean-Baptiste, my younger son, might
be; looking tired, he replies, Well, probably in his room or
watching television. (This exchange takes place within a yard
of the TV set.)

Papa, I say gently, you can see for yourself that he isn't
watching TV.

Well, I said he was probably in his room or watching
television, so if he isn't watching television, it's because he's
in his room.

In the middle of all this tension and stillborn conversation, Jean-Baptiste keeps asking whether I'm okay. I reply
that no, I'm not doing too well, that I will certainly feel better
in time but for the moment I'm not okay, and then a minute
later he asks again: Are you okay? We wind up keeping track,
it turns into a kind of game and gives us a laugh.

Gabriel, his brother, has gone off to climbing camp, so
Jean-Baptiste has been on his own with my parents. I'd come
to see him, thinking to stay two or three days, but I soon
realize that the best way for me to cheer everyone up would
be to leave.

We all go off to swim; the water is rough and full of sea-
weed. A thunderstorm welcomes us back to the house, where
my father puts away the deck chairs as if he were preparing
a corpse for burial, while in the kitchen my mother stares at

the pressure cooker as though stoically expecting its imminent explosion. I tell myself that even if everything had turned out as planned, it was utter insanity to ever imagine that my parents would have taken the story well. What on earth had I been thinking? What possessed me to choose their house as a haven and them as witnesses? Dinner is a silent ordeal, after which, determined to put up a bold front, I go off to Ars to join Olivier, Valérie, and a gathering of mostly mutual friends: a very Île de Ré little group—in other words, Parisian—which hums with curiosity when I arrive. Your absence, my evasive replies to them on the phone—they all want to know what's going on. I cut the conversation short by saying that we're having some problems but they're not important and I don't feel like talking about them. The audience is disappointed. When I won't budge, we fall back on the story. Olivier, whom no one would call a prude, found it—how to put this?—pretty sexy but, well, when you know the people involved, you have to admit it makes you feel weird. Valérie says it's nothing like her fantasies and, in her opinion, waving your dick around like that in front of children and parents is a little immature. Nicole exclaims, I'd love it if a man wrote that to me! François, you'd never do something like that for me, would you? (François shrugs, pours himself another slug of white wine.) Nicole's enthusiasm notwithstanding, the general verdict is that the story is an almost runaway mixture of cleverness and sexual braggadocio that leaves the reader feeling not indifferent but uneasy.

I drink a lot, smoke a lot. When the conversation moves on to something else, I keep my end up as best I can, praising this, belittling that, and I find myself thinking that, although I can sometimes hold my own in this sort of gathering, Sophie, you can't. You'll never fit in, you'll always be jealous of some-

one like Valérie, who is—what?—an editor at *Elle* but can
confidently whip out opinions on everything, not like you,
whose voice quivers with indignation and humiliation. But
it's you I love, for the joy I sometimes glimpse in you, so often
overshadowed by the pain of your illegitimacy, the fact that
when you were born (an ugly baby, apparently, dark and hairy),
your mother cried because she was the only one there to welcome you, my love.

My love.

Holed up inside the house, my mother, Jean-Baptiste, and
I are playing Monopoly. During the game, from which she
is quickly eliminated, my mother breathes heavily, the way
she does when she feels ill. Evenly matched at first with
Jean-Baptiste, I then go down in total defeat (no houses, no
money, no nothing) to double-edged commentary that is
half-conscious on Jean-Baptiste's part and pointedly conscious
on my mother's: Oh, you're really stuck now . . . Oh, now
you're really dead.

You're really dead.

Reading Philippe Sollers in *Le Journal du Dimanche*, I feel
really, truly dead. He's harder to swallow than the ombudsman at *Le Monde*, because Sollers always leads the takedown
pack and sics them on their prey. I who have always had such
fear of ridicule, I would have liked to be that kind of man,
someone who doesn't give a damn about anything or anyone,
especially if they can't hack it as well as he can. Someone

who gazes ironically on the whole world with a thin smile of superiority. And I realize that my unfortunate grandfather, so beaten down by life, would have wanted to be like that as well.

You call me around midnight. A bleak and stormy conversation. You say I'm the only man who ever made you believe in true love. I ask if you still do. You answer that you need time. In the end, I tell you that what's serious isn't the lying, or the accident, or the consequences, but the fact that you slept with another man. That I cannot bear. I don't ever want another man's dick in you ever again.

Are you saying that just to make me feel better?

I'm saying it because it's true. Suddenly the words seem violently erotic to me: no dick inside you ever again except mine.

The next morning, I sit on the terrace with my mother for a last coffee before driving back. Silence, the clink of spoons, tension. Then, abruptly, without looking at me: Emmanuel, I know that you intend to write about Russia, about your Russian family, but I ask one thing of you, and that is not to touch my father. Not while I am alive.

It's strange, but I was expecting this. I'd been waiting for her to say this to me one day, and I was even expecting it just then, as the silence dragged on. After a few more moments of silence I reply that I understand, I know why she's saying that, but her request is devastating, because in effect it kills me as a writer.

Don't be absurd. If you're so interested in your Russian

origins, there are a thousand other stories to tell. I don't see what drives you to dig up this one.

But Mama, if I became a writer it was precisely to tell this very story, to be done with it one day. If there is one thing that *mustn't* be said, you know it is inevitably the only thing that can and must be said.

It isn't your story, it's mine. In any case, you know nothing about it and neither does Nicolas. I am the only one who knows it and I wish it to die with me.

You're mistaken. Maybe I know nothing about it, but it's my story, too. It has haunted your life, which means it has haunted mine and it will haunt and destroy my children, your grandchildren, because that's what happens with secrets— they poison the generations.

Just at that moment, I realize that Jean-Baptiste, lying on his bed in the children's room, which looks out onto the terrace, must have heard the entire conversation, this business about a secret that has poisoned everyone and will poison him in turn. At a loss, I stammer his own words back at him, a pathetic "Are you okay?" Then I put my bag in the car and ask that we all sit down together, following the Russian custom when someone goes on a journey. This gathering doesn't last even ten seconds: my mother jumps up to reclaim Jean-Baptiste, whom I had settled on my lap—quick, get him away from his crazy father—and I drive off without anyone asking where I'm going or when I'll be back. The main thing, for them and for me, is that I disappear.

Driving back to Paris, I think about the first trip I ever made to Russia, with my mother. Invited to a historians' conference in Moscow, she had decided to take me along. I must have been ten years old. I loved Mama—I always thought of her as "Mama" then, never as "my mother"—with absolute, confident love, so traveling alone with her to her family's distant homeland must have been the most entrancing prospect in the world.

We had a room with two beds in the vast Hotel Rossiya, where the conference was held. Mama took me everywhere; I listened politely to the speeches. She was entirely mine and I hers in uninterrupted intimacy, a lovers' voyage. In the morning, walking along the hotel's endless corridors, we would head for one of the many *stolovye*, workers' canteens where breakfast was served under the watchful eyes of professionally surly *dezhurniye*, custodians, whom we made fun of behind their backs. Mama loved to laugh, particularly with me, but she needed to laugh *at* someone. It was important for other people to be a little ridiculous to emphasize how intelligent, cultured, scathing—in a word, superior—we were ourselves. Whenever there was a break in the conference, the two of us took a trip. We visited the Kremlin and the Novodevichy Convent and Zagorsk, and even Vladimir and Suzdal. In Red Square, I admired the monument to Minin and Pozharsky. I don't remember exactly who those heroes were but, finding their names funny, I called them Mimine and Piroshky. I called myself Monsieur Mimine and thought it hilarious whenever my mother used the name. She already called me Manuchok, and the family had also adopted a rhyme Nana had made up, which my father never tired of singing in French: *Manu, viens chez nous*: Manu, we're inviting you. What pleased me the most, however, probably because it was just between the two of us, was being Mama's Monsieur Mimine.

During the conference, Mama met a man; I remember only that he was stocky, with brown hair, and he invited her

to his room for some Dagestani cognac. It wasn't clear
whether the invitation included me, although it was quite
clear that the man would have preferred to drink his cognac
alone with her; in any case, she politely declined the offer.
We ran into him at the *stolovaya*, though, and had tea with
him—so we three were often together. Evidently attracted to
this pretty French brunette, he must quickly have realized
that the son presented an insurmountable obstacle, and had
I been in his shoes I would have detested that clinging and
pedantic little boy. For my part, as I recall, I, Manuchok, Monsieur Mimine, didn't give a hoot. This alluring young woman
was my Mama and I was her favorite. I never doubted that she
preferred to come back to our hotel room and go to sleep
with me rather than drink Dagestani cognac with someone
else. I did not see other males as a threat. I was sure of my
Mama's exclusive love and felt no jealousy. That's still the
way I am—sure that the woman who loves me loves only me
and will never stop, no matter what I do. But if I find out I'm
wrong, I go crazy.

When I arrive home, you are taking a bath. I undress and slip into the tub facing you; we fit together well. The water is hot; I caress your legs, your feet resting on my shoulders; I close my eyes, I feel safe. I must have dozed off for a moment. When I wake up, I remember having a calm conversation, with long pauses, a conversation made gentle by fatigue. But then we go to dinner on the rue des Abbesses, where I ignore my food and knock back white wine until I become unbearable. I tell you that in spite of your possessive jealousy, *you* somehow managed to cheat on me nonstop for a year. And it's not that you've had men but that they've had you—because you're the kind who gets fucked at the end of the party by a drunk who won't remember you come morning. Your friends are jerks and so are your lovers. And then there's Arnaud, such a straight-up guy, so reliable, so sickening. I can just see you in ten years, in your suburban house with your nice husband who waxes his car on Sundays and whom you've been two-timing whenever you can, although—hold on, you don't cheat on him anymore, you're older and you've lost your looks. I say: My love for you, it's like a drug, and it will take me a while to taper off, but I'll get there, don't worry, and I won't worry about you, either, because you'll always find men weaker than you are, pushovers like Arnaud, poor guy, I feel sorry for him. I pour on the hatred and contempt as you listen without a word. Then you talk about the dreadful way I smiled when I returned from seeing Dr. Weitzmann.

But that dreadful smile—it was you and your lies that made me smile like that.

Even so, you seemed so happy to be hurting us . . .

I go home drunk, saying over and over that I don't ever want to touch you again, you disgust me, but when I go lie down in the other room, I feel I'm making a childish scene on principle yet hoping to get out of it without losing face. At dawn, you come get me, you bring me back to our bed, where I fall asleep snuggled up to you, two spoons, your breasts in my hands, and I have a chilling dream in which a little boy discovers he's turning into a congenital idiot. He cries, he rages as I watch helplessly, and all I can find to say is: You won't be unhappy, because you won't realize what has happened.

You leave for work, I'm home alone. I have a hangover and smoke like a fiend. To keep busy, I go through the new e-mails. Almost a thousand. An anonymous woman claiming to be a well-known writer wants to strike up a correspondence on this theme: How far may writers go in exposing those close to them to public scrutiny, sacrificing them for their own pleasure? She is sure that my story must have wreaked havoc in my life and our relationship, if the woman in it is indeed my partner and not just a casual lover. I like neither the anonymity nor the tone, but the message hits home. I wonder if writing, for me, always comes down to killing someone.

In three days we are due to leave for Corsica, where we have rented a house with my friends Paul and Emmie. Will we go? And if we do, what will we do until then? I'm through with my e-mails for the moment; I've answered the few that seemed interesting, and all other work is impossible. It's far too soon to write our story, assuming that I will indeed write it one day. My mother has forbidden me to write about my grandfather, and even though I am sure that sooner or later, one way or another, I will have to defy her to do what I must do, for the moment I can't. I'd often thought I would be set free when I reached my grandfather's age, but perhaps I'll end up fulfilling his destiny instead, perhaps the restless dead will take their revenge and I will disappear.

I'm afraid.

I look up Arnaud's number in the phone book and call it, assuming he is not at home in the morning. I listen to the message on his machine. He has the voice of a very young man, ineffectual but unaffected, the voice of someone who doesn't try to pass himself off as anything other than what he is. There is no irony in his voice, no distance from himself, no awareness that people can assume different roles in society; instead, there's a kind of naïve, enthusiastic immediacy. He sounds like a boy who doesn't gaze at himself in mirrors, a boy who makes rational plans, who trusts other people and inspires their trust in return: the opposite of how I was at his age and how I am today.

I rummage through your things, look in your desk drawer, and unearth a notebook in which you've recorded some to-do lists, titles of books to read, and brief reflections on your deepest anxieties. Last autumn you wondered, in two columns, what you would lose and what you would gain by leaving me for Arnaud. In one column, unique sexual compatibility, moments of intense happiness, and a more glamorous social circle, but also a twisted, egocentric lover who gives you no sense of security. In the other column, tenderness, confidence in the future, loyalty, children—names for our children? Later, we're in June, I'm in Kotelnich, and it's Arnaud's birthday. After hesitating, you call to wish him many happy returns.

You haven't spoken to him since your breakup. You arrange to see each other. He is still in love with you but since you've given him no hope he is trying to forget you and has found himself a girlfriend, which, you note frankly, you find unbearable.

I start in on you as soon as you get home, exhausted, from work. I'm exhausted as well, from obsessing over the same old things, but I've had time to prepare myself. I want to be as wounding as possible, and this evening I'm attacking you through Arnaud. Poor Arnaud: a naïve, vulnerable boy, he loves you to distraction and you use him ruthlessly to deal with your problems with me. A fallback, in case I leave you. When I'm away or things aren't going well between us, you turn to him but give him nothing, nothing but false hope. If he has a girlfriend, you panic, you sleep with him to dig your claws back in. You treat me badly even though you love me, but him you treat like dirt.

You listen to me. You say nothing. You change your clothes, make dinner. I follow you from room to room, hounding you with insults. Finally you say, The one true thing in all of this is that I killed the child in my womb because it wasn't yours.

You weep.

Later, we make love. I tell you I love you, that I love you more than anything. You say you're sorry you hurt me. You want us to go to Corsica as planned. With rest, the sea, bed, and time, we'll relax, we'll talk. I say yes, that's what I want, too, I promise I'll be okay. After we fall asleep nestled together, I wake up in the middle of killing you.

. . .

We're on a motorcycle on a dirt road in the desert. Night is falling. I'm barreling along, you're behind me with your arms tight around my waist. I half turn my head to speak to you; I have to shout because of the speed and the wind. I say it would be good if we left Corsica on Saturday instead of Sunday, to rest for a day at home before you go back to work. You say, also shouting, that if we get back Saturday evening you'll leave me some supper. I'm astonished. What? You won't be there? You're going out? You say yes, you'll have to go out. I feel that you're making fun of me. In that case, I say, furious, this is all I want from you—leave right away, I never want to see you again, and I want every trace of you gone from the house. Laughing, you say that I'm always changing my mind. You add, Kiss me, my love. I turn all the way around, I can't see the road, but I speed up. I kiss you and bite you, I bite the corner of your mouth as if I wanted to tear at your face. You laugh louder and louder. The motorcycle skids onto its side in a spray of sand, it's dark now, you fall off but you keep laughing, your face half torn away, and I begin to kick you. I want to crush you, to kick you to death. You sneer at me and I kill you.

I get up, shaking, to smoke a cigarette in my study. It's still night out. I write down the dream in the file where I'm keeping notes about everything that's happening to us. Somewhat solemnly, I tell myself that it marks the beginning of mourning. I don't want you to die, but I want to kill my love for you, which hurts too much. You will always lie, you will always betray me. When you say "My love," I also hear you saying, "Véro doesn't want to talk to you." I begin to think of nasty things to say to you, but I catch myself: I mustn't be mean, only sad and determined. Sorry about the vacation, it's better if I go to Corsica alone, and I'd like you to move out by the time I return. I hope that your talent for lying to yourself as much as you lie to others will help you slap together a scenario in which you left me because I'm awful—selfish, perverse, whatever you like. Don't worry, I won't deny it. You can think whatever helps you look at yourself in the mirror. I ask only that you leave. If Arnaud still wants you, grab him. Call him up, tell him: My darling, I've chosen, I'm leaving Emmanuel, you're the one I love. Lie and start over again. Really, it's the only thing you can do.

No. Do *not* be mean.

My impulse bothers me: people are mean when they're still in love, and I'm worried that I might start wanting you again, but tonight I feel sure I've made the right decision. I'll tell you in the morning. We won't see each other anymore. I will stay on in the apartment, now cleansed of your presence, your belongings, your smell; it will be painful, but I'll work. I'll write about the last two years: András Toma, my grandfather, speaking Russian, Kotelnich, you, everything. It will be impossible to publish—especially because of my mother and because I don't want to hurt you, either—but not impossible to write. I want seclusion, asking nothing of anyone, not searching desperately for a new woman. Don't be mean, simply say that it's over. Leave it at that.

That's not what happens, of course. Barely have I begun to speak, in the firm, grave voice I've been practicing, when I realize that I can pretend all I want to be unbending, it's still only a game, and in the end I will give in like a child who sulks until his mother takes him in her arms. You listen to my little speech, and although you don't laugh as in my dream I can see that you aren't taking me seriously. First off, you tell me that if you do leave, it will be when and as you please: this is your home. Second, I keep changing my mind; we'd planned to go to Corsica, and we'll do as we planned. I say that it's simple: if you go, I won't. I'll call Paul to let him know. I head for the phone but you tell me calmly not to and I don't push this farce to the point of having to punch in the number to call my own bluff. I've lost, and deep down I'm glad. Still, I say that our love is dead; you say no, that's not true, and I know you're right.

It's been at least a week since the story I wrote for you was published, and you must be the only person I know who hasn't read it. You told me you would read it in Corsica. We get up quite early to pack our bags and I keep a close eye on the special supplement, which I left lying in plain sight on your desk, waiting for you to pick it up. I tell myself that if you take it, if you don't forget my now-pathetic gift that I want you to have anyway, even now, then everything might still work out; if you leave it behind, then we are permanently fucked. You don't seem to notice the supplement. I go out to the balcony to smoke a cigarette, go back into the bedroom, and ask you twice whether you've forgotten anything. You sense the importance of my question but no, you answer, you don't think so.

Emmanuel, what am I forgetting? Tell me.

No, no, it doesn't matter.

I tell you in the taxi, with a cackle of bitter satisfaction. You don't miss a trick, do you? I add.

But why didn't you say something?

It was your job to think of it. I've already read the thing, you know.

I arrive at the airport seething with hatred, and right after we take off I say something hideous. I'm ashamed of it to this day. I say: You know what's going to happen? You want me to tell you? We're going to do what we said. Swim, lie in the sun, smoke joints. It will be nice. I'll be sweet, tender, attentive, I'll make love to you, I'll tell you I love you, but I'm making it clear now: it will all be a lie. I'm going to spend two weeks lying, but the truth will still be all those atrocious things I've said to you. That's what I really think and that's why when we get back I'm going to throw you out. Did you hear me? In five minutes I'll be saying the opposite, begging you to forget what I just said, but you need to know that I'll be lying. Got it?

You close your eyes, you can't breathe for a moment; I see your abdomen heaving with spasms. After half an hour of silence, I take your hand and ask you to forgive me.

Up in a mountain village, the house overlooks the sea. The house is very old, with thick walls, and doors topped with arches; it's cool inside, hot outside. Paul and Emmie welcome us cheerfully, but they are walking on eggshells. Like all our other friends, they've guessed that the story caused some catastrophic fallout; they don't know the details and don't dare ask any questions. One look at us is enough to show that the trouble isn't over yet. As we arrive, they are just heading off to the beach and they invite us along; I say we might join them later, and we shut ourselves up in our room to make love. With quicksand all around us, my only safe place is inside you, and for four days we do almost nothing else. I stay hard for two, three hours and I don't want to leave the bed, go to the beach, have dinner—the only thing I can do is have sex with you, the only reality is my insane and painful desire for you. I tell you again that I don't want you ever sleeping with anyone else, that fidelity is not just necessary but exciting. You say, Yes, my love, yes. I hold your face between my hands, I watch you come, I ask you to keep your eyes open, you open them wide, and in them I see as much fear as love. We sleep in fits and starts, folded together, smelling of sweat and distress. Even sleep is violent. The moment we disentangle, I turn hateful. I tell you over and over that your innocent face is deceitful, that your behavior was appalling, that the cruel coincidence behind our smashup—your abortion and my story, that declaration of love left hanging in suspense—couldn't be more painful. Seeing us so haggard, Paul and Emmie feel lost, wavering between an effort to act normally and the temptation to speak to us—when we leave our room—as if we were survivors of a plane crash. You seem in slightly better shape than I; even during meals, I don't say a word. There are a few moments of respite, though: we go swimming, have a drink on the terrace, where we manage to talk calmly. When people who love each other have gone through this kind of crisis, when they've shared both happiness and horror, then everything is possible, even trust. At that moment, we believe this is true. I tell you I love you and I believe it. One evening, I make ratatouille. You like to watch me dip the long wooden spoon into the pan to taste the simmering vegetables, you love everyday life with me and love that it can be sweet, that it's more than that raging sexual hunger. At some point during the cooking, however, without telling me, you go off to make a phone call in the village, since our cell phones don't work in the house. When I notice that you're gone, I run out frantically to look for you in the two streets and three stairways that lead up to the church, where I find you sitting on the front steps. Tearing the phone from your hands, I accuse you of tormenting me, goading my jealousy, trying to drive me mad. You're stunned, but instead of yelling right back you sit me down on the low stone wall overlooking the village and explain calmly that no, you were not calling Arnaud, you were calling your Corsican friend in Ajaccio, where you'd like us to spend a few days. My fury frightens you but you say you understand it, you were wrong to leave without letting me know, you're sorry. I say that the problem is not whether I forgive you or you forgive me, it's that I can't live like this. I can't bear being this cruel, suspicious person battered by storms of panic and hatred, who goes beserk because you wander away for a moment. I can't stand being this peevish child who longs to be consoled, who plays at hatred to win love, threatens to leave to avoid being abandoned. I can't tolerate being like that, and I resent you for making me like that. Deeply sorry for myself, I sob as you stroke my hair. I feel awful. I detest myself, and it feels good.

Off we go to see your friends in Ajaccio. I drive the entire way without looking at you, and my jaw aches from clenching my teeth. You would like me to admire the landscape; I reply that I don't give a fuck. The Corsican couple are very Corsican, and quite friendly. They plan to take us this evening to a concert of Corsican patriotic songs and Chilean revolutionary songs. I bluntly announce that I don't feel well and would prefer to stay behind, alone. You offer to stay with me; I say no. A house key is left for me, and after I go have a few beers in a café on the main boulevard, the cours Napoleon, I return to smoke a joint on the balcony overlooking the port. I try to sleep, but it's very hot and the noise and music of the cafés drift in through the open window. When my cell phone rings, I see your name come up but I don't answer. I think it would be good to go out again and stay out late, later than you, so you'd get worried, or maybe I should take the car and drive around all night without leaving you a note, but I'm worn out, a bit drunk, and I doze fitfully until you return sometime around one in the morning. I hear you and your friends talking for a moment in the kitchen. You're all laughing, which I resent. And I resent your not coming right away to join me. When you finally enter the bedroom, I'm turned toward the wall, rolled up in a ball under the damp sheet. I hear you undress, I feel you stretch out next to me, you hug me and I push you away with disgust, I push away the woman who has turned me into this wretched man. I'd be angry with you if you gave up the fight and turned away, but you don't, you patiently bring me back to you. A little later, you coax me into the kitchen to have bread and butter and some tea. I haven't eaten anything; you insist that I eat. Your friends are sleeping, the cafés downstairs are closed. We are both naked. The kitchen is pretty, gay, with dappled yellow paint and azulejo tiles. I watch you, naked, brewing the tea, and seeing you move around naked, tan, so lovely, makes me dream about the life I could have with you. We have talked about going to live somewhere in the south. You would find work you liked, I would write, we'd have new friends, my children would come for vacations, our day-to-day life would be so pleasant. I would watch you coming and going, naked, perhaps naked and pregnant, in a house that might look like this one. How nice that would be! And how easy, if we decided to do that! But I know myself too well: before long I'd begin to worry that my jealous and possessive middle-class girlfriend was cutting me off from everything and turning me into a provincial, bitter old fart. That would be horrible. I find everything horrible. We drink our tea, you smile at me, you are beautiful, and I tell you that I just feel lousy, that I don't want to stay. In a little while, after we've slept a bit, I'll take the car and go back to Paul and Emmie in Novella. You sigh but don't argue. Then I say, Listen, if we stay together, you can't keep your emergency exit. Either you use it or you close it. Either you go off with Arnaud or you never see him again, but you stop playing a double game. It's important. I would like you to think about this.

You nod.

We go back to bed. We don't make love. The last time was yesterday, before we left for Ajaccio, and it occurs to me that perhaps it really was the last time.

• • •

In Novella, Paul and Emmie are taken aback to see me return alone. I drink a lot at dinner and tell them the whole story. Even though I haven't told it to anyone before, I already know there are two ways of spinning it. The first way, the listener reacts by saying: You're right, this girl is a liar, she's jealous and unfaithful, and the best thing you can do is leave her. The response to the second version: You've been through something devastating, but you still seem to love her and she loves you, so work this out, move on, be happy. This evening I tell the second version, but I'll shift back and forth between the two in the next few days, depending on my mood swings, the most unbearable of all my symptoms.

It's late when you call me. Your friends have taken you to spend the weekend at their mountain village and you aren't happy there. The house is oppressive, your friends are painfully jovial, you're dependent on them because you can't drive, the cell phone doesn't work, and the only land line is in the middle of the dining room, where the neighbors gather to gab endlessly. They've just gone off to the village fair, you're finally alone for a moment. You're shaking, crying, afraid. You keep thinking about what I said before leaving Ajaccio: either use the emergency exit or close it. You say you can't promise to do that. If you can't trust me, you'll return to Arnaud, it's inevitable.

Then do it now. Go to him.

But Emmanuel, I love you.

You love me, but it's Arnaud who loves you the way you want to be loved, which I can't promise to do. If you leave me for him, you have to take that chance and never look back, and maybe that way you'll find happiness.

I hate it when you talk like that. It's perverse. You can afford the luxury of pushing me toward Arnaud because you know I love you and will come back to you one day. But if I do leave, it will be to come back without always being afraid that you'll ditch me, because I'll have proved that I can ditch you, too.

If you go to Arnaud thinking that, it won't work. But because you're with me, that's immediately how you think! If you were with him, it would be different. Maybe what's going on here is that it's not our story anymore but *yours*, yours and his.

Don't say that. I'm begging you, please don't say that.

Sophie, I'm not being sarcastic, I swear. I want what's good for you, and that's not me. I'm too hurt, too angry, and even before this terrible summer I was never able to make you feel safe. I would like you to be happy and if Arnaud can give you that, then that's what I want. But I swear to you, if you choose to leave me, I won't be here anymore, I really won't. You won't cheat on Arnaud with me. Maybe with other men, there's nothing I can do about that, but not with me. I won't be your emergency exit.

But I don't want you to be my emergency exit, I want to live with you, I want a child with you, but what I think you're saying is that for this to happen, I have to leave you. I think I'm losing my mind. I'm in agony.

So am I, I'll probably wind up in even worse shape than you. You're going to a man who's waiting for you, you'll be starting a new life, while I'll be alone. To me, making love means making love with you; the apartment on rue Blanche was never haunted, but now it has a ghost. Believe me, it's really hard for me to refuse to make promises I can't be sure of keeping. I've made you suffer but I've never lied to you and I won't start now.

I love you. You know you are the man of my life.

You don't know that: perhaps it's Arnaud. Take a chance.

I fall asleep drunk, anesthetized by alcohol. At nine in the morning, I open my eyes; I lie in bed until noon without moving at all, as if my suffering were an animal that might awaken with the slightest movement. When Emmie calls through the door that she and Paul are going out, I reply with a grunt indicating, if nothing else, that I'm still alive.

In the early afternoon, you call. You tell me that you're returning to Paris. You'll move out by the end of the week.

Fine.

We'll still need to talk on the phone, so that you know what I'm taking.

Take what you want. Just leave two or three pictures of us together and you by yourself. And I think it would be better if we didn't talk.

All right. You know, I have the feeling I'm making an incredibly stupid mistake but that there's nothing else I can do.

The days that follow are excruciating. I feel the same way as you, that I'm making an incredibly stupid mistake. I imagine returning to Paris, to an apartment without you, the months of missing you and wondering where you are, what you feel, what you say to Arnaud when he makes love to you. I want to call you, tell you this is impossible, I love you, come back to me, but if you did I know that the infernal machine in my head would start up immediately. I'd drive you away, you'd leave, I'd plead with you to come back . . . This must stop.

. . .

I think about your back next to me when we sleep like spoons. I think about that creepy Philippe from Nice. I'd like to stroke your back, to brush my lips against the downy blond hair between your shoulder blades, gently part your buttocks as you sleep and enter you, you who are always wet for me.

To no longer be seen by you is ugliness, death. I loved it that you found me handsome, and with you I was handsome. I loved my body, my sex—you used to say my *cock*, I said my *dick*, then you started calling it my dick, too. You'd watch me get out of bed every morning to go make breakfast, usually with a hard-on, I was always having hard-ons for you, and you'd say, My dick, that's my dick, and you'd be smiling. Those are the loveliest words of love I've ever heard.

Your face when you climaxed. Your words when you climaxed. Emmanuel, it's rising, can you feel how it's rising in me? I used to think you said the same thing to every man, that your power over men was to make them feel that they could make you come like no one else ever had. Now I don't believe that's true. I really do believe that no one ever licked you the way I did, you've never let yourself go with anyone the way you have with me. You said so, and I know that had you really trusted me you'd have given yourself even more, and it would have been heaven. And I believe that to have had that I would have married you, given you a child. I wanted so much to make love to you when you were pregnant. Someone else will do that, with love, but not like me.

• • •

When I think about Arnaud now, I envy him. He knows what he wants. He knows how to love. He deserves you.

I wish I deserved you, although I know it's too late. In all this absence and loss, I would like to write a book, a book about our story, our love, the madness that came over us this summer, and I'd like this book to bring you back to me.

I would like us to have a second first time.

· 6 ·

It was Sasha Kamorkin who told Sasha, our interpreter, who let Philippe know, and he called me. Anya was dead, murdered with little Lev. Why, how, by whom, Philippe had no idea. He knew only that it had happened the week before and that tomorrow was the ninth day of mourning, an important date in Russian culture. Philippe could take our usual night train from Moscow, where he lived, and reach Kotelnich in time. I told him that yes, that would be a good thing to do.

That same autumn I had begun editing the film. I had resigned myself to it, for lack of any other project, to foil the anguish of Sophie's departure. I didn't expect much but, well, it was work, a reason to get out of bed, go somewhere, see someone. I would come to the studio in the morning, sit down in front of the computer screen next to Camille, my editor, and we'd watch what Philippe had filmed in Kotelnich in June. I had the journals I'd kept while Philippe was filming, and I read them aloud, superimposing on the images my impressions

at the time, so that both words and pictures were now framed
by my commentary in the editing room, because I had to
explain to Camille who was who, what had happened before
and after each sequence, everything that we had taken for
granted while filming but that neither the footage nor the
journals had made clear. I enjoyed giving the commentary
because Camille found it fascinating and because with each
passing day I saw how she became more and more familiar
with Kotelnich, as if she, too, had been there. She learned her
way around the streets, preferred the Troika to the Zodiac,
looked forward to catching up with an entertaining character she'd seen at the village fair. Even without having a sense
of the final form or content, she had no doubt we'd have a
film by the time we were through. I wasn't so sure. I had trouble seeing how all the images, which might make a passable
documentary on daily life in a small Russian town, could ever
be shaped into something that would deliver me from my
obsession and lay my grandfather's ghost to rest, so that when
I reached the age at which he had died, I might at last be
allowed to live.

If Anya had died in a car accident, I would have felt sad, of
course. I liked her a lot. Of all the people we spent time with
in Kotelnich, I grew fondest of her and Sasha, first because I
found them mysterious and then, even after the mystery had
faded, because they were still more complicated, more alien-
ated, more sorrowful than anyone else. Her violent death,
which I suspect was appalling, fills me with more horror than
sadness. At the heart of the horror is the way in which—for
the second time in a few months—reality has matched my
expectations. This spring I had anticipated the realization of

a lover's dream, but reality had savagely destroyed my love instead. In Kotelnich I had been longing for something finally to happen, and voilà, something finally had—something horrible.

Also horrible is that the death of Anya and her son means that the film will work: now it tells a story. We will go back to Kotelnich for the fortieth day, the most important ceremony of the mourning period, when the souls of the dead leave the earth at last and rise into the sky. Right now I don't expect to film Sasha and the family; they won't want us to and we won't dare. But we'll film the town in winter, the snow, the bare trees, the public square near the station where Anya and I sang lullabies to little Lev. These images, shown while I recount what happened, will end the film.

In Moscow we take our usual train, but instead of getting off in Kotelnich we go on to Vyatka, where Anya's mother lives. She has no phone; it's impossible to warn her of our visit. From our hotel in the town center, we take a long taxi ride to an outlying district where clumps of Brezhnev-era apartment buildings alternate with poky little wooden houses half buried in the snow. We spend more time finding the right entrance, the right landing, the door upholstered in torn fake leather. We ring, ring again, in vain, and settle in to wait. Outside the temperature is minus thirteen degrees Fahrenheit, and it isn't much warmer on the landing with its greenish paint feebly illuminated by a sputtering bare bulb. Our faces have a green tinge, as do our jacket hoods; our mouths puff clouds of vapor. In the building we hear sudden rumblings in the pipes, distant voices. Sasha sulks. He's already angry at us, Philippe and me. He agreed to come with us on this third

trip, but he doesn't feel good about it: he'd prefer that Russians deal with Russian business, no foreigners allowed. Even
before the tragedy, during our previous visit, he often made
me feel that I was butting in where I didn't belong. Whenever I asked him to translate, if we were running into some
difficulty, he'd just shrug, suggesting that I wouldn't understand anyway. Now he sighs a few times, saying that the old
woman won't show up, we should go back to the hotel, but
after we've paced back and forth for two hours, the elevator
doors creak open and she appears. A very short woman with
a wrinkled face, engulfed in a heavy, fur-lined coat. Seeing
the three of us on the landing, she takes fright: three strangers at her door, perhaps three enemies. Then she recognizes
Philippe from the mourning ceremony and her face lights up.
She embraces him in delight. He introduces us; she embraces
me as well. Anya talked so much about us! She'd told her
mother that I was the grandson of the last vice governor of
Vyatka, and she is deeply moved to meet me but also ashamed
to welcome such an important personage to her dreary apartment. Excuse me, she keeps saying, please excuse me for my
poverty. I'm a wretched woman, I'm ashamed of myself, I'm
ashamed of my home. As she steps aside for us, she indicates
that we should not make any noise: the neighbors must not
hear us. She is afraid of them, afraid of everyone, and besides,
her neighbors don't know about her daughter and grandson
or about her relations with French people. The mother hasn't
said anything; only the immediate family knows. She prefers
not telling anyone, as if her murdered daughter had killed
someone instead or as if she herself were too poor to rate a
murdered daughter. In the one main room, she has us sit down
around the table, but quietly, as if in secret. She says she'll go
make tea but returns from the kitchen carrying a bottle of

vodka and a large sausage; she pours our drinks into tall glasses she fills to the brim. When I begin to set down my glass after taking a swallow, she frowns and with an imperious gesture orders me to knock it back in one go. Having no choice, I obey; she pours me another. I realize that she's already drunk and we'll have to keep up with her. I miss half of what she says, especially since she talks so fast, and Sasha, who has comfortably ensconced himself in an armchair, determined to get drunk, translates for me only selectively, and sloppily. When Philippe pulls his camera from his bag and begins to film our conversation, she protests, but simply for form's sake, as if it were a game between them. Philippe! Don't film me! I'm old, I'm ugly, my house is awful. She grumbles so tenderly that I'm touched. She hasn't forgotten that he came for the ninth day of mourning, that he stood with her before the grave, that he represented us that day, the French people her daughter had loved. She talked about you all the time, she says, all the time. She used to say that your coming to Kotelnich, it was like a fairy tale, like a Christmas story. She loved you so much, and she was so unhappy that she disappointed you.

Disappointed us? She never disappointed us. What are you talking about?

Yes, yes, of course you know, you pretend to have forgotten because you are a nice man, Emmanuel, because you are a saint, because you are the grandson of the former governor, but she disappointed you. She told me so, when you went to the children's prison, she didn't understand what happened but she must not have translated well, my little girl, because you were displeased, she could tell, and she was so unhappy at having done badly.

I'm struck with dismay. I remember perfectly that visit to

the juvenile detention center where Anya had paid the price for my bad mood. I had told myself it was nothing, a fleeting moment of friction, but if her mother was to be believed, that fleeting moment had cast a pall over her life, and she had never stopped worrying about it, wondering what she had done to deserve my displeasure.

She was ashamed, continues Galina Sergeyevna. She lived through you, she breathed through you, you understand, Emmanuel, and she was ashamed because you paid her two hundred dollars. To her it was as if she'd stolen the money. You already had an interpreter, so what good was she? What good?

No, that's not it at all, insists Sasha, to whom I'm grateful for trotting out the official version. I had other things to do, I had business in town, we really did need her. No one stole anything, don't worry about it . . .

How do you expect me not to worry? She fretted about it all the time. She thought you hated her, Sashulya, because she was trying to steal your place. She thought you took her for a schemer, a girl who sneaks around trying to steal other people's jobs and get paid for doing nothing. You know what she bought with those two hundred dollars? Jeans and cosmetics. And masks, too, paper masks.

Paper masks? What for?

For me, for me to wear when I took care of Levochka. Because I work at the post office, so I see lots of people, behind my service window, and Anyutochka was afraid of germs, so she wanted me to wear a mask when I took care of Levochka . . . like this.

She rummages through a drawer, pulls out some masks, surgical masks. Clumsily, she slips the elastic behind her head, where it catches on her closely cropped iron gray hair, and when she tugs the white mask down over her mouth and chin, suddenly—helped by the freely flowing alcohol—she becomes a living nightmare, this drunken little woman drowning in despair, waving and shouting in her cramped, depressing apartment. And now she bursts into tears: This is how he saw his grandmother, little Levochka, always like this, covered by a mask, never allowed to smile at him, to kiss him, always covering my mouth because of the germs I might have picked up at the post office . . . I scolded my daughter for buying these stupid things. Scolded her, scolded her, I scolded her all the time, my poor little girl. I told her what she should have bought with the two hundred dollars. A door. A new door. That's what she should have done, bought a new door for her apartment. Because that door they had, it was like cardboard. On the ground floor, in Kotelnich, a town of lunatics! I kept telling him: Sasha, you have to change that door, it's dangerous, it's flimsy, and he kept saying he'd get to it. What a laugh! He never had the time. Always working, he said he was, but me, I know the truth: he was off with his girlfriends. I'd told her: Little daughter, don't go with him, he doesn't look you straight in the eye, he's shifty, doesn't give a damn about anything, and he didn't, he just didn't give a goddamn that my daughter and the baby lived in a place with a cardboard door in a town full of madmen . . . The killer, all he had to do was kick in the door, and he took an ax and chopped them both to pieces!

Chopped to pieces with an ax. *Toporom stukat'*: I didn't know what that meant, I didn't understand; looking stricken, Sasha translated for me with his head bowed. Galina Sergeyevna's confused ranting about the murder was interrupted by moans of rage and helplessness, but three days later, with Sasha Kamorkin's help, I was able to put together this: On the afternoon of October 23, a terrified Anya called Sasha at his office. She was alone in the apartment with little Lev and a stranger had just knocked on the door. She had refused to open it, and now he was kicking it in. Sasha calmly told her to stall the intruder, to keep him talking—and he'd be there right away. It took him only five minutes but when he reached the apartment with two colleagues, he was too late: Anya had been strangled with the telephone cord and then she and the baby had been butchered with the ax left in the entryway to chop firewood. Blood, brains, entrails had splattered all over the room. While Sasha collapsed screaming in front of the bodies, his colleagues had rushed out after the killer, who was so blood-soaked that he'd left a clear trail; within another five minutes, they'd found him hiding in a cellar.

The man was known around town: an oven technician at the cake factory, the father of two children, no criminal record. There was no link between him and Sasha or Anya. When he was first questioned, right after the murder, he spoke of hearing voices ordering him to go kill a woman and a child and said that when he entered the apartment they were both shining. They were shining, he repeated: *oni svetilis'*. He said he'd been drinking, but tests showed no alcohol in his blood. The next day, when our old friend Dr. Petukhov conducted a psychiatric evaluation of the suspect, both the voices and the shining had disappeared. He no longer remembered a thing.

At Galina Sergeyevna's apartment that evening, I caught bits and pieces of what had happened. Amid her weeping and wailing, she kept repeating the word *palach*, and when I asked

Sasha what that meant, he shook his head with that exasperated expression I knew so well, indicating that it was none
of my business, and only after much persuasion did he reveal
that it meant a hit man. A hit man? Despite her inebriation,
Galina followed the translation with unusual attention, turning her head from me to Sasha and back again, then nodding in approval, giving me the absurd impression that she
understood what we were saying. Finally she looked me up
and down and with a demented cackle of triumph, as if she
had battled Sasha into submission and the confirmation of
her claims, repeated *palach*, *palach*.

How could that be? *Palach*? What she'd told us sounded
like anything but the work of a hired killer. You'd have to be
insane, I said, or a sadist, or some kind of religious nut to
toporom stukat' a young woman and her little boy.

Fresh cackling from Galina: You trying to make me believe
he's crazy? She pounds on the table, brings her small, pinched
face, ravaged by sorrow, practically nose to nose with mine.
No! Emmanuel, no, he's not crazy! My son tells me: Mama,
shut up. You mustn't say anything because it's too dangerous,
but me, I know what I know. I know that man's pretending
to be crazy. Him, he's the *palach*, but who was it gave the order
to the *palach*? I could tell you his name, Emmanuel. You'd
be surprised to hear it.

She looks at me, searching my eyes, then abruptly straight-
ens up, rises, and solemnly pretends to zip her mouth closed.
She whispers: Now the silence begins.

And silence falls again. Shaken, the three of us sit with this
drunken woman, beside herself with grief, who stands with
her hands on her hips, stretched to her full diminutive height,
daring us to contradict her. At last Sasha shrugs, pours himself another shot of vodka, and in his gravest voice, intones:

So, Galia, you're telling us that it's a put-up job. The question is, who put the killer up to it and why?

She laughs bitterly. You're smart enough to know a question when you see one, Sashulya. Why kill my daughter and Levochka by hacking them up with an ax? Hey? Who would benefit? Think, Sashulya, use your head!

Right, he says, I'm thinking. Who would benefit from that?

Are you a dumb-ass, Sasha, or what?

No, I'm not a dumb-ass. I hope not.

Who, for fuck's sake? Who would benefit from taking an ax to my daughter and grandson? Who's better off?

We don't dare to understand. She presses on: You still don't see?

No, lies Sasha, so that she'll finally spit it out.

Then Galina steps back and says quite clearly, Sashenka.

And immediately collapses in a heap on her chair with her hand over her mouth and her eyes wide with fright. They'll kill me, she murmurs.

I don't really remember what was said after that. She threw us out, but as we were putting on our coats, determined not to hang around any longer, she forgot about having thrown us out and wanted us to drink some more, talk, wanted to show me the curtains. She'd taken the curtains—with a design of red and green circles on a white background—from Sasha's and her daughter's apartment, curtains streaked with blood and brains. Galina had boiled them several times, so that most of the stains were gone, but not all, and she traces with a fingertip the outline of the brownish spots, more visible in the lamplight, and she draws the lamp closer so that I may see them. Look, Emmanuel, look, she says tenderly. It's the blood of my daughter and my grandson. Every time I draw the curtains, which protect my eyes from the moon and the streetlights outside, it's the blood of my daughter and grandson.

I say, Yes, Galina Sergeyevna, yes, I do see.

Back at the hotel, already far gone, we order more vodka and begin to debate Galina's accusations. It's lunacy, says Sasha, shrugging his shoulders heavily. Sickened by the fact that we even consider the idea worth discussing, he soon leaves us for the hotel bar, to pickle himself some more, but in better company. Lunacy, definitely, opines Philippe, but he wonders if this lunacy might not contain a shred of truth.

I object that the massacre had every hallmark of a madman's crime, whereas a hit job means a bullet, and even supposing someone had reason to kill poor Anya, why the baby, too, why such savagery?

Precisely. Perhaps to disguise a hit job. To make it look like the act of a madman. There is no doubt about the identity of the murderer, and Galina isn't saying that it's not him, she's saying that he's only pretending to be crazy.

But why would he want to do that? He's already been caught, and if he doesn't spend the rest of his life in prison, he'll spend it in a psychiatric hospital, which for a hired killer is a bad deal any way you look at it. A hired killer shoots and makes himself scarce, he doesn't let himself get picked up, drenched in blood, just minutes from the crime scene.

Listen, continues Philippe. I'm just tossing this out, but think about it: Sasha wants to leave Anya. We know that's true, he was planning to, and she was miserable about it. So then she threatens him. She threatens to reveal the crooked things he's mixed up in. He's the FSB boss in Kotelnich and, frankly, I don't think he's an honest guy. Anya was no dope: he realizes that she knows a lot more than she should. And he decides to take her out. I'm not saying this is true, I'm just trying to see how Galina's accusations could stand up. Let's say he wants to eliminate his wife. We're in Kotelnich, not Moscow, true, but I've been living in Russia for ten years and I can assure you, this kind of thing happens. Guys willing to put a bullet in someone's head, they're all over the place. Only Sasha doesn't want it to look like a hit. He'd be a suspect. So he thinks about a crazy guy doing it and figures if the baby dies, too, that puts him even more above suspicion. He finds this man, this heating technician, who—let's say—has gotten himself in serious trouble, so Sasha has him by the balls, I don't know how but it's bad enough for him to make the offer: Either I throw you in the hole and make sure you never get out or you do what I ask, you pretend to be insane and we put you in the hospital, first with Petukhov and then someplace out in nowhere where you'll be forgotten, so I can have you sprung in a couple of months. I'm not saying this is true, or even that it's likely, only that in Russia this sort of thing happens.

The next morning, as we treat our hangovers with way too fatty sausage and superstrong tea, Philippe and I don't dare look each other in the face or meet the eyes of our Sasha, who kept going last night even longer than we did and is dosing his own sullen hangover with brown ale. Philippe and I feel a little ashamed to have considered such a monstrous possibility, but the six hours we spent the previous day with Galina Sergeyevna have affected us so powerfully that we now feel wary of Sasha Kamorkin. Without really believing our elaborate scenario, we nonetheless have the vague feeling that there's no smoke without fire, and the old woman made her accusations resonate so dramatically in her tiny apartment that they're still echoing in our muddled minds. When we return to see her early in the afternoon we don't know what to expect, perhaps a chastened embarrassment like our own . . . but she seems to have completely forgotten, if not our visit, at least the gist of the conversation. She is fasting, quite calm, no longer careening between suspicion and gushing gratitude, and when she starts talking about Sasha, which doesn't take long, it's to tell us almost with affection how he and her daughter first met. Anya had just left Vyatka to settle in Kotelnich. She had found work at the cake factory but what kind of work isn't clear; at one point it seems to have involved sanitary and technical inspection, at another, interpretation, although why a baking establishment, even a large-scale one, would require the services of a French interpreter is mystifying. That said, I vaguely remember that during our first meeting at the Troika, the manager of the company, Anatoly, had made slurred toasts not only to Franco-Russian friendship but also to his success in penetrating the African market, which had left me musing on the idea of being in Senegal or Zambia and eating rolls baked in Kotelnich. In any case, it was these connections to abroad that led Sasha, when Anatoly introduced her, to ask Anya sternly if she was authorized to deal in international commerce. He even threatened to have her arrested, says Galina Sergeyevna, but he was teasing her and also trying to pick her up. He pretended to frighten her, she pretended to be frightened, and the next day they went for a walk down by the riverside. They climbed the hill Anya had proudly pointed out on our boat excursion as the Summit of Love, the place where Kotelnichian lovers exchanged sweet nothings, and it was there Sasha and Anya had their first kiss.

Here the plot thickens, because during this walk, Anya told Sasha that she was half French through her mother (dead in childbirth) and that she even owned a house near Paris, where she frequently stayed. Already impressed by her knowledge of French, Sasha was even more intrigued by these revelations. Like me, when I first met Anya, he found her romantic, different from other girls in Kotelnich, and according to Galina Sergeyevna, that's when he fell in love with her. Within a few days, he had left his wife and daughter to move in with the woman he now called *Frantsuzhenka*, little French girl. Anya confided her fabrications to her mother, who advised her to confess everything. Unless she was prepared to hide her family and plunge into a long-term lie, Anya had no choice, really, and resigned herself to taking her new lover to Vyatka to meet Galina Sergeyevna. The resurrection of this mother dead in childbirth had upset Sasha a great deal, and Galina, with her characteristic bluntness, had decided to really stick it to him: So, Mister Big Boss, you make a game of frightening my little girl, saying you're going to put the cuffs on her? You got just what you deserved: she turned the tables on you. France, the house near Paris, that's what you liked about her? But Sasha—think! If she had a house near Paris, you think she'd stay in Kotelnich?

For a man in the secret police, trained in distrust and suspicion, he'd been something of a chump and richly merited that tongue-lashing. Yet what stands out in Galina's story, as well as in the version I later heard from Sasha, is that in spite of feeling foolish after Anya's confession, he still found her mysterious. Several times, he tackled his hostess again: Galina

Sergeyevna, tell me the truth, are you really her mother? No matter how many times she said yes, he didn't fully believe her, and this doubt, paradoxically, worked in Anya's favor. She had been deeply afraid of losing his love by confessing her lies. If she was simply herself, neither very pretty nor rich, with no distinction other than her command of French, then she might well expect a man like Sasha to tire of her. But without believing her lies, he kept believing in them just a bit, kept believing that the mother and daughter hadn't told him quite everything, that beyond the mystique of Anya's French and her trips to France there was something they were hiding from him—in short, that there really was something special about Anya. She did in fact speak French, even if he had no way of knowing how well. She had really been to France, as the visa in her passport showed, and he would take it out of the drawer to marvel at it and dream about it. She really had received letters from a French girlfriend and cassettes of French songs. I think Sasha was proud of all that and had not completely given up on what he imagined lay behind it.

He arrived from Kotelnich on the morning of the fortieth day, driving a van loaded with Anya's possessions, which he was returning to her mother. There were boxes of clothes, but also her guitar, wrapped in plastic, which made it look like a sinister exhibit in a criminal case, and a piece of kitchen furniture we had a lot of trouble getting into the tiny apartment. Galina Sergeyevna fluttered around protesting against this invasion, but Sasha paid no attention and piled everything up, precariously balanced, in the only corner where there was still a bit of space. Beneath his fur-lined coat he was dressed in black, and his face was pale and puffy. He was being heavily medicated, he explained to me. In the days following Anya's death, he had gone seriously off the rails: he'd roamed the town armed with a revolver, threatening to break into the cell where the murderer was being held and let him have it. Sent to a clinic, he'd spent three weeks there doing a sleeping cure. He'd just left the FSB, and I decided not to ask him if he'd quit or been pushed, given his erratic behavior and the suspicions about his actions. He, too, was touched to see us, and we warmly embraced. Seeing an opening, Philippe asked if he would agree to being filmed on this solemn occasion. Raising his faded blue eyes to stare at the camera's lens cap, which Philippe was gently tapping as if waiting for the signal to pop it off, Sasha laughed. It was one of the saddest laughs I've ever heard. What the fuck do you think I care now? he said. Film whatever you want. As for his mother-in-law's insane accusations, if he was putting on an act, I thought, he was doing a good job, but I no longer believed that he was pretending. I remembered the arrogant, secretive FSB officer we'd found intriguing and tried to catch on film; I remembered how pleased we'd been on the evening when we tricked him and snagged a three-quarter view of his face; now he was a haggard, beaten man who hugged us like old friends, and I realized that in spite of our earlier suspicions, and our morbid, childish excitement over them, we had indeed become old friends who embraced him with no other thought in mind but the horror of his nights and the enormity of his sorrow.

Waiting for us at the cemetery is Galina's brother, Sergey Sergeyevich, a man of about fifty who has never been the same, she tells us, since the time two years ago when a couple of strangers pulled him from his car in the middle of town, beat him senseless, and left him for dead in a ditch without robbing him of a single kopeck, just for the fun of it. Galina's son is also there, Seryozha, a noncom in fatigue dress with a shaven skull. He's serving in Chechnya. He keeps bursting into thunderous laughter, thumping everyone on the back, and his alarmingly effusive cordiality strikes me, given the circumstances, as slightly out of place. Since it's minus twenty-two degrees Fahrenheit, the ritual is reduced to the strict minimum: we light two candles, stick them in the snow, take a bottle of vodka and a few slices of sausage from a basket, hurriedly do the honors, then retreat to the warmth of our cars. We would leave immediately were it not for Galina Sergeyevna, who lingers alone, moaning, pacing around the grave, picking up snow that she packs distractedly in her gloved hands. I watch her from the window of Sasha's van, where I have taken refuge with him and Sergey Sergeyevitch, who fatalistically recites the litany of deaths endured by the family. He himself, thank God, has two living sons, but out of his three sisters' six children, the only survivor is Seryozha, the soldier. The other five, the whole young generation, died violent deaths: Afghanistan, a blow to the head from a falling stalactite, a drunken brawl, Chechnya, and for Anya, the ax.

Sasha, who'd seemed to be dozing behind the wheel, turns to me and demands point-blank: Emmanuel, tell me the truth. How well did she speak French?

Quite well, I reply, but like a foreigner who speaks it well.

Like a foreigner? Not like a Frenchwoman? You would never have taken her for a Frenchwoman?

No, I tell him. I'm sorry—I can see my reply disappoints him.

But don't you think, he continues, that she might have pretended not to speak perfectly?

Pretended? What for?

So no one would suspect her.

Suspect her of what?

Well, of being French.

I look at him in confusion. Perhaps, I reply, perhaps, yes . . .

What else could I say?

The meal that follows lasts three, four hours, during which Galina Sergeyevna becomes severely drunk. She started out with good intentions, drinking only water, knowing that her brother and son would be watching her. She wants to behave well, like a lady receiving her guests, and she plays this role carefully for half an hour. As soon as Sasha Kamorkin decides the time has come to make a toast, however, she begins sniping at him, even though she's been read the riot act where he's concerned. Having doubtless spread her accusations against him far and wide, Galina Sergeyevna has been told to shut up, not just for decency's sake but to avoid getting the whole family in trouble. Even if he has been fired from the FSB, the family still sees Sasha as an intelligence agent, and they're afraid of him. So all day Galina has been kissing him, joking around, calling him Sashulya, Sashulenka, but when he stands up, raises his glass, and in a flat voice sluggish with drugs, begins a long speech about his love for Anya and their mutual devotion, Galina can't help making bitter comments. Sasha, however, does not claim to have been a model husband or insist that his life with Anya was one of undiluted harmony. On the contrary, he speaks of his remorse, saying he truly loved her but did not learn how to love her as she deserved. He says that when we're sure we have something, we neglect it, only crying once we've lost it, and he begins to cry in a way that seems sincere and moving to me—but not to Galina Sergeyevna, who with every other sentence calls him a lying asshole. For the moment she's just accusing Sasha of neglecting Anya, of making her unhappy, and especially of making her live in Kotelnich, a town of madmen. The miserable Hungarian is cited as a prime example of what goes on in Kotelnich, but soon, in the welter of words, I recognize the term *palach*. That's it, she's off: a *palach* killed Anyutochka and Levochka. The two Sashas shake their heads miserably, as if pained by some endless litany of reproach they no longer have the heart to deal with. Sergey Sergeyevitch, who must also have had more than his share of this, sighs and breaks in: Galina, you're talking nonsense. If your daughter had been a millionaire or someone important, I wouldn't rule it out, but she was a young mother in Kotelnich, why would anyone have her killed? Galina explodes:

Sergey Sergeyevitch, look who you're sitting next to! Since Sergey Sergeyevitch is sitting next to Sasha Kamorkin, a sinking feeling tells me that we're heading for a recap of her earlier accusations, and since the man in question is right here, this might well do some damage. But she takes a new tack: You think he hasn't got enemies? You think nobody has it in for him?

So now she's saying that whoever killed Anya and Lev was aiming at Sasha, who listens without saying a word. He bows his head and, his hand trembling, pours himself a big glass of vodka, enduring the storm with such a guilty, shame-faced look that I suddenly think: That's it. He's the one they were after. By massacring his family they've hit at him, and he knows it but there's nothing he can say. He simply turns to me and in a faint voice asks: Emmanuel, can we go? Go back to Kotelnich?

I really want to go, too, I'd like to stop drinking, but the meal isn't over, Galina has more dishes coming, we can't just slip off like that. Then it's Seryozha's turn to make a toast. He rises, throwing out his chest in his military uniform, but hardly has he begun to invoke the memory of the dead when his mother starts cursing a blue streak. No more sarcasm, nothing about her son's speech—what pours from her mouth is her despair, her rage, and her shame. She shrieks as if she were about to grab plates from the table to smash them against the wall. She shrieks that no one wants her anymore, she's been tossed aside, good for nothing but to croak in her corner, and no one will come to her funeral because she's a poor old woman, crabby and ugly. She shrieks that it's her own fault that her daughter and grandson got killed because she should have stopped them from going to Kotelnich. She shrieks that

Seryozha is a bastard because he has abandoned her as well as his wife and children, going off to strut around his barracks in Chechnya instead of chopping wood for the winter. The idea that Seryozha is skipping off to Chechnya to lead the soft life and escape his firewood duty is so outrageous that everyone cracks up, especially Seryozha, and Galina, sensing that she's hooked her audience, piles on the hysteria, until it seems she might almost get up on the table and dance. Then, abruptly, she falls silent, crumpling into her chair, where she dissolves in tears and in a tiny voice, to herself, murmurs: Why?

Right, says Sergey Sergeyevitch, *na posashok*, one for the road. We raise our glasses, we drink. Galina Sergeyevna, who missed this turn of events, doesn't understand what's going on or why, having drunk the toast, we're putting on our coats and beginning to kiss good-bye. Going through the motions of departure, it's as if we're doing something unfathomable that completely bewilders her. When at last she understands, she takes it very, very badly. She begs us to stay just a little longer, she clings to our sleeves to detain us, one after another, saying that there's still so much to eat—and I feel awful abandoning her, leaving her all alone with a meal prepared for three times as many guests, alone with her drunkenness, her shame, and her grief. It would be nice of us if we stayed until the evening, had some more to eat, and helped her clean up, accepting the inevitable packages of food. But Sasha doesn't want to stay, he wants to go back to Kotelnich.

It's probably his relief at having managed to get away: he's particularly merry in the car. After four hours spent bearing up, enduring the reproaches and insults and even affection

I expect he would rather have done without, Sasha relaxes. He'd grabbed himself a sausage, along with a bottle of vodka from which he takes huge swigs and, driving along, he begins to bray a cynical song about eternal love, "Comme d'habitude," in French. Too bad, he sighs, that I didn't bring Anya's French cassettes with me. You remember, Emmanuel, the evening we met, at the Troika? She brought them especially for you.

We'd danced to songs by Claude François, Adamo . . . "Tombe la neige" . . . "Vous permettez, monsieur" . . . Snatches come back to him, he starts to sing, urges us to join in. I try to sleep during the trip, surmising correctly that the coming evening will be as trying as the afternoon, but Sasha doesn't want me to sleep, he wants to sing and talk. He is counting on us to introduce him to new women, Frenchwomen like Juliette Binoche or Sophie Marceau, and in fact why not Juliette Binoche or Sophie Marceau? I disappoint him by admitting that I know neither one and so cannot be his go-between. I have the impression my prestige has been tarnished, and perhaps my ancestor the vice governor's as well. Later Sasha returns to the question that obsesses him: Could Anya have been French? But he doesn't linger over the question or my replies (which haven't changed since the morning), for he actually has something else to tell us. A revelation. We aren't to make fun of him, he knows perfectly well it is unlikely, that there's a 99 percent chance it isn't true, but, that 1 percent of uncertainty won't let him rest. It's something Anya said shortly after they met, something that happened, it seems, in East Germany, where her parents were stationed at the end of the seventies. Something about children being switched. From what I can understand, Galina Sergeyevna and her husband entrusted their young daughter to a French family and received a little French girl in return. And that French girl, raised as Anya, was trained to be a spy: that was the only reason for the exchange, organized by the French intelligence agency. She had grown up in the household of a Red Army noncom and later studied at the military interpreters' school, all the while sending information back to her native country. Of course, the meeting with Sasha was part of her mission. What better prey for a Western femme fatale than an officer in the FSB? I am drunk, so is Sasha, and I'm listening to all this in a fog, but with an increasing feeling of dismay. I know from my own experience and her mother's stories that Anya was something of a pathological liar, but the thought of her pillow-talking Sasha into believing such a concoction . . . Because deny it though he does, part of him—more than 1 percent—still believes that Anya was a French spy because she'd told him so, she'd told him that while he was courting her, she was drawing him into her net, because the head of the FSB in Kotelnich was a high-priority target for the French intelligence agency. She had confessed all this to him in the end because she'd fallen in love, and her crazy love for him had proved stronger than her mission. By revealing the truth, she was betraying her handlers and running an enormous risk. By falling in love with a spy, he, too, was putting himself in danger within his own organization. Well, I had clearly been right on the mark the first time we'd met when I'd pegged the two of them for romantics, when I'd called Anya the Mata Hari of Kotelnich. Together, they had constructed a living fiction, with Anya spinning the fabrications and Sasha eagerly accepting them because deep down, as I had guessed, they pleased him. But did he still believe in them enough to think that the double murder of his wife and son had some connection to that story? I didn't dare ask.

There isn't much left for me to say about the last three days we spent with Sasha in Kotelnich. We helped him pack and move the boxes from his FSB office to the creepy studio apartment where he'd taken refuge after the tragedy. In the evenings, we drank and listened to the tapes of French songs. He'd tell us about Chechnya. I remember that at some point we had a contest to compare the merits of tai chi (which I practice) and karate (his martial art), but the results were inconclusive (we were both too drunk). I told him about a Chinese martial technique called drunken kung fu, which involves imitating the erratic movements of a drunk before delivering a swift and efficient blow. We played around a bit with drunken kung fu, laughing, drinking some more, crying. Now and then we'd go out to get more booze. It was minus thirty-one degrees Fahrenheit and had been pitch-black since three in the afternoon. Every evening, toward midnight, we'd leave Sasha and return to the barely heated Hotel Vyatka, where we'd roll ourselves up in our blankets fully clothed, boots and parkas included. In the mornings, I'd drag myself over to the frost-covered window, where I'd watch the trains go by behind a screen of bare trees. I'd look at the trains, at the wretched room where I'd slept, and without really understanding it, I would remember the path that had brought me there. I used to wonder what I had come looking for in Kotelnich and what it was I had found.

. . .

I thought: I came to dig a grave for a man whose uncertain death has weighed on my life; I find myself before another grave, that of a woman and child who were nothing to me, and now I am mourning for them as well.

Perhaps that's it; that is the story.

· 7 ·

I say that is the story, but I'm not sure, either that it really is the story or even that it amounts to one. I tried to set down what happened during two years of my life—Kotelnich, my grandfather, Russian, Sophie—in the hope of determining just what is eluding me and eating away at me. But it still eludes me, still eats away at me.

When I returned from my trip in December, Camille and I went back to editing the film. Now it was a film, no longer a chaos of scattered moments. The events of that week largely escaped me at the time (because I was too drunk, because everything happened too fast), but the legacy of that brief, intense experience was Philippe's images, which fell naturally into a narrative. The film became the story of mourning for Anya, our various visits to Kotelnich, everything that happened to us there on our voyage of discovery. The only thing missing was what I had wanted to add before we left: some shots of the town in winter, the square where Anya and I sang lullabies to her son.

One morning when we were still at the beginning of our work, Camille—to whom I had never mentioned my Russian lullaby—came into the editing room saying: I had this dream. You know what it was? That you end the film by singing a song in Russian.

I laughed, it seemed ridiculous. But three months later I found myself in a studio recording a dozen sentences about the fate of my grandfather, followed by my lullaby. I sang it for him, for Anya and her son, for my mother, and for me. It was the end of the film and to me it seemed like a victory. Something that had never been said before had been said at last. My grandfather had been named, mourned, and if not buried, then finally declared dead. I had performed the exorcism; I could begin to live.

I invited my parents to the first screening. I sat behind them. My mother is not a woman to display her emotions, but as the end credits were rolling, she turned halfway around and I leaned toward her. She gripped my arm and murmured: I understand now, I understand that you did it for me. When the lights came on, all trace of the tears I had seen gleaming in the darkness were gone. She had pulled herself together; she and my father left quickly.

After that, nothing more.

Since the summer of my short story and our breakup, I had seen Sophie again, a few times as an ardent lover, a few times as an uneasy analyst of our relationship. As always, I prevaricated. She had been living alone since our separation, but I knew that Arnaud was waiting for her, waiting for her to have truly broken with me. I knew that she still loved me, that I still loved her, but I could not bring myself to suggest that we live together again. I didn't trust myself, feared promising things I could not deliver and, by making her sacrifice a love more certain and straightforward than mine, ruining her happiness. She suffered cruelly from this hesitation, drawn out for months, between two men: one who waited patiently and tirelessly and one who made her wait, repeating just as tirelessly that she'd be better off not trusting him.

And yet, I wanted to be a new man, not that old one. I had finished the film with a gesture I deemed decisive, liberating, and I believed myself capable of an equally significant gesture in the realm of love. I bought a ring, a very lovely antique ring, and during a meeting I'd suggested with a hint of mystery, I slipped it onto Sophie's finger after having her close her eyes. The gesture was emphatic; I liked that. I wasn't shying away anymore: I asked her to be my wife. I expected her to burst into tears; she burst into tears. But she was holding back a part of herself: I sensed reticence and didn't know whether she was only half pleased by the ring or whether she only half-believed in my sudden proposal. I had told her often enough that sincerity and truth are two different things, especially with me, so I could hardly hold it against her when she didn't simply let down her defenses.

When I look back, I realize that it was a strange idea to have taken her that evening, the evening I had chosen for our engagement, to the premiere of a play adapted from my book *The Adversary*. It should have been a flattering advertisement for myself, but as testimony to the authenticity of my feelings, I could have chosen something better. Throughout the play, I held Sophie's hand. I felt the ring against my fingers. The play was drawing to a close when reference was made to the present Jean-Claude Romand had given his mistress a few days before he tried to murder her. The gift was a ring described in my book and now by an actor onstage: a white gold ring set with an emerald surrounded by little diamonds.

Sophie looked at her hand.

I looked at it, too.

The ring on her finger was a perfect match.

I had given her Jean-Claude Romand's ring.

I will always wonder what made me choose that ring. I hadn't been thinking about the other one, of course, I hadn't remembered that detail from my book, but as Sophie told me after the play (which we both sat through to the end, in icy misery), the unconscious does exist. How could I claim otherwise? In offering her that ring I couldn't have said more clearly: I ask you to believe me, but don't believe me, I'm lying to you.

She gave me back the ring. And that evening, even if there were other vacillations later on, other delays and excuses I won't go into, I learned that I had lost her and that I had arranged to lose her without wanting to, but that was even worse than doing it on purpose—it was the cleanest, most surgical strike I could have made.

Shortly after that, she went to live with Arnaud.

The following year, they had a child.

She never did read my story. It remained a dead letter right to the end.

About a year after Anya's death, I returned to Vyatka. Now that she was gone, my plan to organize a huge celebratory

showing for everyone in Kotelnich was no longer appropriate: they were not in the film and had nothing to do with it.
The only people concerned were Galina Sergeyevna and Sasha
Kamorkin. I dreaded their reactions. Galina Sergeyevna's
didn't surprise me: she wept when her daughter appeared on
the screen, and cried out loudly when she saw herself in her
rage and drunkenness. She cursed and blessed me, and in the
end the blessing won out. With Sasha, things were different.
He was sober, extremely attentive. I did my best to translate for
him—the sections of French dialogue and the commentary—
and several times he stopped the film to have me repeat something, to make sure he'd understood. At the end, he said: It's
good. And what's particularly good is that you talk about
your grandfather, about your own story. You didn't just come
here looking for our unhappiness, you brought your own
along. And that I like.

I've spoken to him a few times since then on the phone.
He is usually drunk, maudlin, in despair. His life in Kotelnich
is miserable. His daughter and ex-wife have gone to live in St.
Petersburg. He remains alone with his grief, his French tapes,
and his hopeless questions about Anya's past, which he still
believes is wrapped in mystery. Now he works as a judicial
assistant, a low-level position, and although he doesn't say so,
I suspect that the people he dealt with in his days of power
never miss a chance, now that he's down, to give him a swift
kick. He's not yet forty, but whenever he's been drinking he
talks about things he'd like to do before he dies: see Paris and
embrace us one last time, Philippe and me.

A few days before my forty-sixth birthday, I met a new
woman. If this were a novel, I would bring things full circle

by making this new woman an avatar of Mme Fujimori, the intriguing trollop of the dream that started everything three years earlier. But this isn't a novel, and the woman's name is Hélène.

We, too, have just had a child. A girl. Her name is Jeanne.

On Wednesday, April 19, 2006, François, the elder son of my uncle Nicolas, committed suicide. I did not know him well; we hadn't seen each other for at least fifteen years and what I feel, something violent and profound, is empathy not so much for the suffering that made him jump from his apartment window but for the unbearable pain Nicolas will now face for the rest of his life. I spoke to him on the phone the next day. In his quavering voice, shaken by sobs, there was something more than sorrow: horror. I can't forget what he said: It's the family curse. Hélène and I, we are monsters. We should never have had children. She made three unhappy souls, and I two. For years, I knew that one of you five would kill yourself, I knew it would happen one day. I was afraid it might be you, and it's François who did it first . . .

He said the same thing, almost word for word, to my mother, and she mustered all her strength to reject the tragic vision toward which he is drawn, impelled by his overwhelming grief. Our father did not kill himself, she said, he was not suicidal. François's suicide is a shocking tragedy, but it has nothing to do with our father's death. François was going through a separation from his wife, he couldn't bear the breakup of his family, and there's no need to point to his grandfather to explain what he did. Insisting on that, she—so superstitious—seemed to argue against magical thinking. Well, I believe that what's involved here is not magical thinking but history and the obscure workings of the unconscious through two generations. All five of us are unhappy—all four of us, now, steeped in shame and fear, haunted by a ghost. The shadow of our grandfather looms over us and I can't help thinking—along with Nicolas and in contrast to my mother (or rather, in contrast to what my mother would like to think, with an energy all the more desperate because in her heart of hearts she believes otherwise)—that when my cousin killed himself, it was the shadow that won.

While we await the forgone conclusion of the inquest, the body lies in the morgue, where Nicolas takes his two grand-children, who are nine and eleven years old. He never saw his own father's body and he wants them to see theirs. The head sticks out from under the sheet at one end, the feet at the other, and between them is the shape of a body, but it is a fiction, says Nicolas, a mannequin charitably put together at the morgue, because a man crashing down from the thir-teenth floor no longer resembles a man. François's mother and wife say his face is peaceful, but Nicolas does not find it so at all. He says it is the face of a monster, the face of the adversary his son tried to defy, only to lose in the end.

Last year François kept a notebook, which Nicolas deci-phers with feverish patience. As the pages progress, the tiny handwriting fractures, breaks up. What's there is a mixture of hairsplitting ratiocination, megalomania, and paranoia that is chillingly familiar to Nicolas. The more he studies the notebook and compares it with his father's letters, the more he realizes that he's been blind to a vast and terrible thing: the madness of his own son. François was gentle, François was calm, François was noble, François was loving, François was a great thinker, and François was mad. Which means that a sneering, cruel, vicious enemy lived inside him, an enemy who hurled him out the window, who wrote horrific letters before he died, and that enemy, says Nicolas, glared at the world like poor François's grandfather—with that evasive, hunted look, the oppressively black look of a man who did not love life and whom life did not love, the gaze that stares from all his photographs. When I showed these photos to Hélène, she, too, was struck, appalled by that gaze, which can inspire only fear. Nicolas says François had that same look in his eyes.

Mama,

I'm writing you from Kotelnich, where I returned in search of a coda for this book. I spent yesterday drinking with Sasha, drinking from noon to midnight. He's doing worse and worse, although he has found himself a new woman, pretty, gentle, delicate, an angel who puts him to bed dead drunk every night. He's a mean drunk. He calls her a whore as she's tenderly unlacing his shoes before getting him under the covers. I can guess this doesn't much interest you, what's happening to Sasha, but imagine: he takes a great interest in you. He saw you on Russian television, he admires you, would like to discuss the fate of his country with you. He'd like me to give him your phone number, the way he used to want Juliette Binoche's or Sophie Marceau's, and I promised I would, but don't worry—in the eddies of intoxication, the promise was swiftly forgotten.

I woke up at around two this afternoon in my room at the Hotel Vyatka. It's snowing. I'm sitting at the table by the window. This evening, I'll take the train back to Moscow. I know that it's the last time, that I will never come back to Kotelnich.

In the deepest clutches of the depression triggered by writing this book, I'd thought to end my tale with François's suicide and say that your father's ghost had won, and that he'd beaten me as well. I kept hearing his voice—not his spoken voice, which I never knew, but the written one, the one that speaks through his letters—and it was saying: You believed your plan would work. You believed that Sophie's love, learning Russian, looking into my life and death were going to deliver you, let you make peace with a past that is not yours yet repeats itself through you all the more ruthlessly because it is not yours. But love lied to you, and you still don't speak Russian, and what was broken in me goes on breaking you, killing you, my grandchildren, one by one. No need to jump out a window; people like you can die just as well while alive. There is no deliverance for you. Wherever you go, whatever you do, horror and madness are waiting. You can flap your arms around all you want, my little falcon: you will not escape. Go film trains in Kotelnich, try writing your book to be done with all this, to move on, to live. Go ahead, believe that, flap your arms. We'll always be here, your mother and I, to crush you with our fate.

I wrote the above—or something like it—before coming here to Kotelnich, even though I knew it could never be the ending I wanted, because it is not the truth, or at least not the whole truth. There is something else. Something else: Hélène and Jeanne, of course, Gabriel and Jean-Baptiste, but I cannot write about them. I have no words to describe the joy of spending hours with a five-month-old baby girl, bringing my face up close to hers—once, twice, ten times—to make her laugh. Perhaps one day I will find the words, I don't know, but the ones at my command can speak only of tragedy and sorrow.

And once again, they've done their job. I did not jump out a window. I wrote this book. Even if it has hurt you, you must admit that is the better choice.

You know, there's one thing I often wonder about. You're busy from seven in the morning until midnight—meetings, conferences, trips, books to write and read, grandchildren you somehow find time to care for with love, the Académie, receptions, premieres, grand dinner parties—and in that packed agenda there is not a single moment of solitude and introspection. Your mind is always occupied, and I think if I tackled a fourth of what you do, I'd drop from exhaustion in a week. But at night, when you go home and go to bed, in the moment between turning out the light and falling asleep, what goes through your mind then? A few thoughts about your whirlwind day, probably, and the one awaiting you in the morning, and what you'll have to do, say, write. But that's not all, I'm sure. So what else? Do you think about your father, whose letters you sometimes reread and who you sometimes dream has come back home? Or the son you so loved and who loved you so but who seems so distant today? The young girl you once were, little Poussy? The hard, triumphant journey of your life? What you have accomplished and where you have failed?

I may be wrong, Mama, but I believe that in those rare moments when you face yourself alone, you suffer. And in a way, you know, that reassures me.

That's what I wanted to talk to you about in this letter: our suffering. Night is falling, there are few passersby in the street below my window; the grocery store across the way is about to turn off its lights and close, but I still have an hour before I leave for the station. What I believe is that you had to deal with appalling suffering at a very early age and that you suffered not only because of your father's tragic disappearance but also because of the darkness inside him, his torment and his horror of life, a horror you, his confidante, knew well. The man you loved most

in the world saw himself as irredeemably rotten—a judg-
ment I pass on myself at times. That is a burden you must
have carried. And you decided, also at an early age, to
deny the suffering. Not just to bury it and follow your
life's motto, "Never complain, never explain," but to *deny*
it. To decide that the suffering must not exist. Your choice
was heroic. I think you were heroic. That poor, radiant
young girl whose photographs I so love to look at walked
her road without faltering, all the way to social success
and academic triumph, with breathtaking courage and deter-
mination. Along the way, however, you inevitably caused
a great deal of damage. You would not allow yourself to
suffer, but you would not allow those around you to suffer, either. Well, your father suffered, poor damned soul
that he was, and it is the silence over his suffering, even
more than the silence surrounding his disappearance, that
created the ghost haunting all our lives. Your brother,
Nicolas, suffers. My father, your husband, suffers. I suffer,
too, and my sisters, although I don't claim the right to
speak for them. You did not deny us, no. You loved us,
you did everything you could to protect us, but you denied
us the right to our suffering, which so surrounds you that
someone had to take charge of it one day and give voice
to it.

You were proud when I became a writer. There is nothing
better, in your eyes. You are the one who taught me to read
and love books. But you have not liked the kind of writer
I've become, the kinds of books I've written. You would have
preferred me to be a novelist like, say, your fellow *académicien*
Erik Orsenna—a happy guy, or at least so he seems. That
would have been fine with me, too. I did not have a choice.
My inheritance was horror, madness, and the injunction

against speaking of these things. But I have spoken of them. This is a victory.

I write these final pages and imagine you reading them, in a few months, when this book comes out. I'm sure they have caused you pain, but I believe you suffered more while you knew I was writing the book, even though I never mentioned it to you. We didn't talk, or hardly ever. You were afraid and so was I. Now it's done.

I'd like to tell you about a childhood memory. It was at a pool, on vacation, in the sunshine. I must have been five or six years old and learning to swim. The instructor, supporting me, helped me cross the kiddie pool. You were sitting on the steps at the other end with your feet in the water, and while I was having my lesson you never took your eyes off me. You were wearing a one-piece suit with black and white stripes. You were young, beautiful, and smiling at me, and I loved you the way I have never been able to love any woman since. None of them have measured up, except, now, my daughter. Crossing the pool meant going toward you. You watched me come closer, and chin above the water, the instructor's hand below my tummy, I watched you watching me and was deeply proud and happy to be swimming to you, to be watched by you as I swam.

It's strange, but while writing this book I sometimes recaptured that unforgettable feeling: swimming toward you, crossing the pool to join you.

It's time for me to go. I will close this notebook, turn off the light, return the room key. The receptionist who welcomed me like an old friend yesterday will smile and say, *Do skorogo*, See you soon, and I'll reply, *Do skorogo*, but it will be a lie. For the last time, I'll walk through the snowy streets of Kotelnich on my way to the station. I'll wait in the cold for the train. Tomorrow morning, I'll be in Moscow; the next day, in Paris, with Hélène, Jeanne, and my boys. I will go on living and struggling. The book is finished now. Accept it. It is for you.

ABOUT THE AUTHOR

EMMANUEL CARRÈRE, novelist, filmmaker, journalist, and biographer, is the award-winning internationally renowned author of *Class Trip*, *The Mustache*, and *The Adversary*, a *New York Times* Notable Book. Carrère lives in Paris.